'A charming mix between A................. .... Bailey … exquisitely opens the door for readers on the history and traditions of the Inns and legal world' *The Times*

'It is rare that an original protagonist appears in historical crime fiction but Sally Smith has created one in Gabriel Ward … a delight from first page to last' *Sunday Times*

'Whip-smart whodunnit … a guaranteed page-turner with secrets, twists and turns throughout' *Woman & Home*

'A triumph of ingenuity' *Daily Mail*

'A guaranteed page-turner with secrets, twists and turns throughout' *Woman's Weekly*

'I loved it! … A whiff of Shardlake and a pinch of Rumpole. The plotting is brilliant and it's a joy for any lover of literature … or justice' S.J. Bennett, author of *The Windsor Knot*

'A cunning and delightful mystery with rich, wonderful characters and period detail so vivid, you can touch it' Ian Moore, author of *Death and Croissants*

'The world of barristers living and working in the Temple in 1901 is perfectly evoked, and Sir Gabriel Ward KC is endearingly eccentric. Intriguing, engaging, and thoroughly satisfying' T.E. Kinsey, author of the *Lady Hardcastle Mysteries*

'This was a total delight! An intriguing, intelligent, insightful mystery, giving a glimpse of a secretive society in the heart of London, all skilfully woven together with a poignant, human story. I devoured this in one sitting!' Sarah Yarwood-Lovett, author of the *Dr Nell Ward Mysteries*

SALLY SMITH spent all her working life as a barrister and later KC in the Inner Temple. After writing a biography of the famous Edwardian barrister Sir Edward Marshall Hall KC, she retired from the bar to write full time. *A Case of Mice and Murder*, her first novel, was inspired by the historic surroundings of the Inner Temple in which she still lives and works and by the rich history contained in the Inner Temple archives. It is the first in a series starring the reluctant sleuth Sir Gabriel Ward KC.

A Case of

MICE
AND
MURDER

SALLY SMITH

RAVEN BOOKS
LONDON · OXFORD · NEW YORK · NEW DELHI · SYDNEY

RAVEN BOOKS
Bloomsbury Publishing Plc
50 Bedford Square, London, WC1B 3DP, UK
Bloomsbury Publishing Ireland Limited,
29 Earlsfort Terrace, Dublin 2, D02 AY28, Ireland

BLOOMSBURY, RAVEN BOOKS and the Raven Books logo are
trademarks of Bloomsbury Publishing Plc

First published in Great Britain 2024
This edition first published in 2025

A catalogue record for this book is available from the British Library

ISBN: HB: 978-1-5266-6873-8; TPB: 978-1-5266-6870-7; PB: 978-1-5266-6872-1;
EBOOK: 978-1-5266-6871-4; EPDF: 978-1-5266-6868-4

2 4 6 8 10 9 7 5 3 1

Typeset by Integra Software Services Pvt. Ltd.
Printed and bound in Great Britain by Clays Ltd, Elcograf S.p.A.

MIX
Paper | Supporting
responsible forestry
FSC® C018072

To find out more about our authors and books visit www.bloomsbury.com
and sign up for our newsletters
For product safety related questions contact productsafety@bloomsbury.com

For Roger

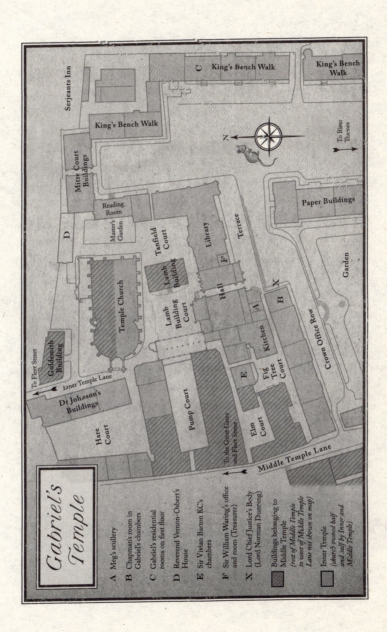

Gabriel's Temple

A Meg's scullery
B Chapman's room in Gabriel's chambers
C Gabriel's residential rooms on first floor
D Reverend Vernon-Osbert's House
E Sir Vivian Barton KC's chambers
F Sir William Waring's office and room (Treasurer)
X Lord Chief Justice's Body (Lord Norman Dunrong)

▨ Buildings belonging to Middle Temple (rest of Middle Temple to west of Middle Temple Lane not shown on map)

☐ Inner Temple (church owned half and half by Inner and Middle Temple)

King's Bench Walk
King's Bench Walk
King's Bench Walk
Serjeants Inn

Mitre Court Buildings

Reading Room

Master's Garden

Tanfield Court

Library

Terrace

Paper Buildings

Garden

Lamb Building

Lamb Building Court

Hall

Kitchen

Temple Church

Crown Office Row

Fig Tree Court

Pump Court

Elm Court

Goldsmith Building

To Fleet Street

Inner Temple Lane

Dr Johnson's Buildings

Hare Court

To the Great Gates and Fleet Street

Middle Temple Lane

N

To River Thames

It is anybody's guess what went through the mind of Lord Norman Dunning, Lord Chief Justice of England, on the evening of 20 May 1901, in those frantic seconds when he knew that his death was inevitable. Did his life – successful, conventional – flash before his eyes as some suggest it does? And, if so, did he have time to register the irony of the startling and exotic circumstances of its end?

Very occasionally, over the centuries, society had been shocked to hear of more disreputable and lesser judges who had died in beds other than their own, with lovers who were not their wives or, even worse, were not women; or in taverns or gambling houses; or once, in an opium den. But Lord Dunning, the most senior judge in the country, was the sort of man to conform with all society's expectations: to administer uncontroversial, unimaginative justice for at least twenty years, and then to die in his bed of high blood pressure brought on by one too many rich dinners.

He was the very last sort of man to be murdered.

His body was stumbled upon, quite literally, by Sir Gabriel Ward KC, early on the morning of 21 May. It could not be said that Sir Gabriel had spent his career as a barrister in the pursuit of truth, or even of justice, since he never gave much thought to either. He had only an immense respect for the rule of law and for the necessity for precision in its application and certainty in its results.

He was the very last sort of man to become an amateur sleuth.

Gabriel lived alone in the Temple, that cloistered fifteen-acre London bubble in which lawyers have lived and worked undisturbed since the 1300s, amongst the gardens and squares and alleyways huddled around the Temple Church. Every morning, at two minutes to seven, a time when the Temple had scarcely awakened to the working day, Gabriel closed the door firmly on his small set of rooms in King's Bench Walk and, just to be sure, pressed it three times, although he knew when he first shut it that it was securely locked.

Walking his familiar route, secure within the Temple gates, to the professional chambers from which he practised the law, the real world was both close by and far distant. To the south lay the River Thames, the masts of barges and the funnels of steamships just visible; the seagulls just audible. To the north was Fleet Street, and the throb and rattle of immediacy in its many newspaper offices and printers as the sale of the morning editions began. But Gabriel was scarcely aware of either; he emerged only occasionally and with great reluctance into the world outside the Temple gates. Within them he had all he wanted. Looking from the great dark bulk of the library looming in front of him to the green slope leading from the Terrace to the wide expanse of the lawn, he would often murmur to himself the words of the great Roman advocate Cicero: 'If you have a garden and a library, you have everything you need.'

Sometimes, on those mornings when the necessity to finish writing a judgment before court led the Lord Chief Justice to arrive early in the Royal Courts of Justice, he and Gabriel would meet as their paths across the Temple intersected. Gabriel was indifferent to the Lord Chief Justice as a personality and despised him intellectually. They had known one another since the future Lord Chief Justice was eight and Gabriel himself was seven. From prep school he had followed Dunning to Eton, and from Eton to Christ Church, and from Oxford to their pupillages in the Inner Temple. They had both had long legal careers, leading in the Lord Chief Justice's case to his present position of national fame and distinction, and in Gabriel's to a reputation for being the ultimate opinion on those most intractable legal problems despaired of by his colleagues at the Bar.

The world considered Lord Dunning to be a sound judge and a decent enough man. Gabriel thought him stupid. Although he was well aware and often said, in his dry, snuffly way, that stupidity was only too plainly no bar to becoming a High Court judge, in the case of the position of the Lord Chief Justice he felt that a little more than being 'sound' (a word he always associated with furniture and horses) was required. Despite these feelings he had great respect for office and would not have dreamed of showing any familiarity or discourtesy to the incumbent of the most senior judicial post in England, second in rank only to the Lord Chancellor.

When their paths crossed, therefore, he would unfailingly raise his top hat and say 'Good morning', and then after a little pause 'Lord Chief Justice'. The pause was intended to convey a subtle note of incredulity, combining deference for the office with contempt for the individual. He would have been infuriated to know the depth of the Lord Chief Justice's indifference to it. Dunning never noticed Gabriel's pause at all, or indeed Gabriel himself, except as someone who gave him a vaguely comfortable feeling of familiarity. The old chap had never changed, he thought, since he was seven years old: shy, bespectacled, hesitant (that was the nearest he got to noticing Gabriel's pause), self-contained.

Very occasionally, as Dunning also raised his top hat and called his usual cheery 'Morning, Ward', for reasons he had never analysed the Lord Chief Justice would picture the scene at his home. The opulent breakfast room in Stafford Terrace, Kensington with its groaning table; his large family seated there amidst the claustrophobic splendour of mahogany and silver and brocade and mirrors and mezzotints. And if somewhere deep in his subconscious he felt a twinge of indefinable yearning that a more introspective man might have recognised as envy, then he did not analyse that either. Good God, the last thing he would ever want was poor Ward's lonely life.

That memorable morning of 21 May 1901 started much like any other. Because his routine never varied, Gabriel always found that his mind was one step ahead of his physical actions. So, as he walked across the Terrace to his Chambers in Crown Office Row, he seemed already to feel under his hand the black iron doorknob of number 1, its contours rounded with centuries of paint; and when his hand was indeed on the doorknob, in his mind he was already seating himself at his large mahogany desk with its faded green leather writing surface, and its immaculate piles of papers all neatly tied with pink ribbon.

It was for this reason he at first failed to notice, as he attempted to step over the threshold of his chambers, that lying across it was a body. It was only when his toe encountered an odd, soft obstacle that, coming back from the desk he was already mentally occupying, he found his entry barred. He was at the narrower end of what was only too plainly a corpse, lying on its left side, its face pressed close against the wall, a dark coat covering its torso and a top hat wedged down over its head. Its feet, dusty though well cared for, were bare. It was not difficult to step over the immaculately trousered legs, ending in those naked pink incongruities, and so gain access to the hallway. Instinctively, he did so and, as instinctively, though afterwards he felt a little ashamed of his action, slammed the door on the atrocity on the doorstep.

2

Paralysed by this intrusion into the predictability of his routine, he stood frozen in the familiar hallway. He knew of course what he should do: call the police. His lack of familiarity with the workings of the telephonic communication system, newly installed in the clerks' room by Chapman, was really no excuse; he could, as Chapman had not infrequently pointed out to him, at least try. And if the attempt were to be unsuccessful, an errand boy would be readily available in Fleet Street to convey a message by hand to the City of London police station.

As he wavered between two courses of action, two things happened simultaneously. From the clerks' room he heard Chapman's voice, raised and imperative, speaking on the telephone; outside, scream after scream tore through the peace of the early morning, shrill, uncontrolled, unrelenting. 'Oh no, oh no, oh no,' on and on, until they ceased to be words and became instead a meaningless howling mantra: 'Ohnoohnoohno.'

Involuntarily he opened the door again, to reveal the corpse and also the chambers laundress who now stood there, her way barred, face distraught and mouth open, calloused hands uplifted in a curious gesture of supplication.

'Oh no,' she screamed. 'Oh no, oh no.'

And Gabriel, unthinking, wanting only that the penetrating noise should cease, bent forward. Placing his hands on her upper arms, he half-lifted, half-pulled her over the legs of the corpse and into the hall, where he guided her to the chair upon which his instructing solicitors would sit while waiting to consult him.

By then Chapman had emerged from the clerks' room. Insofar as it was possible to apply the word 'ruffled' to the stately Chapman, he looked ruffled.

'I have called the police, sir,' he said. 'They will be here shortly.'

'But what has happened, Chapman?'

'I've no idea, sir.' Shaken out of his normal deferential urbanity, Chapman sounded almost sharp. 'I have only been here five minutes. It was there when I arrived.'

The two men had to raise their voices above the screaming, which continued unabated.

Gabriel looked with distaste, not untinged with alarm, at the streaming eyes and the running nose. Dredging his memory for the correct response, he found at last somewhere in its deepest recesses his nanny's words to his small self, a phrase he had never understood or responded to.

'Come,' he said. (And what on earth did that mean? asked his inner lawyer. Come where? He did not want her to come anywhere; he wanted her to desist.) 'This will never do.'

And as in a miracle, she stopped after one last heaving gulp. Emboldened by this extraordinary success, and by the restored quiet, Gabriel rummaged through his memory for what Nanny had done next. But this time Nanny failed him. Turning instead to a lifetime's experience of judges' reactions to distressed witnesses (not uncommon since Gabriel's cross-examinations were legendarily excoriating), he suggested she might like a glass of water. This, too, judging by her whispered assent, was the right thing to do.

It was then that Chapman asserted his sense of the proper order of things.

'Now, Annie,' he said firmly, 'into the clerks' room, if you please, and there you may have a glass of water. And no more troubling Sir Gabriel with your hyst— with your distress. We have all had a shock.'

Gabriel hovered anxiously. But Chapman was now back in his familiar role of barristers' clerk, one of that faithful band of special servants who combined the loyalty and discretion of a good butler with the business acuity and power of a theatrical agent. Gabriel's peace of mind was Chapman's peace of mind; Gabriel's career, Chapman's career; each guinea that Gabriel earned was a shilling in Chapman's pocket. Corpses on door-steps, however shocking, must be dealt with and the business of chambers must move on. At all costs Sir Gabriel's distinguished practice must be protected.

'Your coat and hat, if you please, sir,' the clerk said. 'I will call you, sir, when the police arrive. The papers in Cadamy and Moore are on your desk. There is nothing more you can do here until the police come. I will look after Annie, sir.'

Meekly, Gabriel took off his coat and hat and, entering his room, sat at his desk. This time in the morning was normally his special quiet time. Now the body that lay unseen on the doorstep seemed to make the peace ominous and the quiet had a temporary quality.

But seconds passed in the still room, marked by the ticking of the clock and the dripping of the tap in the cupboard in the corner that housed a sink. Then the seconds became minutes and slowly the beating of Gabriel's heart resumed its normal pace, in time with the tick and the drip, and, for all that could be seen and heard, normality was re-established. He checked his desk. Was his inkwell placed so that the hinges on the silver top were precisely aligned with the edge of the perpetual desk calendar that stood next to it? Was his gold pencil (with the lead pointing towards the window) tucked away in its shallow tortoiseshell case?

All was in order. And it no longer felt impossible to him to reach for the new set of papers in the intractable case of *Cadamy v Moore* and to untie the fiddly knot in the pink ribbon that bound them. Even to feel, as he always felt, the little thrill of adventure as a thorny new legal problem, despaired of by lesser barristers, unfolded itself to him like a rose at last encountering the warm sunshine of genuine interest.

It was seldom that any legal problem nonplussed Gabriel for very long, but the extraordinary facts of Miss Cadamy's claim against his client Mr Herbert Moore, the publisher – a claim worth huge sums of money, with profound reputational issues at stake – had already engrossed him for some hours. He was looking forward to many more, snuffling happily away amongst ancient legal precedents that might or might not be of relevance, and ferreting in the forgotten corners of his own mind for inspiration.

Peace wrapped itself like a blanket around Gabriel and his room.

It was not to last. Only twenty minutes later he was forced to tear himself away from his notes to give a thought to a very different question, from a newly arrived police constable. 'Did you recognise the deceased, sir?'

'No,' said Gabriel. 'His face was turned to the wall. And his top hat covered his head.'

'Would you look for me now, sir? I have turned him over and removed his hat.'

As slowly as the tortoise he resembled, Gabriel followed the police officer to the door and just as slowly blinked down at the body, in full white-tie evening dress under the open overcoat. The long, elegant corpse now lay on its back, the top hat placed almost reverently beside it. On the immaculate white dress shirt was a small circle of bright deep scarlet. Extruding from this was a large carving knife, embedded to within an inch or so of the hilt. Inlaid into the handle was the image of a silver-winged horse. Gabriel said nothing.

'Well, sir?'

And Gabriel then articulated a fact so staggering that he heard his own voice, as he sometimes did in court, and had time to register its quiet, dry cadences, its clarity and precision.

'It is Lord Dunning.'

'Lord Dunning, sir? Not the Lord Chief Justice, sir?' The policeman's tone suggested the attempted soothing of a lunatic.

'Yes,' said Gabriel firmly. 'The Lord Chief Justice.'

3

'But he has bare feet.'

'Even the Lord Chief Justice has feet, officer,' said Gabriel. 'And in this instance,' he added with the characteristic little snuffle that indicated a witticism, 'they were feet of clay.'

'Clay?' said the struggling policeman.

And suddenly, despite the satisfying reference with its apposite metaphorical and literal meaning, Gabriel felt ashamed of the cheap joke, the error of taste. Dunning had been a decent enough chap really, he supposed. And into his mind there came the image of the eager boy who had been good at cricket and average in class, whose knees had been permanently scraped and whose generosity amongst his classmates with the contents of his tuck box had been legendary.

Gabriel's own knees really felt quite wobbly and, seeing at last a sign of what he regarded as the right reaction to the circumstances, the policeman became more solicitous, putting his hand under Gabriel's elbow and steering him back across the hall to his room, Chapman hovering protectively behind.

Sitting behind his own desk, Gabriel felt more secure. But Constable Maurice Wright, who had been a mere two years in the City of London Police Force, fervently wished himself back on the beat in Fleet Street from which he had been so hastily summoned. As he contemplated the enormity of the information given to him, the ghastly embarrassment if the identification were wrong, its staggering impact if it were true, he felt for a moment quite overwhelmed. He removed his helmet and mopped his brow.

'Are you sure this is Lord Dunning, sir?' he ventured.

'I am quite sure,' said Gabriel, and then, obscurely feeling something more was required, 'I appeared in front of him only yesterday.'

'In front of him, sir?'

'I mean that I appeared as counsel in his court,' Gabriel explained meticulously. 'I lost,' he added.

Now why had he referred to that still raw experience? His beautifully analysed short legal application, Dunning's brisk pragmatic rejection of it, the hefty costs award to his smug opponent; and all so utterly wrong, so illogical, so lacking in rigour and purity and all that made the law beautiful.

But to Constable Wright, something was at last beginning to illuminate this funny old cove's impenetrable observations.

'Were you upset when you lost, sir?'

'Not enough to want to kill the judge, if that is what you mean. We would have few judges left if we were to kill one each time we lose.'

'Do you recognise the knife, sir?'

'It has the silver Pegasus motif inlaid into its handle,' said Gabriel sadly. 'As does all the Inner Temple cutlery. Pegasus is the symbol of the Inner Temple. He is our icon, the winged horse of divine inspiration, flying heavenwards: *Volat ad aethera virtus.*'

Constable Wright, lost again, heard with a spasm of relief the scrape of confident boots that heralded the arrival of his superior officer. Sergeant Rayner's bursting self-confidence and contempt for the emergence into detective work of what he sneeringly referred to as 'them scientists' was usually a great trial to Constable Wright. Now the sergeant seemed to him a profoundly welcome sight. Wright hurried to the door where two young police officers stood waiting with a stretcher. The sergeant was bending over the body, one large leather-gauntleted paw outstretched towards the knife.

'Perhaps we shouldn't touch the handle,' said Constable Wright, hovering anxiously at his shoulder.

'Not touch the handle? What the deuce do you mean? Do you imagine we could do him any harm? The man is as dead as a doornail,' said Rayner irritably.

'The murderer may have left fingermarks on it, Sergeant,' said Constable Wright. Not for nothing had this ambitious young policeman, yearning for transfer to the Detective Division, pored over the new handbook on criminalistics.

'Yes indeed,' said Gabriel appearing in the doorway. 'Dactylography.'

'I beg your pardon, Sir Gabriel?'

'Dactylography,' said Gabriel happily, losing himself in intellectual interest. 'Fingerprints used to establish identity – a most fascinating and ancient subject. The Babylonians, you know, in two hundred BC, and indeed Quintilian, the great Roman advocate in the second century AD, who used the bloody handprints at the scene of a crime to secure his client's acquittal…' His voice tailed off.

'Yes,' Constable Wright chimed in enthusiastically, 'and they say that the Assistant Commissioner of the Metropolitan Police is going to open a fingerprint bureau at Scotland Yard very soon. Like the one in Calcutta, you know.'

'Nonsense,' said the sergeant sharply. A City of London policeman to his marrow, any mention of the Metropolitan Police at Scotland Yard evoked hostile rivalry. 'Calcutta! The Assistant Commissioner of Scotland Yard has a bee in his bonnet. I may be old-fashioned but I say the old ways are the best ways. Fingermarks are bosh, my lad.' And grasping the hilt in one meaty, leather-clad fist, he gingerly withdrew the blade, worn from centuries of sharpening into a narrow, stiletto-like point. He placed the knife in his bag and turned his attention to the body.

'Now pick up his feet,' he ordered Wright as he lifted the shoulders of the corpse, 'and help me bung 'im on the stretcher.'

'I did turn him over to identify him, Sergeant,' confessed Constable Wright unhappily, 'but perhaps we should now leave him where he is for the police surgeon to examine him.'

'Leave him where he is?' barked Rayner. 'Lying across a doorway?'

'Yes indeed,' put in Gabriel. 'Maintenance of the *locus in quo*. The work of Edmond Locard, you know… a most interesting French criminologist… has shown that every contact leaves a trace. He is gaining great authority.'

Rage caused Sergeant Rayner's face, already scarlet with exertion, to deepen further in colour.

'Never mind Latin and Indians and Frenchmen.' The sergeant's cockney tones were withering. 'Good English policemen and some straightforward detective work are good enough for me. I don't need a doctor to tell me he's been dead for hours. The police surgeon can have a look at him in the mortuary.'

He redoubled his exertions to drag the body onto the stretcher. As he did so, a shard of glass tinkled to the ground.

'Wait, sir,' cried Constable Wright.

He slipped his hand into the dead man's inner pocket, just beneath the wound in his chest, and withdrew from it an open-case pocket watch. The face had broken in the impact between body and ground and through its shattered glass the hands were still; frozen in the moment that life had been extinguished. For Lord Dunning, time would never continue beyond twenty-five minutes past eleven on the evening of 20 May 1901.

4

An hour after the discovery of the pocket watch, a police van was pulled slowly up Middle Temple Lane, the ancient cobbled little roadway that divided the Temple and the two ancient societies of lawyers who resided within it, the Inner Temple on one side and the Middle Temple on the other.

The horses' hooves slipped and clattered over the cobbles, waking all those remaining residents not already peering open-mouthed from the windows. The Temple porters, custodians of the Great Gates that gave onto Fleet Street, dragged them slowly open to allow the van through. And so Lord Dunning, Lord Chief Justice of England, took his last journey past the Royal Courts of Justice over which he had presided.

Meanwhile within the Law Courts there was tumult. The administrative implications of the news were mind-boggling. The Lord Chief Justice's list of court hearings was full for the morning on which his body was found and for many thereafter. Litigants who had waited for months were even now anticipating decisions in their various disputes. Two KCs were waiting, fully robed, outside Lord Dunning's court, accompanied by their respective commercial clients who had paid enormous fees for the privilege of hearing a forensic legal battle of the highest order before the Lord Chief Justice. The next most senior judge, hastily consulted, decreed the closure of the Law Courts for that day.

Bewildered judges, suddenly liberated from their duties, emerged from their rooms and as they met in the judges' corridor, the unimaginable horror of the news spread. Dunning, by now several years in office, had been a popular man, but like many universally popular men had not made intimate friendships. The predominant emotion was one of incredulity that such a crime had been committed rather than of grief. When all his colleagues had congregated, driven by some strange collective impetus they made their way down into the vast entrance hall and out of the building, a small group walking as close together as dignity and bulky robes allowed.

Arrayed on the stone steps, a defiant bulwark against lawlessness, united in discipline and restraint, they arranged themselves instinctively in order of seniority. First, the five judges of the Court of Appeal, and behind them the twenty-one judges of the King's Bench, Chancery and Probate divisions – all encased in exotic combinations of black and gold and scarlet and mauve and ermine for that morning's sittings. They stood with bared heads, wigs in hand, gathered in a spontaneous display of respect as the Lord Chief Justice's body was driven slowly out through the Temple gates and down Fleet Street.

Amongst the rarefied group of judges of the Court of Appeal stood Lord Justice Wilson and Lord Justice Brown, shoulder to shoulder, heads bent in prayer. There is something about all-enveloping robes trimmed with ermine and adorned with sashes that makes all judges look the same, and Lord Justice Brown and Lord Justice Wilson seemed at that moment to be the twin embodiments of the judicial authority that transcends all personal characteristics. In fact, although each possessed a keen intellect and fierce professional ambition, they were very different men. Lord Justice Brown was tall, thin-lipped, reserved and patrician. Lord Justice Wilson was shorter, rather red in the face, and inclined to both stoutness and pomposity.

Both of them at this moment appeared to be caught up in the tragedy of the extraordinary event; but in the heart of each was the same quiet jubilance. For each of them knew, absolutely knew, with a glorious, singing certainty, that he was going to be the next Lord Chief Justice of England.

All His Majesty's judges, released from the ritualised drama of the moment and imbued with a new and deep sense of vulnerability, found themselves unaccustomedly at a loose end. They used this tragically acquired freedom in their own individual way, the studious making for the library, the gregarious for their clubs, and the uxorious for home. Each found in these various refuges their own particular kind of solace.

Lord Justice Brown's immediate impulse was to return to the comfort of his wife. But then he recalled that Tuesday was Lady Brown's orphanage day and so instead he first headed for the library and spent a conscientious hour ruminating over the subtleties of the new Railway Employment (Prevention of Accidents) Act, the provisions of which he anticipated would loom large in his next case.

When he eventually arrived home, Lady Brown still had not returned from her morning visit. Childless herself, she was devoted to the orphans of St Saviour's whose stiff-uniformed, disciplined little beings soaked up like hungry sponges all the pent-up love she had to offer. Every Tuesday, for years now, she had made her way to the cheerless institution in Shepherd's Bush, bringing with her the softness of her silks and furs and embraces, and the sweetness of her personality and her toffees, to enrich the lives of the orphans with stories and games. Every Tuesday afternoon she returned to her silent home appearing especially bright and cheerful, so that her beloved husband should not know the depth of her sense of loss.

But he did know. Offering to accompany her one day during the legal long vacation, he had watched as she sat under the single note of hope in what the orphanage called the garden, the great spreading chestnut tree in the middle of a meagre lawn. Surrounded by rapt children, she had recounted one of her little made-up stories about a garden that was quite different, in which flowers and rabbits and fairies flourished. And he had seen her transformed, as indeed the orphans had been.

'I am sorry, my dear,' he said stiffly, on their way back in the carriage. And it was all they had ever said on the subject.

Now, the judge prowled his drawing room until at last he heard, in unison with the booming of the luncheon gong, the sounds of her return. Her response to the news was all he had come to expect: solicitousness as tender as though he himself had been threatened with the Inner Temple carving knife; horror at how close he must have come to danger on the night he had dined with the Lord Chief Justice; ready warm sympathy for Lord Dunning's family.

'I simply cannot believe it,' she said. 'And what is so sad is that this very morning I met Amelia Murray at the orphanage. She can have known nothing of it.'

'Who is Amelia Murray?'

'I am forgetting you would not recall. She was one of the orphans, some years ago. Such a clever, determined, ambitious little thing. But the point is, she is now the Dunning family governess.'

'What time was this?' said her husband, looking perplexed. 'The family must have been in absolute shock. What on earth was she doing at St Saviour's?'

'Oh, it was very early. I got there at eight. I do so love to see the little ones at breakfast. Amelia cannot have known of it. And then she must have returned to news of this dreadful tragedy – I can hardly bear to think of it. Those poor bereaved little Dunning children.'

'But why was the young woman there?'

Lady Brown shook her head. 'My dear, I really do not know. She merely said she felt she would like to help with the little ones. I thought… I wondered if she might be unhappy. But she said nothing. I am probably being silly. She has done so well. We are all so very proud of her. Anyway, she helped with breakfast and then she came and sat in the garden and listened to my first story and then she just slipped away.'

She looked wistfully at her husband. 'I never stop thinking of them all, you know, and hoping they go on to lead happy lives. I feel so sad if our orphans do not settle in the outside world. They have such a dreadful start in life. Sometimes I have wished… I have wished we could provide a home for one of them.'

Lord Justice Brown looked at her in mild surprise. 'My dear Maria, you know you have complete responsibility for the servants. When a vacancy arises, you may of course offer the position to a suitable orphan.'

'Oh,' said Lady Brown, 'I did not mean as a servant. I… I meant perhaps to… to… be with us.'

'With us? What can you mean? You mean as a ward? That is quite out of the question!'

Lady Brown stared fixedly at her plate.

Lord Justice Brown was very fond of his wife. He said more gently, 'Maria my dear, these children — you know nothing of their backgrounds. Their heredity may include anything: criminality, drunkenness, madness… anything at all. Good God, you of all people know there must not be the slightest question of anything of that sort connected however remotely with us.'

Lady Brown was well aware of her husband's shyly shared but entirely confident plans for professional advancement. It had at first seemed tasteless to refer to the implications of Lord

Dunning's death. But now she ventured, very delicately and obliquely, to approach the subject.

'I suppose, my dear,' she said, 'that you may be particularly busy very soon?'

But even that seemed to him a trifle too close to a topic of such sensitivity and he flinched from the gentle hint like a frightened horse.

'I anticipate there will be many questions to answer in the next few days,' he said evasively, 'in relation to the death. I must have been one of the last to see poor Dunning alive, at the Treasurer's Little Dinner, you know. I hope it does not cause… difficulties for me.'

'No, no, my dear,' said his wife soothingly. 'Dear Lord Dunning, your friend and colleague, everyone will understand how hard this is for you.'

Lord Justice Brown, looking into those devoted trustful eyes that saw only good in people, wondered why he felt like a betrayer.

He said uneasily, 'Maria, my dear, you must understand that murder investigations are exhaustive. The police will ferret everywhere. With regard to my anticipated new appointment – I – we must be very, very careful what we say.'

'You mean – do you mean – but surely that can have nothing to do with the death of Lord Dunning?'

'No, no,' he said hastily. 'Though there was something he said at the Little Dinner…'

Maria Brown's eyes widened in alarm.

'Oh, it was nothing. *Nothing.*' The uncharacteristic violence of the emphasis made her gaze even more anxiously at him.

Luncheon was finished in silence.

———

Meanwhile Lord Justice Wilson had gone straight home, compelled by a desire greater than any immediate need to see his formidable wife. The steps that led to his Hampstead house were steep and the morning now hot. As the portly Lord Justice Wilson plodded towards his front door, no one would have known that his apparently pragmatic progress was conducted to a running poem in his head, a kind of interior music that propelled him as though on wings: 'Leda', 'Charles de Mills', *Rosa* 'Alba', 'Old Blush', 'Nuits de Young', 'Cécile Brünner', 'Reine des Violettes...' And then he was home, reunited with the budding, tumbling ecstasy of his roses.

Access to these required walking through the conservatory and the inevitable encounter with his wife, also a keen horticulturist, who sat writing invitations to her next At Home amid the glories of her immaculately tended palms and jasmine. Her eyebrows shot up enquiringly at his unexpected appearance in the middle of a Tuesday morning, but she assimilated his astounding news with great speed. Her response, however, though predictable to her husband, was less edifying.

'Did they speak to you about the job?' she demanded. There was in her voice a note uncomfortably close to triumph.

Lord Justice Wilson had also confided his hopes and expectations to his wife. He was not a sensitive man; but even he flinched at the tactlessness of this direct approach.

'My dear Louisa, of course not. Good God, the place was in an uproar. I hardly think that I can expect to hear quite so soon. It is the most shocking tragedy.'

'Nonetheless,' she said, 'life goes on.' She uttered this platitude as though she had just thought of it. 'And inevitable as the outcome may be, I would not wish us to lose any opportunity to advance your cause.'

At the luncheon table she continued, 'I think perhaps I should have a word with the Lord Chancellor's wife as to when her husband expects to make the announcement.'

Lord Justice Wilson looked appalled. 'My God, no, Louisa! Do not even think of it, I beg you.'

'But why not? She is a charming woman. I have met her frequently at receptions. It seems to me a good idea. Really, I sometimes think I am more ambitious for you than you are for yourself.'

Lord Justice Wilson's chest swelled with pomposity so that the rose in his buttonhole quivered in synchronicity. 'My dearest Louisa, this is not a matter for the ladies. I think you may leave to me and the Lord Chancellor my imminent elevation to high office. I really must ask you not to interfere.'

Rather huffily, Lady Wilson rang the bell for the butler. 'Very well. I have already done my best to advance your interests. From now on I will do nothing more but wait for the announcement to be made. And it had better be soon.'

Her husband looked anxious. He wondered uneasily why an expression had fleetingly crossed her face that could only be described as shifty. And what on earth had Louisa meant when she said she had done her best?

'I am more concerned at present,' he said, 'by the fact that I must have been one of the last persons to see the Lord Chief alive.' And then, unknowingly echoing to the letter the sentiment of the colleague he did not even consider to be his rival, 'I hope it does not cause… difficulties for me.'

'Why on earth should it?' demanded his wife. 'You do not imagine that anyone will think you murdered the Lord Chief Justice, do you?'

'My dear Louisa! I meant merely that it would be a happier circumstance if I were not associated with what in any estimation is going to be a major scandal in the Temple. I must expect the most minute questioning as to the events of last night.'

'Then it is fortunate,' she said with a snort, 'that I collected you from the Temple after the dinner and we went home together, is it not?'

'Yes,' said her husband meekly, 'of course.' But he still felt a little uncomfortable. There had popped into his mind, quite uninvited, a memory of the time ten years or so ago when he had taken Louisa to the Lyceum to see Henry Irving play Macbeth. He dismissed the memory hastily. He could not begin to imagine what had made him think of it.

5

'Bare feet?' It was said in a tone of the most withering contempt. 'Why on earth did he have bare feet? And where the devil are the man's shoes and socks?'

Gabriel shook his head unhelpfully and wriggled a little on his hard upright chair. The speaker was Sir William Waring, Master Treasurer, the head of the Inner Temple. The chair on which Gabriel was seated in Sir William's elegant office had been deliberately placed directly facing the enormous sash window, to ensure the incumbent's maximum discomfort. Through the sunshine pouring in, Gabriel squinted at Sir William who sat comfortably behind his desk with his back to the light. Beyond him, Gabriel could see across the Terrace to the blaze of laburnum in the gardens that formed, as in some early devotional painting, a kind of halo of hazy gold behind the Treasurer's sleek, dark head.

Sir William Waring found Gabriel incomprehensible. Everyone in the Temple was aware of the rigidity of his routines, and jokes were made that you could tell the time by his lamplit window in 4 King's Bench Walk: from six o'clock until six-fifty-eight in the morning and from six o'clock in the evening until half-past midnight every night. That steady, scholarly light shining each night from Gabriel's window somehow infuriated vain, frivolous, gregarious Sir William Waring past bearing.

'What the devil does the chap *do*?' he would ask his companions at convivial evenings in the Garrick Club. 'Work,' came the answer, and Sir William Waring would shake his head, more in sorrow than anger.

'I need not tell you, Ward,' he said now, scowling at Gabriel, 'that this is all extremely unfortunate for the reputation of the Inner Temple. The timing could not be more inconvenient.'

Catching Gabriel's quizzical expression, he hastened into a more appropriate comment. 'All very dreadful of course, and naturally, I am greatly concerned for the safety of our members and servants. I am very aware of the sense of fear that is pervasive. I have instructed the porters to be extra vigilant and ordered the lamplighter to ensure all the lamps are lit at night, rather than only those in the more populated areas.' And then, his true concerns surfacing once more, 'We simply cannot have this sort of scandal just now, with the summer calendar in full swing. The Middle Temple, of course, is gloating over it.'

It was midday on the day Lord Dunning's body had been discovered and Gabriel, submerged once more in the still intractable case of *Cadamy v Moore* in which he had a consultation that very afternoon, had obeyed Waring's mysterious summons with extreme reluctance. He now made a non-committal noise and wondered if he could somehow look surreptitiously at his pocket watch.

Sir William glared at him. 'It is vital for our standing in the eyes of the world, I am sure you will agree, that we all pull together.'

Dreadful clichéd expression, whispered Gabriel's inner lawyer. Other than its obvious nautical origins what *does* it intend to convey? He shook his head again, this time at the vagaries of metaphor, and then, recalling the question, nodded it hastily instead.

'I will not have policemen crawling all over the Inner Temple, nosing into the business of those who reside and work here,' said Sir William severely. 'There is enough anxiety as it is. The servants are insisting that they will not walk about alone, barristers are locking their chambers for the first time in history, and as for the judiciary... there is little short of panic in the Law Courts.'

He fiddled with the paperweight on his desk and looked slightly defensive. Gabriel waited, not without curiosity; Sir William never fiddled and his inner confidence was such that he seldom seemed to feel the need to defend himself. Previously a judge of the High Court, he had retired early because he had wanted very much indeed to be Treasurer. It would not be quite fair to say he had worked hard for the appointment, since the necessary qualities came so naturally to him. He was by nature a courteous juggernaut, the preservation of the reputation of the Inner Temple coming second only to that of himself. Diplomatic, even emollient, so long as he was not crossed. Ruthless if he was.

Under his rule, the Inner Temple had flourished: its estate beautifully tended, its historic portraits and silver immaculately restored, its dinners grander, its wine cellars increasingly distinguished, its gardens lusher, invitations to its social events more eagerly sought after. If there were those (and Gabriel was one) who thought wistfully of gentler days when the gardens, though beautiful, were overgrown and the sense of history in the dilapidated buildings seemed strong enough to touch, they were in the minority. On the whole, it was felt, Sir William was doing a good job. And sunning himself in this approval Sir William sought to consolidate his position with larger and larger plans for aggrandisement.

Now he said, 'You are aware of the very special status of the Inner and Middle Temple, are you not, Ward?'

Gabriel was now on firm ground. 'Yes indeed, Sir William, I have studied it in some depth. The Temple, Inner and Middle, was owned by the crusading Knights Templar in the twelfth century and thereafter inherited by the lawyers. It is within the boundaries of the City of London, yet it is an independent enclave in rather the same manner as the Vatican is in Rome. It is one of the ancient so-called Liberties: by law, free from the jurisdiction of the Mayor and Corporation of London. It is exempt from all civil and ecclesiastical jurisdictions and governed by its own parliaments. Our own little world. It holds great romance, does it not?'

Sir William did not have a romantic bone in his body.

'Yes, yes,' he said testily. 'But more to the point, flowing from its special status has been a responsibility for our own policing. The City of London Police enter only with our consent. My view is that this appalling crime should, initially at least, be investigated internally by a senior member of our community. It is a sensitive matter, of course. We would not wish to be seen as usurping the role of the police and nor do I wish the Inner Temple to be seen as a backward-looking institution in this modern era. Progress, that is the word that must guide us. Progress and prestige!'

Gabriel was silent.

Sir William slid effortlessly into one of his remorseless diatribes from which, famously in the Inn, there was no escape.

'We know, do we not, that no member of the Inner Temple, far less one of the senior members with whom the Lord Chief Justice dined, could have committed this outrage? Our security must have been breached. However, we must concede that the weapon was one of the Inner Temple carving knives and the body was found here. All timings and opportunities within our community must be checked, for appearances' sake. I have expressed these views to the City of London Police Commissioner, with whom, fortunately, I have some acquaintance through dinners in the City. I am pleased to say the Commissioner has agreed with me that we should make some brief initial enquiries with the family and amongst our own members, and he has assigned a constable to assist us, if necessary. All relevant findings will be reported to the City of London Police, who will then take over the external investigations, which will no doubt lead to the discovery of the intruder. The press, meanwhile, must be kept at bay for a few days. I shall have a notice posted.'

He paused for breath. 'We take the view that the appropriate barrister to make these initial enquiries should be one who has an alibi, rendering him above even notional suspicion. I have chosen you.'

'Me?' Gabriel's voice rose in horror.

'Yes, Ward, you.'

'But I couldn't possibly.'

'You are a barrister with a highly trained analytical mind and a reputation for exceptional forensic objectivity. Furthermore, I understand that at the scene of this appalling murder you betrayed some considerable knowledge of crime detection. Though how,' said Sir William tartly, 'since you have specialised in only the most arcane subjects of civil law, I cannot imagine.'

'I have just read about it,' said Gabriel meekly. 'I have read about most things.'

The Treasurer snorted.

'And I have no alibi,' Gabriel added hopefully.

Sir William smiled grimly. 'You have an alibi, Ward, of a nature that I believe policemen refer to as cast-iron. Your habits are well known in the Inn and your profile seen through your window as you work is very familiar to us all. I am informed by one resident of Paper Buildings, a most reliable member of the Bar whose windows overlook your own, that last night you were seen working as usual from six o'clock in the evening continuously until half-past midnight, when you rose from your desk and extinguished the light. The light in your bedroom was then seen to be lit and you were observed standing at the window in your nightshirt.' He paused triumphantly.

'Sir William, I am no detective but if we do not know when Lord Dunning died, how does that assist in providing me with an alibi?'

'Aha!' Sir William liked to be the one to provide answers. 'It so happens, Ward, that the same gentlemen who observed you going to your bedroom at twelve-thirty also saw that lying outside One Crown Office Row was a long dark shape. He is quite certain that it had not been there when he looked out at about eleven o'clock. However, he was aware that some gentlemen were moving from their chambers at Two Crown Office Row and the porters were working late. I fear he mistook Lord Dunning's body for a roll of carpet and thought no more of it until he heard the tragic news. Then he came to me with the whole story. You are therefore exonerated, and ideal for the role of investigator.'

Gabriel opened his mouth to ask how Sir William knew the mysterious shape had *not* indeed been a roll of carpet. But he quickly realised that it would be dangerous to reveal even the smallest talent for detection. Instead he said: 'Investigation? You mean like Sherlock Holmes?'

'Who is Sherlock Holmes?' said Sir William, who never read anything but the *Law Reports*.

'He is the hero in the novels and short stories by Mr Conan Doyle. Very good they are too. I recommend them.'

Sir William snorted again, this time dismissively. 'No one is asking you to emulate a fictional hero. We are merely asking you to do a little gentle questioning within the Inner Temple community, and to report your findings to me and to the police. We know that Norman Dunning dined last night in the Inn and that his body was found by you this morning, yards from the entrance to the Great Hall. He had dined with me. It was one of my Little Dinners, you know.'

He said it in the capital letters it deserved, and Gabriel did know. All the Inner Temple knew about the Treasurer's Little Dinners. These occasions took place in circumstances of extreme formality regarded by the more irreverent members of the Inner Temple as close to ludicrous. The guests, never more than six, sat in the Great Hall, closed to lesser members of the Inn for the occasion, all ninety-four feet of it stretching in cavernous emptiness before them. They sat at High Table, designed for forty dining in comfort. White-tie evening dress was worn. The food was excellent, the wines sublime; the port, in particular, legendary. The price extracted for these pleasures was high. Sir William's strategies for manipulation of power in the Inner Temple were discussed and those present implicitly charged with carrying them out.

'The guests were the Reverend Master of the Temple Church Reverend Vernon-Osbert, Lord Justice Wilson, Lord Justice Brown and Sir Vivian Barton KC. The Lord Chief Justice was our guest of honour. We had a delicate matter to discuss, which had no bearing whatsoever on the subsequent tragic event and with which you need not trouble yourself. However, I suggest you obtain information as to our movements from each of the others before you do so from me. Justice requires detachment and independence of thought, eh?'

Gabriel bowed in silent response to this observation. Despite its triteness, it happened to be one he agreed with.

'You will of course verify this, but I can tell you that Lord Dunning left my Little Dinner at about ten-forty-five. The period we must investigate is between that time and half-past midnight. You have one week. You will report back to me next Tuesday.'

He paused to allow comment, but Gabriel was speechless. It occurred to him that throughout their encounter, Sir William had not expressed the slightest personal regret for the murder of the Lord Chief Justice, a man he had known personally for many years.

'May I suggest you begin by talking to the cook in Inner Temple kitchens to verify the timing of dinner and the whereabouts of the knife,' Sir William continued. 'You can follow this up with a visit to Lady Dunning and that eccentric sister of his to ascertain such matters as what time they were expecting Dunning home and whether they can shed any light on his footwear, or indeed lack of it. They live in Stafford Terrace. Kensington, you know.'

'Kensington!' cried Gabriel, who, save for professional attendances across the road at the Royal Courts of Justice, had not left the precincts of the Temple for some years.

'Yes,' said Sir William inexorably, 'Kensington.'

'And they are both women!' cried Gabriel miserably. To him, all women were rolled together into one bewildering being comprising the stifling love of his Nanny and the neglect of his mother.

'Really,' said the Treasurer (who had two daughters, a wife and a mistress, not to mention the occasional diversion), on recounting this interview to his cronies with a sneer, 'the man couldn't have sounded more appalled if I had suggested he popped across to a brothel in Paris to interview the inmates.'

In his horror Gabriel became resolute. 'I am sorry, Master Treasurer, I cannot do this. I am quite exceptionally busy. I have a most interesting and difficult new case. It will require an enormous amount of preparation. In fact, I have a consultation this very afternoon. I must respectfully decline to conduct the investigation. There is absolutely no question of it.' And this time he did look at his pocket watch.

In the silence that followed, the Treasurer bowed his head in seeming acquiescence and slowly swivelled his desk chair until he was able to gaze obliquely across the Terrace.

'What a beautiful afternoon,' he observed urbanely, 'and how delightful the soft red brick of King's Bench Walk looks in the sunshine. Wren designed it, I believe?'

'Yes indeed,' said Gabriel, happily returning once more to firm ground. 'Little is known about the architects responsible for most of the buildings in King's Bench Walk, but Sir Christopher Wren almost certainly personally designed Number Four where I am fortunate enough to live.'

'Fortunate indeed. A tenant of the Inn for over thirty years, are you not? Many would envy you your residence. Indeed, many do. How comfortable and settled you must feel there after all this time. But,' and here the Treasurer swivelled his chair back to face Gabriel's, 'it is a fact of life, I'm sure you'll agree, that all good things may come to an end?'

It seemed to Gabriel that the sunshine pouring through Sir William's window had suddenly dimmed, although there were no clouds to be seen in the flawless blue sky.

Sir William rose from his desk and Gabriel rose too, as though they were attached; the Treasurer made for the door, and Gabriel followed; and there Sir William turned so sharply that Gabriel stumbled backwards. The Treasurer laid a hand on his arm to steady him and smiled.

'I have enjoyed our talk, Ward, and I shall look forward to hearing of your progress with Mrs Bugg, who is expecting you. We have reached an understanding, have we not?'

And he opened the door and ushered Gabriel out.

6

At first the reality was far, far worse than any imagining. Trapped against the cold stone wall of the ancient kitchen, Gabriel gazed transfixed through the steam at the Inner Temple cook, twice his size in every direction, her face red and shining, a rough protective covering wrapped around her ample waist over the immaculate white of her apron and a meat cleaver dripping blood in one hand. When she spoke, however, her voice was surprisingly cordial.

'I am very grateful to you, Sir Gabriel,' she said, 'for being so kind to our Annie this morning.'

'A-Annie?'

'Yes, my sister, you remember? What a terrible thing to see, bless her. Quite distraught she was when your Mr Chapman brought her here, sobbing and shivering and not much sense could I get out of her, but Sir Gabriel Ward, she said, had been that kind and told her there was no need to take on…'

'Annie!' said Gabriel in triumph as he at last identified the name. Surely, his inner lawyer thought, he could never, ever have told Annie not to 'take on'? Take on what? Or was it where?

Mrs Bugg now beamed at him and put down the meat cleaver and he felt a little more confident.

'I hope she is recovered,' he ventured.

'She is still beside herself.' (Be quiet, said Gabriel to his inner lawyer.) 'She's not stopped crying since. Annie, I said to her, it's not as though you knew the poor gentleman and now you must put it out of your mind. But there, she has always been a one for getting in a state and so I said to Mr Chapman, we must just let her rest at home for a day or two. It was the feet that upset her most, you know. On and on, she kept sobbing: "The feet, the feet." Quite spooky it was. Thank gawd she never saw the knife.' She looked at Gabriel round-eyed. 'My gawd, the knife, Sir Gabriel! No doubt about it, one of ours. Many's the time I've seen it, dripping with blood from the gentlemen's beef! And now it is not the beef.' She shuddered, with some fear and not a little relish. 'Murder on our doorstep! Horrible to think of.'

'Yes, the knife. It is the knife that Master Treasurer has asked me to speak to you about.' Gabriel shifted hastily away from the dangerous bog of human emotion and onto the firm ground of fact. 'Where did you last see the knife?' He felt quite proud of this resolute and professional-sounding question.

'I had it sharpened only that morning and it went up as always with the joint for the gentlemen's dinner.'

'How is the food sent up?' asked Gabriel curiously. During the many dinners he had attended over the years, he had never really given a thought to the process by which his exquisitely prepared food had arrived from the cavernous kitchens to the silver and crystal and candlelight of the Hall.

Mrs Bugg gestured towards a short passageway, in which could be glimpsed an elaborate contraption operated by ropes on pulleys.

'Our service lift,' she said proudly.

'And the time of dinner?'

'Seven-thirty to sit down at eight,' she said. She nodded towards the large wall clock. 'We always begins when Reginald says it is eight o'clock. I winds him every week, bless him.'

'Reginald?'

'After my husband,' said Mrs Bugg with a beam. 'Always right. And a good thing too, until Sir William at last gets the library clock repaired.'

Gabriel nodded appreciatively. The Temple's days had been punctuated for centuries by the sonorous chime of the clock on the library tower. Two weeks ago, however, the great hands had stopped and the clock had lapsed into uncanny silence. Always on the lookout for a bargain, Sir William had employed a series of incompetent workmen who had so far elicited only intermittent and undignified chirrups from the timepiece, to the hilarity of residents and staff.

'The china and cutlery comes down after the meal for Meg to start the washing-up and we leaves the gentlemen with the cheese, and port in the decanters ready for when they want it.'

She led him through the service-lift passage to the small scullery adjoining the kitchen where Gabriel saw a wispy girl bent over the vast Belfast sink full of pans, her arms deep in suds, head almost lost in clouds of steam. At the cook's command she turned reluctantly, dripping, from the sink to face her questioners. She seemed, thought Gabriel, as nervous as he was.

'And did you wash up the carving knife?' he asked her.

Meg nodded vigorously. 'I washed it up along of the others, and I polished the horse on the handle like I always do, and then I put it all away like I always do.'

She indicated the narrow, mullioned window above the sink behind her, the only ventilation in the scullery. Beside it hung a huge rack with the knives of the Inner Temple *batterie de cuisine* arranged in regimental rows of diminishing size, each carefully inserted so that facing outwards on each handle shone the inlaid silver Pegasus emblem.

Gabriel walked over and peered through the window. It looked out onto the long passage between the wall of Crown Office Row on one side and that of the kitchen on the other. At the end of it was poky medieval Fig Tree Court.

The passage was barely wider than a man's shoulders, the back kitchen door and window being the only feature on the north side. Directly opposite was the equally small window of the clerks' room of his own chambers on the south side.

The kitchen window was ajar, detritus on the ledge suggesting that this was a long-standing state of affairs. The knife rack was easily accessible to any passer-by.

'Who closes this at night?' asked Gabriel.

'It's never closed, sir,' said the girl, looking astonished. 'Why should we close it? There's only the barristers and the servants here. The porters are at the gates. We never need to worry when we are in the Temple, sir.' She hesitated. 'At least up until now. Mrs Bugg has told us kitchen staff that we must always be in pairs. That doesn't seem right, does it, sir, here where it has always been safe?'

Gabriel warmed to her; this child, it seemed, felt the same trust in the sanctuary of the Temple that he himself felt, and like him, perceived in this horrible crime the loss of its innocence.

'Have you worked here long?' he asked.

'I lives in Clifford Alley off Fleet Street. My father is one of the Temple porters and my mother is Violet, the laundress who cleans Fig Tree Court. I've allus known the Temple.'

'And what time did you leave last night?'

'A quarter to midnight,' she said promptly.

'How are you so sure of the time?'

'I looked at the clock,' she said simply. 'I left to meet my father so he could walk me home. He finished his duty at eleven o'clock and then he went to the Cock in Fleet Street for a drink in the landlord's back room. "You make sure you're at the gate at midnight," he says to me; yes, I thought, and you'll get to drinking and talking and you'll be late. And he was.' She smiled at Gabriel with kindly womanly wisdom. 'He'll be late for his own funeral, my mother says, bless him.'

Working in that airless kitchen until late at night... how old would she be? Fourteen? Perhaps fifteen? Gabriel looked at the wispy, determined little figure and thought of his own life at fourteen.

'Did you see anything after you left?' he asked uncomfortably.

Meg shook her head. 'I didn't see nothing. I came out the scullery door and went through Fig Tree Court and Elm Court up to Middle Temple Lane, and then I waited by the gate for my father till he came.'

Gabriel was no detective but he was a barrister of thirty years' standing. Now he looked at her and saw what he had seen in a hundred witnesses in a hundred courts: the little mottled flush of pink at the base of her throat; the eyes that slid sideways; the slightly too quick answer; the hands that gripped her apron, as he had seen hands grip the rail on the front of the witness box countless times. And because he was not a detective but a barrister, he left it just where it was; pressing witnesses too far only served to entrench them. Far better to come back to it later.

But he knew that she was lying.

7

In the early afternoon of the day that Lord Dunning's body was found, the publisher Herbert Moore gazed out from his first-floor office on the eastern corner of Chancery Lane and Fleet Street across the manure-strewn road, over the dense traffic of horse-drawn omnibuses and hansom carriages and down towards the Great Gate that led into the Temple. He was contemplating with foreboding his consultation at four o'clock that afternoon with Sir Gabriel Ward KC in connection with an appalling situation for which Moore had only himself to blame.

He had feared, when the news broke, that the death of the Lord Chief Justice on the very steps of Sir Gabriel Ward's chambers might have resulted in the cancellation of this anxiously awaited meeting. But the Temple, although its business was strife, stood serene above the dramas and scandals of the outside world, unmarred by the crime, commerce and human conflict over which its occupants arbitrated; not even violent death would disturb, more than momentarily, its seven hundred years of tranquillity. And if Sir Gabriel Ward had a consultation in his chambers at four o'clock in the afternoon on 21 May, then he would be there, and no death but his own would prevent it.

Moore was a legal publisher and bookseller, the fifth generation of his family to inhabit this eighteenth-century office above a picturesque little shop. With its panelling and corner fireplace and its run of three tall windows looking over Fleet Street, the office summed up the business; the top half of the walls was lined with the leather-bound, gold-tooled spines of the *Official Law Reports*, and beneath them, in cloth-bound covers, was a string of academic legal titles each running into several editions. Moore's published them all, a monopoly that had earned Herbert's family a comfortable living and a solid reputation for the past hundred and fifty years.

It was a room that held all the confidence of tradition: its partners' desk solid and square, its two wing chairs comfortable without being self-indulgent, its Turkish carpet cheerful but restrained, even its coal fire well behaved. On the only portion of wall that was not covered with books was displayed the sole incongruity in this most congruous of rooms: a large painting of a mouse with its inquisitive little head tipped to one side, an expression of slightly cloying sanctimony on its face and, around its neck, nestled in the soft grey fur, a small gold cross. And this mouse, whose expression Herbert had come to loathe, was the problem that now confronted him.

It was a problem that would have caused his father and grandfather great distress but little surprise. 'He has an odd kick in his gallop,' his grandfather, a racing man, had said in his hearing, and the eighteen-year-old Herbert, already feeling the oppressive responsibility of the family firm, had been flattered to think that no one felt he was very reliable. But over the next twenty years he had settled down under the family expectations, and the odd kick had manifested itself only very occasionally in little flashes of defiance. The mouse had been one of them.

Four years earlier, a plain paper parcel had been found on the doorstep of Moore & Sons. A secretary, opening it and discovering what was plainly a manuscript, had deposited it on Herbert's desk. It proved to be a book for children by a Miss Harriet Cadamy, engagingly written, though to Herbert's eyes with rather too obvious a moral message. No explanation was provided as to how the clear error of delivering it to the door of Moore & Sons had come about, and Herbert, having flicked through it, deposited it in a wastepaper basket.

That would have been that, had it not been for the afternoon visit of Herbert's adored daughter Elsie, then eight years old, taken by her mama to a tea party in the Temple and afterwards brought to see Papa in his office. While Mama and Papa discussed the dismissal of the new and already unsatisfactory coachman who on being instructed to take Elsie and Mama to the Temple had gone halfway to a synagogue in Whitechapel before his mistake was noticed, Elsie was left to her own devices. She had retrieved *Millie the Temple Church Mouse* from the ignominy of the wastepaper basket and had sat enthralled as the simple plot unfolded, ultimately begging not to be parted from the volume. She was allowed to take it home. Millie became her world, and her father, exhibiting his odd kick, decided to publish it in the face of astonished disapproval from his staff, and to display it beside the usual legal tomes in his shop window as a Christmas gimmick.

Millie the Mouse, born in a hole in the round nave of the Temple Church to loving mouse parents, had grown up to become, thanks to her early exposure to the beauties of the Temple services, a devout mouse dedicated to performing acts of kindness for the congregation. These acts, necessarily limited in scope by her species and size, nonetheless assumed saintly proportions in the hands of Miss Cadamy. A little child who had been cold during a winter service had her feet warmed when Millie curled up on her ankles; an unhappy man was consoled to discover Millie sitting comfortingly in the pew beside him; a lost hymn book was found by Millie whose heroic and ultimately successful attempts to push it out from under the choirstalls took up quite two pages. All church festivals provided Millie with the opportunity to contribute to the beauty of the service in one way or another. She was a Christmas mouse, a Harvest Festival mouse, an Easter mouse. Her surreptitious attendance at a christening and a confirmation had resulted in both these blessings being bestowed upon her as well as on the official recipient. Each chapter was moralistic, educative, redolent of the tenets of the Anglican tradition.

The book had been an instant, raging success. No child could resist it; mothers and governesses endorsed it. Herbert's tentative first print run of two hundred and fifty copies sold out in a few days. He printed more and more. He printed thousands. He could not print enough. An artist had painted a picture of Millie, the original of which had been presented to the firm. It now hung on Herbert's wall, while prints of it held pride of place in children's bedrooms everywhere. Within six months the Temple Church congregation had swelled to become almost unmanageable. Children from all over England begged to be taken there in hopes of encountering Millie, and the bewildered Master of the Temple Church, the Reverend Vernon-Osbert, now had to adapt his sermons to the needs of large families.

It was, said *The Times* newspaper, one of the greatest (if rather unaccountable) publishing phenomena of the century. Sales of Mr Kipling's *Jungle Book* were rapidly overtaken by those of *Millie the Mouse*; the famous German toymakers, Steiff, had purchased the rights to make Millies; and Mr Hamley, the proprietor of the great London toyshop, had paid very handsomely for the sole right to display in his Regent Street windows the resulting irresistibly dumpy, furry Millies, with their boot-button eyes, wire whiskers and small crosses of real gold. The queues to buy a Millie had stopped the traffic up to Oxford Circus. One of the most famous impresarios in London was even now preparing for the West End opening of a musical play of the book. And then, only a couple of days ago, had come another significant endorsement: Mr George M. Hill, Chicago publisher of *The Wonderful Wizard of Oz*, which was currently captivating America, had paid a vast sum for the right to publish *Millie the*

Temple Church Mouse throughout the USA. Millie was soon to become an international success, announced the newspapers.

Before publishing the book, Herbert Moore had placed a discreetly worded advertisement in *The Times* in a genuine attempt to trace Miss Harriet Cadamy, who had written upon the manuscript nothing but her name. The attempt had failed. Anticipating the modest sale of a few hundred copies and with a passing resolution to set aside a small sum for royalties should Miss Cadamy eventually turn up, Herbert had gone ahead and published.

Millie had made Moore & Sons a fortune. Miss Cadamy had never materialised; and gradually Herbert had become inured to the doubtful legality of signing contracts in her name. It all happened with a speed that made his head spin but soon the prim signature became as familiar to him as his own and, having invented for the increasingly rapacious press and public a reclusive, devout Miss Cadamy who shunned all publicity and lived in an unspecified and conveniently remote village, he really grew quite fond of her.

The solicitor's letter had therefore come as something of a shock. Couched in highly technical language, the underlying threat was clear. The writer had the honour to act for Miss Susan Hatchings, the creator of *Millie the Temple Church Mouse* written under the pseudonym Harriet Cadamy. Miss Hatchings, then resident of the Hebridean Island of Mull where she had been wholly devoted to the care of her now sadly deceased mother, had mislaid her manuscript four years ago while in London. She had only recently, upon her remove to Edinburgh, and to her great astonishment, become aware of its wholly unauthorised publication and its great success. She felt now, mingled with her pride as an authoress, an (in the eyes of the writer) understandable outrage that this had come about with neither her knowledge nor her consent, and a not unnatural interest, it was suggested, in the whereabouts of what must by now be astronomical sums of money arising therefrom.

It was seldom that Herbert Moore felt real panic, but he had felt it then. The proceeds of *Millie the Temple Church Mouse* had rescued Moore's at a difficult time. The centuries-old lease on the building in which the firm was housed had come to an end, and the booming newspaper industry had rendered Fleet Street property surprisingly expensive; but, with new-found financial confidence, Herbert had fought off hot competition from the *Sunday Post*, negotiated a new lease, and then gone on not only to buy the freehold, but to expand into the house next door.

The business had also expanded. He thought with a shudder of the numerous highly complex contracts into which he had entered in Harriet Cadamy's name, the huge sums of money involved and the renowned companies who had relied upon those contracts to enter into further transactions in their turn. An obligation to recompense both Miss Hatchings and the businessmen who had trusted him could ruin Moore's. The publicity and reputational damage did not bear thinking about.

'What can I have done wrong?' In his anxiety, he said it aloud. Millie had not been his creation. He had acknowledged that. He had tried unsuccessfully to find the author; but had he done enough? What was enough? He had had no contract with her. He had made all the decisions relating to the publication of her book with no authorisation of any kind. The many agreements he had signed had been not in her name but in that of Miss Cadamy, who did not, apparently, exist. Was that dishonest? Could it be fraud? What about all the subsidiary profits that had arisen, from the prints, the toys, the foreign rights? All those had been obtained by his own skilful negotiations when he recognised the book's potential. Were they therefore Moore's or were they Miss Hatchings'? Visions of a prison sentence with hard labour, of disgrace, of little Elsie's trusting face, swam before Herbert's eyes.

8

When he sat, at four o'clock that afternoon, with Anthony Dawson, his sleek, unsympathetic solicitor and senior partner of Dawson, Dawson & Dawson, in Gabriel's comforting higgledy-piggledy panelled room in Crown Office Row, with its crooked door and window frames contrasting with the immaculate tidiness of the desk, with its wide dark oak floorboards, its ticking grandfather clock and its dripping tap, it was the first thing he asked.

'What exactly have I done wrong?' he enquired plaintively.

Gabriel snuffled approvingly.

'That, if I may so,' he said, 'is a very good question. Indeed, it goes to the heart of the matter. It might be argued that, morally, you have done nothing wrong. Legally, the question becomes more difficult. Whose book is this? That is the question. As Mr Dawson will have told you, the copyright principle is nearly as old as time: sixth-century Irish law, you know, and the judgment relating to the Cathach psalter: "*To every cow belongs her calf, therefore to every book belongs its copy…*"'

Dawson shifted impatiently in his chair and scowled. That was the trouble with instructing Ward: he had the infuriating habit of coming up with the most obscure legal knowledge accompanied by an even more infuriating assumption that everybody else shared it; he made one look a fool.

Gabriel continued pensively, 'So the first question in your case, Mr Moore, relates to the identity of the author. It could be the plaintiff, Miss Hatchings, writing under a pseudonym; or

Miss Hatchings could be an imposter, in which case the name Harriet Cadamy may be a pseudonym for someone else; or there could be an author who really is called Harriet Cadamy. So the first thing that Miss Hatchings must prove is that she wrote the book using that particular pseudonym. And to do that, she must explain the very odd circumstances of its reaching Moore & Sons. Did she abandon the manuscript? Or lose it? Or leave it deliberately? If she cannot explain all these things satisfactorily, the book is really the equivalent of an anonymous manuscript. In that event, the law is that the publisher is ultimately deemed to hold the copyright.'

Herbert Moore sat up in his chair and began to look a little more hopeful.

'I fear there will be little real difficulty about establishing authorship,' said Dawson. 'Of course, we are at an early stage. I must carefully investigate Miss Hatchings' case to see if her story holds water. But she is represented by very respectable solicitors and by Sir Vivian Barton KC. Surely she would have to be mad to think she could get away with a claim like this if it is false? So far, we have found no reason to doubt she is the author writing under a pseudonym.'

Herbert's hopes began to fade and he wilted.

'But even if Miss Hatchings does prove she wrote the book,' Gabriel continued, 'it is still by no means clear upon what she bases her claim. What kind of legal right or remedy is triggered by these unusual circumstances?'

Herbert began to feel as though he was on a switchback railway in a fairground. Did lawyers always change direction in this dizzying way?

'I wish there were fewer questions and more answers,' he said, and put his head in his hands.

'Well,' said Gabriel, 'what I am saying is that even if she did write the book, she must have a proper remedy in law and at present I am not sure what it is. You simply came by the book. It is not a breach of contract between author and publisher since there was no contract. There is no indebtedness between the parties. There is no claim on the basis of undue influence, nor mistake—'

'But I don't want to know what it *isn't*,' said Herbert miserably. 'I want to know what it *is*.'

'Well,' said Gabriel, 'if Miss Hatchings can establish that she is the author, I cannot conceal, Mr Moore, that I think your situation will be very grave. A judge would undoubtedly be sympathetic to her position and would look for a way to compensate her. But he must do so within the parameters of existing case law. He cannot just make it up as he goes along. He has to find a precedent for the decisions he makes. My researches into whether such a precedent exists have so far been preliminary. That is why I say I am uncertain as to the basis of her claim. It really is a unique case that will require many hours of thought and research prior to trial.'

'But how much?' persisted Herbert, anxiously going to what seemed to him to be the heart of the matter. 'How much will the judge make me pay if Miss Hatchings proves she wrote the book?'

'I fear,' said Gabriel patiently, 'that even that is hard to answer. There have been so many complex contracts with totally innocent parties. A court would have to attempt to trace the proceeds in their entirety…'

Herbert remembered with awful clarity the distinguished businesses who might have a claim against him, all lining up…

And as though reading his thoughts, Gabriel said soberly, 'Mr Moore, Mr Dawson will, I am sure, do all he can to check on the veracity of the claim and I will do my best in court, with the material he provides, to try and establish that it is unfounded. But if we do not succeed, I must warn you that Miss Hatchings' case may only be the first in a long chain of litigation.'

'And all this,' said Dawson sourly, 'is no doubt going to cost my client another vast sum of money in fees?'

This was a truly frightful professional solecism. Dawson knew very well that no barrister played any part in the negotiation of his fees.

'I could not possibly discuss that matter,' said Gabriel, retreating firmly into his shell like the tortoise he so closely resembled. 'You must talk to Chapman.' And he shook them both by the hand and ushered them out.

Dawson left Gabriel's door wide open and flung across the hallway into the clerks' room.

'Well, Chapman,' Gabriel heard his raised voice say, as he was intended to, 'your master is far too grand to discuss his fees. What extortionate amount are you going to extract for him to represent Mr Moore when his case comes to court?'

Gabriel closed his door firmly on the discussion, only to have it opened a few minutes later by Chapman.

'And after all that,' said his clerk without preamble, 'there is now a policeman waiting outside chambers for you.'

'A policeman?' Gabriel snuffled. 'Good heavens, Chapman, surely you did not ask Mr Dawson for so much money that we are to be arrested?'

'Very amusing, sir. I imagine the officer has called in connection with the Lord Chief Justice's death.'

It was nearly six o'clock. Gabriel always went home at nearly six o'clock. Not even the death of the Lord Chief Justice could break his routine. He tidied the papers on his desk, turned the inkwell so that the hinges on its silver top were precisely aligned with the edge of the perpetual calendar that stood next to it, placed his gold pencil (with the lead pointing towards the window) in the shallow tortoiseshell case that housed it, put on his top hat and emerged blinking into the early-evening light.

9

Standing by the wall outside was a solid figure in policeman's uniform who now removed his helmet and approached, blushing and diffident.

'Constable Maurice Wright, sir, of the City of London Police. From this morning, sir? The police surgeon has examined the body of Lord Norman Dunning and I have been asked to bring you his report. And I am told to assist you.'

'Assist me? With what?' said Gabriel.

'With your enquiries, sir.'

'Good heavens,' said Gabriel mildly. 'What am I supposed to do with you?'

'Well, sir, I can accompany you when you interview members of the Inn and discuss it with you afterwards. Two heads, you know, sir.'

'I have never thought that the remainder of that expression was necessarily correct,' said Gabriel, diverted. 'Does it not depend wholly on the quality of each of the heads?'

Police Constable Wright shook his in bewilderment.

'I don't quite understand you, sir.'

'I will let you know if you can help me with anything,' said Gabriel dismissively, taking from him the slim report; he was turning away when Wright, pinker than ever, laid a hand on his arm to detain him.

'And I wanted to show you something, sir, because of what you said this morning – about the Roman chap?'

'The Roman chap?'

'Yes, sir, and the fingermarks?'

'Ah, yes,' said Gabriel, the light dawning. 'Quintilian, one of the greatest orators of them all. Are you familiar with his wonderful work *Institutio Oratoria*?'

'I don't know any foreign langwidges, sir, but after what you said I went to have another look. I want to show you something,' Constable Wright persisted. 'Right here, sir, by the door.'

He pointed to a spot bare of the ivy that festooned most of the doorway to 1 Crown Office Row.

Gabriel peered around the old stone pillar, and there, on the back of it about five feet from the ground, was a handprint, reddish-brown on the pale surface. The imprint of a palm, scored with lines, was discernible, though the fingers, obviously applied to the surface with less pressure, were mere ghostly outlines.

'It is blood, sir,' said Wright. His voice sank almost to a whisper. 'Do you suppose it is the Lord Chief Justice's blood, sir? Or that of the murderer himself?'

Gabriel shook his head. 'I fear there is no way of telling whose blood it is, though I believe science may one day be able to assist us. Certainly, it seems…' He paused, while his inner lawyer ran through the possible standards of proof: possible? Probable? Beyond doubt? 'Highly probable,' he concluded carefully, 'given where the body was found, that it is the blood of one or the other.'

'I took a picture of it, sir, and I developed it this afternoon,' said Wright eagerly. 'I have just bought one of the new Brownie box cameras. I saved up for it for months.'

'How very modern of you, Constable Wright,' said Gabriel. He looked curiously at the grainy little black-and-white print proffered to him on which the image of the hand appeared with surprising accuracy.

Despite the warmth of the evening sun and the grace of his surroundings he felt something close to a shudder. He wanted urgently to be at home in King's Bench Walk, in his familiar room, in the wing chair that had been in his family for centuries, surrounded by his books, in the safety of solitude. He gripped his fingers firmly around the envelope he held, lest the policeman had noticed the shudder; brought back to reality, he remembered the nature of its contents.

'We had better open this report,' he said. And then added in his quaint, courteous way, 'Perhaps you would care to come back to my rooms where we can study it in privacy?'

Constable Wright followed him readily across the Terrace, noticing as he did so Gabriel's slow and careful negotiation of the paving stones. Then they were at the doorstep of 4 King's Bench Walk. It was not the poky old building the policeman had been expecting: in front of him were a generous, light-filled hallway and a broad staircase. On the first floor Gabriel fumbled in his waistcoat pocket for the iron key that opened a vast oak door under the legend *Sir Gabriel Ward KC* painted across the lintel, and thus revealed the inner door – complete with doorknocker and letterbox and a brass sign engraved: *All telegrams to the Porters' Lodge* – which he edged open.

'You'll have to breathe in a little, I fear,' he said.

Obediently squeezing after him into a small hallway, Constable Wright gave a gasp of astonishment. Ranged in teetering mountains to three sides of them were books. Through the open door that led to the large, square-panelled drawing room, he could see occasional pieces of once elegant furniture emerging like the tops of wrecks from an undulating ocean of volumes on shelves until they had run out, on tables until they were full, in piles on the beautiful old rugs so that they covered all but the meagre amount of floor space absolutely necessary to permit a small man to move around.

For Gabriel was a traveller. Not of the pith helmet and bamboo stick variety, nor even of the Baedeker guide and Gladstone bag kind, but a traveller in the mind, scaling the mountains of learning created by historians and philosophers, scientists and poets and novelists. The books in Number Four King's Bench Walk were friends into whose warm embrace he fell every evening and who held him until bedtime at half-past midnight every night. Few knew of these travels, since Gabriel read not to acquire knowledge, nor to impart it, but simply because he could not help himself.

'Crikey, sir!' said Wright. 'The books!'

'Do you feel there are too many?' he said. 'They accumulate, you see, and I like to revisit them.'

'I like them,' said Constable Wright unexpectedly. 'They give me a funny feeling. All those people who have learned things over hundreds of years and written them down.'

Gabriel nodded approvingly.

'Of course, I couldn't read them myself, though I really want to know things, sir. But it is hard for a man like me. How do I find things out? I was only taught my letters and my sums at school, and I never owned a book.'

Gabriel found his own world hard enough to fathom; this glimpse into another was so alien to him he found nothing he could contribute.

'Please do sit down,' he said, removing from the seat of what turned out to be a chair four volumes of the complete works of Shakespeare, which he piled on top of Phipson on *The Law of Evidence* upon the floor. Wright sat down and removed his helmet, placing it awkwardly on his knee.

'Would you care for a small sherry?' Gabriel enquired, reaching for the decanter and glasses balanced on top of an improbable pile consisting of Chitty on *The Law of Contract*,

Alice's Adventures in Wonderland and a little-known three-volume biography of Lord Melbourne.

Now off-duty, it was time for Constable Wright's nightly beer, but he gingerly held out his large pink hand to take the exquisite stem of the eighteenth-century sherry glass proffered to him. Sipping the pale liquid, he tried to hide a slight grimace.

'I do hope it is not too dry for you?'

'No, sir, thank you,' said Constable Wright, whose mother had brought him up to be polite. 'It is really quite wet.'

Gabriel looked at him rather sharply; Constable Wright looked back. And suddenly Gabriel chuckled. He did not often chuckle, but when he did, it was immensely charming. Without knowing why, Wright beamed, and they sat for a few seconds in a silence that was of a different, almost companionable, nature.

Gabriel withdrew the report from its envelope and began to read aloud the contents.

'"*At the police mortuary I examined the body of a well-nourished man in his fifties…*"' He broke off. This then, ultimately, was Lord Norman Dunning, Lord Chief Justice of England, all his fame and hard work and ambition and wealth now reduced by death to this simple categorisation.

'Claudian,' he said softly to himself. '*Omnia mors aequat.*' And to the policeman sitting expectantly awaiting the rest of the report, 'Death levels all things.'

He resumed reading.

'… *The body was attired in full evening dress. The feet were bare. Examination revealed no injuries of any kind save for:*

'*1: very minor abrasions on the soles of the dusty feet, consistent with walking barefoot on a rough surface;*

'*2: a single stab wound to the chest just below the left nipple;*

'*3: a small linear wound on the palm of the right hand, consistent with a gesture of self-defence just before or at the time of the infliction of the stab wound referred to above.*

'*The weapon that had reportedly been removed at the scene was a very narrow carving knife, the blade worn with age and sharpening, and both the wounds were consistent with infliction by this weapon.*

'*With regard to the main stab wound to the chest, the knife had penetrated between the underlying ribs, pierced the intercostal muscles and directly entered the left ventricle of the heart. The pericardial cavity contained some blood.*

'*The wound had been inflicted with great precision and at close range, and its angle is suggestive of a tall assailant who inflicted it while face to face with the victim.*

'*Death would have been close to instantaneous, although the deceased might have been able to stagger a few steps after being stabbed. I am informed that the body was found at seven a.m. I estimate that death would have occurred about six to nine hours prior to that.*'

Gabriel looked quizzically at the police officer. 'Death between ten in the evening and one o'clock the next morning according to the medical professional, and between ten-forty-five and half-past midnight according to Sir William Waring. But we can do better, can we not, Constable? Thanks to your sharp eyes?'

Wright blushed. 'Yes, sir. Death at eleven-twenty-five.'

'Last seen by Sir William at ten-forty-five. Though the "last seen" may become closer to the time of death as we question the other guests at the Little Dinner and the porters. But at least we know he was dead at eleven-twenty-five.'

'And killed by a hand that was either very lucky or very skilled,' Wright added. 'Stab wounds are usually a messy business. This was a very efficient job; no blood anywhere, sir, except for that handprint on the doorway.'

'Perhaps,' said Gabriel slowly. 'And since it was inflicted face to face, and apparently with no struggle, it suggests, does it not, that Dunning knew the attacker and had no cause to fear him.'

'But it seems from what the doctor says that he was barefoot prior to his death,' mused Constable Wright. 'That's odd. I thought someone had pinched the shoes off the corpse.'

'Yes,' said Gabriel. 'I confess I had made the same assumption. Unlikely though it seemed that anyone could have done such a thing, the alternative seemed far odder.'

'Could the murderer have made him take his shoes off first, sir?'

Gabriel snuffled. 'I have no doubt they were handmade by Lobb in St James', Constable, but surely not so desirable that someone would murder for them?'

'I wasn't thinking that, sir. I was wondering whether someone could have wanted to – to humiliate him, like? Was he the kind of man someone might want to make look a fool, do you think, sir?'

Gabriel looked at him with a dawning respect. 'Yes,' he said, 'I think it could be the case that someone might have wanted to do that. Though I cannot imagine who, nor how it could have come about that he would have acquiesced without a struggle.'

'I will have a search around for those shoes and socks, sir, though I doubt we will find them until we find the murderer. And I will keep an eye out, sir, for anyone who looks as though he might be the culprit.'

Gabriel raised his eyebrows; it seemed to him a naive remark coming from a policeman, even a young one. 'I do not think,' he said, perhaps rather more dismissively than he intended, 'that you can just wander about hoping to identify a murderer, Constable.'

But Wright stood his ground. 'Large jaws, low foreheads, handle-shaped ears, upturned noses – they need to be looked out for, sir, so I have been taught. That is how you spot the criminal type.'

'Ah,' said Gabriel, enlightened, 'Cesare Lombroso.'

'Pardon, sir?'

'He is an Italian doctor who has claimed to be able to identify links between physical appearance and criminal behaviour, although I have to say his evidence is not wholly convincing. Many scientists have expressed doubts about Lombroso's theories.'

'That's it, sir!' exclaimed Wright enthusiastically. 'Lombroso! Funny how all these scientists are foreigners, sir, but that is him and Detective Inspector Hughes told us all about it.'

In his enthusiasm, Gabriel noticed, the young policeman had gained confidence.

The chimneypiece clock chimed the hour. Constable Wright put on his helmet and rose to go. He hovered awkwardly. 'You will tell me, sir,' he said eagerly, 'if you want any other help?'

Gabriel hesitated, and then surprised them both. He spoke shyly. 'I wonder, Constable Wright, would you perhaps be able to assist me tomorrow in finding my way to Stafford Terrace in Kensington?'

IO

The journey to Kensington was an ordeal. On leaving 4 King's Bench Walk the next morning, Gabriel checked three times that his front door was securely closed and felt, along with the familiar little release of tension that followed this long-established ritual, a new sensation. The security of his home seemed suddenly less absolute. Sir William's threat, veiled but unmistakable, was still in the back of his mind. Just the once (he had rules for just the once) he pressed the door three more times. And then he descended the steps to meet the world outside.

He rejected with horror the idea of horse omnibus or underground train, upon neither of which he had ever ventured; finally he and Constable Wright resorted to a hansom cab.

Rattling and swaying along the thronged Strand, Wright silent and respectful beside him, Gabriel looked out on the outside world he so seldom saw. Here, in the packed roads and teeming pavements, in the shouts of the costermongers, in the garish colours of the sea of shop awnings, was a life he did not know or want to know.

Others might have labelled his life short on love, or lonely, or impoverished in a more profound sense than the material. But the fact was that it had suited Gabriel down to the ground, and he was grateful for the empty rooms and rolling parkland of his childhood country home; for the ancient squares, the cloisters, the rickety staircases up to the double oak doors of school and Oxford and the Temple, all so alike that they had been almost indistinguishable; grateful for that seamless life in a changeless environment; grateful for his peaceful sanctuary behind the closed and guarded gates. For the quiet. Above all, for the quiet.

That predictable, privileged background and the substantial trust fund that had come with it had enabled him to give no thought to the necessity of earning a living and set his mind free to revel in the purity of learning.

He had hedged around him in that safe little world many rituals and routines. He did not know why; he knew only that they were a part of him. A grotesque form of superstition in which the order and touch of things insured against failure? A yearning for control over the important things by maintaining a rigid grip on the unimportant? A manifestation of what was, in his working life, such a virtue: his minute attention to detail, his exquisite precision? He could not say. He knew only what he had to do. *Had* to do. He had read, of course, the renowned Mr Sigmund Freud's analysis of *Zwangsneurose*. Read it, as he read everything, with the interest of a scholar. But it had not been in any sort of personal quest for diagnosis, let alone cure. Years ago he had ceased to try to rationalise his inner compulsions and allowed himself instead to be carried along with them like a man floating in a current, wrestling with it only very occasionally when the force threatened to overwhelm him. And so, by accommodation, he had found his own kind of contentment and no longer knew or cared if those rituals and routines were prison bars or crutches.

He seldom thought back, as he was doing now, to his youth – a time, it seemed, spent largely in waiting to be a grown-up. He tried to remember what he knew of Norman Dunning's background. It had been very different from his own. Gabriel's family had been landowners who had held their vast acres for centuries, but the Dunnings were Londoners; Norman Dunning's father and grandfather had both been senior judges. Neither had advanced legal principle by a jot, nor rocked any boat of legal convention, nor expressed an idea relating to the law that was not in accordance with the understanding of his predecessors. Both had by this means secured lasting legacies.

Dunning, as Gabriel recalled, had been a confident, extrovert little boy, the kind who was popular with boys and masters alike: tall, good-looking, brilliant at sport, bumping along somewhere around the middle in class, with a ready loud laugh that hid his lack of any sense of humour, a superficial sympathy that masked his egotism, and a deep sense of entitlement that enabled him to float through all adversity.

Gabriel, firmly on the side-lines in all but lessons, and sometimes even in those, when his questing, maverick intellect took him outside the confines of conventional learning, had grown up alongside Norman Dunning without envy, malice or interest. He was unsurprised when they both fetched up at the Bar: it had been a career preordained for both of them. In Gabriel's case this was because, rejecting his destiny as custodian of the family estates, it was the only place he wanted to be; in Norman's because he had never thought it possible he would do anything else but follow in his father's footsteps. It was ironic that, in ending up in the same place, the brilliant Gabriel had disappointed his own father, who had taken his revenge by disinheriting him and leaving his estate to a nephew, while the (at best) average Norman Dunning had fulfilled his father's fondest dreams and thereafter he had basked in the vicarious worship of his family. But not even that irony caused Gabriel more than a momentary snuffle when he thought of it.

As young bachelors, Gabriel and Norman Dunning had both lived in the Temple (Gabriel securing the beloved rooms in King's Bench Walk that he had never left since), and their paths had crossed frequently. They managed to display the same tolerant indifference they had shown towards each other at Eton and at Oxford. Then, as Norman had embraced all things worldly with increasing fervour and success, Gabriel had retreated as fast in the opposite direction.

After years of what he described as 'playing the field', there had been the lavish wedding in the Temple Church when Norman had married one of the meringues of that season, fifteen years younger than himself, had moved out of the Temple and had dedicated himself to the production of two little male Dunnings, who were also destined to become sound judges, and one little girl who would become, like her mama, a meringue.

Gabriel had always thought of them as the meringues, those all-the-same girls dressed in the pastel-coloured frills and crinolettes and bustles of that long-ago time, with their piled-up hair and docile demeanour, all rigidly schooled into a uniform sweetness: light, insubstantial and unsatisfying. Norman Dunning's bride, he recollected, had been a prime example of the type.

The carriage jolted to a halt in Stafford Terrace. Alighting with Constable Wright, Gabriel reflected on the vagaries of life thirty years on: Norman Dunning, that most conventional of men, was now dead in these extraordinary circumstances, the girl Gabriel had long forgotten was now a grieving widow, and he himself had been cast in the unlikely role of detective.

The two men stood by the red-carpeted staircase in the oppressive mahogany-panelled hallway, waiting for the butler to announce them. Looking down upon them were not only the ponderous portraits of Norman Dunning's long-dead father and grandfather, but the owlish and very much alive face of a small boy framed by the balustrade two floors up. He had round spectacles, a round head and an unblinking gaze.

'You,' he said conversationally to Gabriel, 'are a man I do not know. Nor do I know why you are in my house. And you,' transferring his gaze to Wright, 'are a policeman. You have come to see my mama because my papa has been murdered.'

Constable Wright looked horrified by this unfilial detachment, but Gabriel, to whom it never occurred to speak any differently to children than he would to adults, and who in addition had no expectations about the proper level or expression of emotion, answered promptly.

'That is an admirable summary of the circumstances confronting you.'

The little boy went on speaking without pausing for breath.

'Papa went out, even though it was my sister Seraphina's birthday. And Seraphina cried and Mama said she should remember that Papa was very busy because he was a very important person, and she asked Aunt Theodora if that was not so, and Aunt Theodora said, "Certainly very self-important," and then Mama cried too and told Aunt Theodora she should not be unkind about Papa in front of us. And Aunt Theodora went to her bedroom and slammed her door and didn't come out again until breakfast. And then, Miss Murray was late for breakfast when she never is, and Papa never came at all, and Mama says she is prostrate. Why do you suppose she said that when she was standing up?'

Gabriel could not suppress a snuffle. Police Constable Wright looked dumbfounded.

The account seemed set to continue, but at this point the round head veered rather comically sideways, boxed on the ears by a pair of disembodied hands in starched cuffs, and the boy was carried off shrieking. The butler reappeared to conduct them to the ladies of the household.

———

In the overstuffed drawing room two women rose to receive them. Both were wearing mourning dress. One of them was as far from a meringue as it was possible to imagine. Like her brother Miss Theodora Dunning was tall, thin and dark. In an era of elaborately embellished fashions and contorted female curves, her appearance was curiously plain and columnar. It was she who took charge, motioning Gabriel to an armchair and Constable Wright to a rather far-off wooden chair, to which he meekly retreated.

'I am Theodora Dunning, the Lord Chief Justice's sister. This is Lady Dunning, his widow. The Treasurer Sir William Waring has explained your role to us.'

She folded thin hands in fingerless black embroidered gloves upon her black lap, and waited.

Gabriel blinked at this unexpectedly business-like greeting, momentarily lost for words. It was almost with relief that he turned to the predictability of Lady Dunning. She was plump and fair and fluffy; her mourning attire, while also unrelievedly black, was covered in the frills and bows of haute couture. A lace handkerchief hid most of her face, though from behind it peered a dry eye. It was she who rushed into the tumbled, inconclusive speech Gabriel had been bracing himself for.

'This dreadful thing, Sir Gabriel, oh, this dreadful thing. And, oh, the manner of it and the disgrace! He never came home. And Theodora and I sitting at the breakfast table and the children there and then his clerk came with a policeman… Oh, dear, a *policeman*. And I have been prostrate, *prostrate*. My migraines are bad at the best of times, but now—'

'Sir Gabriel does not wish to know about your migraines, Charlotte.' Theodora's voice was acid with contempt.

'Oh,' Lady Dunning rode unheedingly through and over the reproof, 'and my poor chicks… Seraphina's birthday, and Percival going to school in the autumn, and dear little Claud still in the nursery. Will they remember their papa? Nanny says they are such dear, good little children, although Percival—'

'He does not wish to know about the children either,' said Theodora.

Afraid he was losing control of the questioning, Gabriel resorted to the familiar rules of advocacy that had been drummed into him: let the witness talk, make them a little comfortable, bide your time.

'We met a little chap in the hall,' he interposed politely. 'With spectacles?'

'Oh, yes indeed. Percival. Just nine, and should be at school by now, but he was not well and is a little delicate, so he will not be able to go away until next year and the governess says so clever, although—'

Percival's name, it seemed, was always accompanied by 'Although—'

'It occurred to me,' he said, 'in our brief interchange, that he would make a good barrister.'

Lady Dunning smiled. 'Of course he will be a barrister, and one day a judge,' she said complacently.

'Oh, of course he will,' echoed Theodora Dunning with clear sarcasm.

His gentle tactics thwarted by these hostile interventions, Gabriel fell back on his prepared questions.

'I wonder if you would be kind enough to tell me about Lord Dunning's movements that last day?'

Lady Dunning looked at him helplessly, as though the intellectual demands of the task were beyond her. Again, Theodora intervened.

'My brother was adjudicating in the Royal Courts of Justice all day. As was his custom, he rose at four-fifteen in the afternoon. He arrived home at five o'clock and rested until six. He changed into evening dress. He left in a hansom cab at seven o'clock. He was expected back at about midnight. He did not come home. Unsurprisingly, since he had been stabbed to death in the Temple. We had all retired. He had his own front-door key. The staff had been instructed not to wait up. His absence was not detected until the next morning. What else would you like to know?'

Blimey, thought Constable Wright, shifting on his very hard chair, you can see where that little blighter Percival gets it from.

'You must forgive me,' Gabriel said politely, 'for asking the unlikely, but are you aware of anyone who might have wished Lord Dunning ill?'

To his utter astonishment it was Lady Dunning who answered him, her high, querulous voice suddenly firm with conviction.

'Of course we know who did it!' she cried indignantly. 'It was that dreadful man. Over and over I have said to Norman to be careful, to go to the police. And would he? No, he would not. That dreadful, rough, dirty brute.'

'You too would be rough and dirty if you were compelled to sleep in a shop doorway,' said Theodora crisply. And turning to Gabriel: 'The man to whom my sister-in-law refers had indeed pestered my brother on numerous occasions. His name is Broadbent and he was a clerk in a City bank. He was prosecuted for theft from his employer and was unwise enough to represent himself. My brother was the judge. He sent Broadbent to prison for two years and so he was ruined; he is now a vagrant, poor man, and has harboured a grudge ever since. You may possibly have seen him; he sits outside the Law Courts, bearing offensive placards. Most are without literary merit, though one I recall read "Vermin in Ermine", which I thought rather apposite.' She smiled for the first time.

'Broadbent,' said Gabriel, incorrigibly diverted by this mention of litigation. 'Wasn't there some public feeling at the time that an injustice had been done?'

'Yes,' said Theodora. 'In 1897. An unfortunate sentence, given the equivocal nature of the evidence against him, though one could not actually say it was wrong. However, it takes an unusual man to appreciate the abstract notion of legal decision-making if the result of it is contrary to his own interests. Mr Broadbent was not such a man; he knew only that he had lost his case and my brother had sent him to prison, and therefore he burns with a misplaced sense of injustice.'

Gabriel's eyebrows rose a little but he said nothing.

'What is the matter, Sir Gabriel?' she said sharply. 'Do you imagine no woman can take an interest in the law?'

'No,' he said mildly, 'it is merely that it has not so far been my, admittedly limited, experience that they do. No doubt because they have not been encouraged to do so.'

'Precisely.' Theodora rose in the manner of one indicating that the conversation was at an end. 'If there is nothing else we can help you with, no doubt you have other commitments.'

Gabriel hesitated; there was one subject of such sensitivity he was uncertain how to approach it. 'One last matter,' he said. 'May I ask if Lord Dunning was – was conventionally clad when he left home for the dinner?'

'Certainly he was,' said Theodora Dunning, quite composed. 'He was in full evening dress. Why do you ask?'

Gabriel hesitated and then took the plunge. 'When his body was found, his feet were bare and there was no sign of his shoes and socks.'

There was silence until Lady Dunning, having assimilated the information, broke into a fresh wail of dismay. 'Oh, the shame! Oh, what can it mean?'

Theodora made an odd sound and Gabriel looked sharply at her; in any other context it might have sounded like suppressed mirth. Perhaps, he thought, it had been distress; her expression was quite grave. 'I can only say that my brother was a man who was always immaculately and suitably dressed for every occasion, Sir Gabriel,' she said. 'If there is nothing further…?'

Herded out into the hall by the butler, they once again encountered Percival, now hanging with simian ease from the first-floor balustrade.

'... Mama said,' he continued, as though there had been no interruption, 'that on no account was I to tell if I was asked where Papa was. But how am I to know whether to obey her or a policeman?'

'We know where your father was and no policeman has asked you anything, so you can obey your mother, as all boys should,' said a thoroughly exasperated Constable Wright as he made for the door.

'Was that quite wise?' asked Gabriel mildly on their return journey to the Temple. 'We do not now know why his mama instructed him not to tell us where his papa was.'

'The little devil,' Wright retorted. 'Delicate indeed! I would have had my backside tanned if I'd dangled off a staircase like that. And he fair riled me, sir, so I could not give him the satisfaction of questioning him. My, sir, what a family!'

'Did they seem so bad? I agree the atmosphere was a little tense but they seemed to me reasonably typical of the upper professional classes.'

'But that dreadful child, sir, his father not cold and not a tear for him! And Lady Dunning, sir: "The governess says... the nanny says..." Doesn't she know her own children? And then that sister!'

'The boy probably lives very much in the nursery, I imagine, until he goes away to school. I recall when I was that age, during holidays, it was my nanny on the top floor and the kind cook in the kitchen who mattered most to me. I saw my mama once a day for half an hour after tea and my papa very seldom. It did me no harm. And strained relations between a wife and a spinster sister-in-law living in the same household are not uncommon.'

Constable Wright thought of the overcrowded kitchen at home over which his mother presided, doling out wonderful meals, and his father by the fire doling out stories and wisdom and occasionally blows when deserved, and of Aunty Violet next door – all of them equally doling out fierce love to him and his four sisters and two brothers, and warmth and rough sympathy and timely praise he had had automatically as his right since the day he was born.

'Poor little blighter,' he said. 'I wonder why they call it privileged.'

Gabriel chuckled.

'At any rate, it appears we have a suspect. I know Broadbent, sir, I've had him in twice for drunk and disorderly and three times for begging.'

'Nonetheless, I very much doubt that he is the culprit,' said Gabriel. 'How could he have got into the Temple at night? No, I think you will quickly be able to eliminate him. In any event, I am thankful it is not my task to interrogate him. I have been charged with investigating within the Temple and I shall, as I always do, adhere strictly to my brief. I have Lord Justice Wilson and Lord Justice Brown to see, and the Reverend Vernon-Osbert and the porters. And, of course, Sir Vivian Barton KC. Then the Treasurer to report to, and my duty, I profoundly hope, will be done. It cannot be too soon for me; Miss Dunning was certainly correct in that regard. I have other commitments – a big case next week and a lot of preparation to do beforehand.' And he felt a little squirm of tension at the prospect of the looming trial and the present unwelcome demands that were eating into his normally sacrosanct preparation time.

'I shall have to report back to the inspector at headquarters, sir, and we will have Broadbent in,' said Constable Wright soberly. 'This puts a different light on things to my mind. Now we have an outsider with a grudge. Broadbent could have sneaked in somewhere, sir, and he obviously has a motive. And after all, who else could want to stab the Lord Chief Justice? There was only the grand gentlemen and the servants in the Temple at that time of night.'

'I never thought to hear myself say it, Constable Wright,' said Gabriel, 'but you put me strongly in mind of Sir William Waring, Master Treasurer of the Inner Temple.'

11

In anticipation of their interviews, Lord Justices Wilson and Brown sat in their private rooms in the Royal Courts of Justice in the Strand. These rooms, like those of all the judges, were designed so that the occupant could materialise through his private entrance into court and directly onto the bench. By this means the judge was uncontaminated by the common herd of clients and lawyers who had entered through a door on the other side of the court and congregated in its well. This literal and spiritual elevation, while beneficial to the abstract concept of justice, was not so good for the humility of the judges.

Both men had greeted with the same combination of relief and contempt the news that they were to be questioned by Sir Gabriel Ward KC, accompanied by a mere police constable. Of course, Ward was known to them as an opponent in their old days at the Bar, and, now they were judges, as a result of his frequent appearances before them. In both these contexts the brilliance of his mind had always made them nervous. He did not, however, strike either of them as convincing in the role of detective, even if he had been appointed by the Treasurer of the Inner Temple with the connivance of the City of London Police, and his being accompanied by a lowly constable seemed almost insulting.

Only by invitation could the Bar penetrate the exclusive precincts of the judges' corridor; for consultation, for a dressing down, for the occasional convivial glass of claret. But all these Gabriel had experienced over his long career, and the corridor held no mysteries for him as he made his way along it to Lord Justice Wilson's room and knocked firmly on the door.

Lord Justice Wilson had divested himself of his robes and Gabriel noticed in his buttonhole a budding yellow rose. This seemed a good sign. Irreverent young members of the Bar, he knew, judged Wilson's mood by the rose in his buttonhole. The crimson 'Charles de Mills', for instance, was a very bad sign indeed.

'Extraordinary business,' observed the judge in a tone more curious than regretful. 'Can hardly believe it. Known Dunning since we were youngsters. Did pupillages in the same chambers, you know. And after such a good evening at the Treasurer's Little Dinner…'

'May I ask what the purpose of the Little Dinner was?' Gabriel asked, more as an opening gambit than anything else.

The judge immediately looked smug. 'You must ask the Treasurer if you really feel it is your business to know. It was a matter very personal to him. I can tell you it is wholly irrelevant to your… investigations.' He delivered the last word with something close to a sneer.

'As to what *is* relevant, I have written a short statement.' He handed Gabriel a single sheet of paper.

Gabriel read it quickly. Lord Justice Wilson's recollection was that Vernon-Osbert and Barton had left together, at around ten o'clock, bound first for the church where Vernon-Osbert had left some papers, and then for their respective homes. The Lord Chief Justice had left three-quarters of an hour later. He said he was leaving by the Terrace entrance to the Hall rather than the main entrance leading into Lamb Building Court. It was a glorious night and he was going to look at the garden in the moonlight on his way home. Lord Justice Wilson recalled that the Lord Chief Justice had looked at his pocket watch and mentioned the time as he left. He had no further knowledge of Dunning's movements. He had himself left after his wife's arrival was announced. She had been visiting Mrs Maud Rentoul, a widowed friend living in Bloomsbury, and came to pick him up in the carriage. Brown must have left a few minutes later. They saw him in Middle Temple Lane when they were getting into their conveyance; Brown had strolled beside it up Middle Temple, at which point he had walked away down Fleet Street.

'Did Lord Dunning seem quite himself all evening?' asked Gabriel.

'Quite himself and quite sober, as were we all, if that is what you were about to ask,' said Wilson sharply. 'Not,' he added, 'that Brown could ever be accused of being anything else.' He lowered his voice. 'Teetotal, you know.' He managed to make it sound like a rather grubby character defect.

'Was it a convivial occasion?'

'Perfectly so. Though Brown – ' Lord Justice Wilson seemed unable to refrain from constantly making disparaging comments about his colleague ' – was downright rude to the Lord Chief Justice. Bad form. Can't think why. Chap should be able to put up with a bit of ragging after a lifetime at the Bar, eh?' And he gave a little bark of laughter.

Gabriel, looking at the little eyes in which he now detected a hint of the bully, remembered, quite suddenly, his own school-days during which he would have traded an entire year's tuck box for half an inch in height. He rather wondered about the nature of that 'ragging'. But for now, he changed the subject.

'May I ask,' he said in his mild way, 'about the arrangements you had made with your wife in relation to the timing of your journey home?'

But at this, Wilson swelled like a particularly indignant bull-frog. 'Really, Ward, what possible business of yours are my domestic affairs?'

Before Gabriel could reply, Constable Wright, relegated once again to a hard chair by the wall, intervened.

'Sir Gabriel is investigating the movements of those in the Temple that night, sir.' And then, looking doubtfully at the judge, 'My lord. We need to know exactly what time you left the Lord Chief Justice so as to calculate the latest time he was seen alive.'

Lord Justice Wilson scowled. 'He left before me.'

Wright persisted. 'Yes, my lord, but Sir Gabriel has asked you what time it was that Lady Wilson arrived to collect you.'

'It was about eleven o'clock. The time was not prearranged. Her ladyship simply said she would ask the coachman to drive home via the Temple and would see if the dinner was over and I was ready to accompany her. Had I not been, I would have obtained a hansom cab later. As it happened, I was ready to go home.'

'And how did she convey to you her arrival?' asked Gabriel.

'How do you imagine? She sent the coachman in to inform the butler and the butler conveyed the message to me. And now,' he ended rather testily, 'if there is nothing else?'

Gabriel bowed. There was, as far as he could see, nothing else. But a thought occurred to Lord Justice Wilson. The little eyes gleamed unkindly. 'Is it true,' he asked greedily, 'that Dunning's feet were *bare*?'

'I am afraid so.'

The judge blew out his cheeks. 'Shocking!'

'It does not seem to me so shocking as the fact that he was found stabbed to death in the Temple,' said Gabriel mildly.

'Well, that too,' said Wilson. But he said it in the tone of voice that suggested Lord Dunning had in both respects committed an error of taste.

As Gabriel and Wright walked to the door, it seemed to occur to Wilson that he had struck the wrong note. He clapped Gabriel on the shoulder with highly uncharacteristic camaraderie.

'A tragedy for the Bench, of course. Big shoes to fill.' He caught himself up. 'Sorry. Tasteless phrase in the circumstances. You know what I mean. Well, well, Ward, you and I have known one another a long time. No friends like old friends, eh?'

In an identical next-door room sat Lord Justice Brown. Though he had had time to change, he was still robed from the day's session in his wool and ermine, as though he subconsciously felt that, thus armoured, he gained protection.

He greeted Gabriel with his usual quiet reserve, ushered him to an armchair and indicated a bench by the door to Police Constable Wright. Peering in his myopic way across the judge's desk, littered with the predictable piles of paper, the weighty legal textbooks ranged like a barricade in front, the wig negligently tossed on top, Gabriel's eye was caught by something rather less expected: a copy of *Millie the Temple Church Mouse*.

The judge, following the direction of his gaze, seemed to think an explanation was called for.

'For my wife,' he murmured. 'Another copy for Sunday School. I happened to see it in Moore's window. St Saviour's Orphanage, where Lady Brown is a devoted volunteer, has a copy, and she finds it is most instructive for little children.'

'So I believe,' said Gabriel noncommittally. 'It has certainly acquired a quite astonishing renown.'

'And an astonishing amount of money for a lady author,' added the judge drily. 'Shall we turn to the business in hand, Sir Gabriel?'

The interview was formal and civil. Lord Justice Brown confirmed the attendees at the Little Dinner. It had been a perfectly convivial occasion, he said. And in answer to Gabriel's question, yes, the Lord Chief Justice had seemed his usual – er – genial self.

'Were there any tensions?' asked Gabriel, noting the hesitation, and with Wilson's remarks fresh in his mind.

Brown raised his eyebrows. 'None of significance,' he said coolly, 'that I recall.'

Otherwise, the judge's recollections accorded with those of his colleague. Vernon-Osbert and Barton had left together, at around ten o'clock, he thought. Dunning had left three-quarters of an hour later, at about ten forty-five. Lord Justice Wilson was called for in his carriage by his wife who had been visiting nearby. Brown believed that to have been about eleven o'clock. As for himself, he had a few further brief words with the Treasurer and left minutes after the Wilsons. He had encountered them both outside, in Middle Temple Lane, getting into their carriage. He had strolled beside it as far as Fleet Street, where he had waved goodbye to them and then returned to his own home.

'By hansom?' said Gabriel.

'No. I walked.'

'Where do you live, sir?' enquired Constable Wright. It was his first contribution to the conversation. The judge addressed himself very pointedly to Gabriel.

'Chiswick.'

Wright, Gabriel noted with some approval, was not going to be dismissed.

'Quite a long walk, sir,' he said, 'at that time of night.'

Lord Justice Brown began to acquire the look that had caused thugs and fraudsters to quail in the dock.

'I like walking,' he said. 'I think I would be in a position to know if there was a law against it, Constable.'

'About seven miles, isn't it, sir? What time did you arrive home?'

There was a prolonged silence.

Gabriel intervened gently. 'We can ask Lady Brown, of course, if you are unsure in your recollection, Judge.'

The silence continued.

Then Brown said evenly, 'It was about two-thirty a.m.'

'You left around eleven? Did it take you three and a half hours to walk home, Judge?' asked Wright.

The silence deepened.

At last the judge said, 'I sat on the Embankment for a while. And I walked about a bit. It was a beautiful night.'

Wright opened his mouth, caught his companion's eye and subsided.

'Indeed yes,' said Gabriel. 'May I turn to the purpose of the Little Dinner?'

'I think, Sir Gabriel, that you must discuss that with the Treasurer,' said Lord Justice Brown firmly, confidence restored. 'If, that is, you really feel it is relevant to your enquiries. I can assure you that it is not.'

He hesitated before he added, 'Is it really true that Lord Dunning was *barefoot* when he was found?'

'I fear so,' said Gabriel.

'Poor fellow,' said Brown. The sensitivity in his voice was in marked contrast to the prurience of Lord Justice Wilson. 'I have asked my wife to enquire how the family are getting on. Dreadful for the young children. My wife knows the governess. She was one of St Saviour's orphans. Maria says she is one of their greatest successes.' He hesitated. 'I am sure it is of no relevance, but Maria saw her at the orphanage yesterday morning. Tuesdays are her day to help with the children there. It was before the news of the tragedy had broken. She gained the impression the girl was not very happy. But there, not so surprising perhaps. Lady Dunning and that sister… Not an easy family.'

'No,' said Gabriel unexpansively, and he got up and retrieved his hat. 'Thank you, Judge,' he said, 'for your time and help.'

Lord Justice Brown shuffled the papers on his desk unnecessarily.

'It is all very dreadful,' he said. 'And of course leaves a gap in our judicial brotherhood which, tragically early as it is to discuss it, will need to be filled.'

Gabriel bowed slightly.

Lord Justice Brown unbent a little. 'It is good to see a friendly face from the old days, Ward. We must not forget old friends, must we?'

12

'Well, Constable,' said Gabriel as they walked back to the Temple, 'did you notice any prominent jaws or handle-shaped ears adorning His Majesty's Judiciary?'

Wright grinned sheepishly. 'No, sir, but they are a funny pair, aren't they?'

'Funny?'

'Well, yes, sir. Here we have a man dead in terrible circumstances. You would think they would want to help, wouldn't you, sir? But Lord Justice Wilson behaved as though he thought it was a fair cheek to ask him anything. And Lord Justice Brown, sir, he seemed a decent enough chap, but choosing to walk all that way home sounds a bit rum to me, and what was he doing until two-thirty in the morning? And he only told us that because he didn't want us finding out from his wife.' He went rather pink. Well, that's what I thought, sir.'

'That is exactly what I thought too, Constable,' said Gabriel. 'But I doubt if Brown spent the time murdering the Lord Chief Justice. There are many reasons why a man shuffles a few hours out of the pack, so to speak. You will find, should you have further acquaintance with them, that all of His Majesty's Judiciary react to all possible circumstances with instant concern primarily for their own reputations. That is how they have reached the elevated positions they hold, and why, in living memory, none of them has ever been dismissed for any scandalous reason. They make very unlikely murderers. Before they are appointed to the judiciary in the first instance, they are judged by the Lord

Chancellor to possess great personal probity and respect for the law.'

'Who is to be the next Lord Chief Justice, sir?' enquired Wright guilelessly.

Gabriel paused. 'Do you know, Constable, I had not given the matter much thought until they both seemed so anxious to ingratiate themselves at the end of our interviews. Traditionally, the post goes automatically to whoever is the Attorney General at the time. But in this instance, he is known to prefer to remain in his present job. So now you come to mention it, it will, I suspect, be a matter of very great interest to a considerable number of His Majesty's judges of the Court of Appeal, those two among them.'

'A good motive to get rid of Lord Dunning,' offered Wright hopefully.

Gabriel chuckled. 'Rather a risky one. They cannot both be Lord Chief Justice and each of them has four rivals.'

'Who decides, sir?'

'The Lord High Chancellor in consultation with the Prime Minister and the senior judges, who themselves take informal soundings from the KCs.'

'And who chooses all the judges, sir?'

'Well, the Lord High Chancellor, in consultation with the KCs and the other judges.'

'What, the Lord Chancellor and the judges choose who at the Bar is to judge alongside them, and then they all decide which of the judges is to be in charge?'

Gabriel chuckled again. 'When you put it like that, Constable, it sounds a rather dubious practice. But yes, something along those lines has been the case for many centuries. I doubt it will ever change.'

'Well,' said Wright, abandoning his pursuit of information, 'I think we should remember they both want to be Lord Chief

Justice, sir, and Lord Justice Brown hasn't a shred of an alibi nor any reason I can see for sitting about on the Embankment half the night.'

'Indeed yes,' said Gabriel. But he wondered whether another piece of information they had heard might prove illuminating in this regard.

They had reached the Temple Church. The interior was lofty, the light dim, the holiness palpable. Through thin beams of sunshine, dust motes danced, and details on the monuments were delicately illuminated. All was a deep silence and not even the rustlings of Millie, or any other more corporeal mouse, could be heard.

Entering from the brightness of Church Yard, they were momentarily blind and then eyes and minds adjusted to the dimness and enveloping peace. While Wright disappeared into the shadows in search of their quarry, Gabriel pottered gently into the round nave, where the stone effigies of the brethren of the Knights Templar lay supine on the floor, frozen in history, in some sense still custodians of the church they had built in 1185.

What would they, who had lived and died by passionate personal belief in their God and their Holy Land, have thought of the battles fought by their successors? he wondered. The barristers of the Inner and Middle Temple may have occupied the church and surrounding land since the 1300s, but they were mere new boys by comparison. They fought their battles with words rather than swords; and unlike the Crusaders, they fought not because they believed passionately in a cause, or even because they thought that right was on their side, but because they represented their clients, whether in the right or in the wrong, bad, mad, innocent or guilty, in accordance with the strange ethics of their profession. What would the Crusaders have said about that deliberate moral detachment? Would they have recognised it for the clean virtue it could be?

'You are looking for me?'

The Reverend Vernon-Osbert thought well of his fellow man without reservation or suspicion, and sometimes in the teeth of evidence to the contrary. All his long life as a clergyman he had spent living in the Reverend Master's house next to the church, long widowed, alone now with his cat, tending his garden and the spiritual needs of the Temple. He loved God and the church he had served for fifty years with fervour, reverence, and without ever having suffered a scintilla of spiritual doubt or despondency. He knew Gabriel well, revered his intellect, and pitied and deplored his agnosticism. He had never despaired of converting him and saw in Gabriel's attendance in church not the respect for the traditions of the Temple that it in fact represented, but a quest for religious enlightenment that Vernon-Osbert fervently believed would be bestowed upon him at the very next service he attended.

Now he positively beamed at this unexpected weekday visit. 'You were deep in thought, Sir Gabriel.'

'Yes,' he agreed, 'but not, I fear, communing with my soul. I was contemplating the nature of moral ambiguity.'

Vernon-Osbert looked bewildered.

Gabriel took pity on him. 'And I have come to speak to you about the death of the Lord Chief Justice.'

'Oh, indeed, indeed.' Vernon-Osbert led him into the small office by the vestry, on the wall of which was displayed the ubiquitous picture of Millie the Temple Church Mouse. Constable Wright was motioned into a chair as comfortable and central, he was pleased to note, as that to which Sir Gabriel was ushered.

'Sit down, sit down. A dreadful, dreadful tragedy. That evil of this kind should come to the Temple! People are afraid, Sir Gabriel! Afraid within these beloved environs! And of course

I am deeply shocked at the loss of so great a man to our small community. He will be sorely missed. A towering figure in the law. And his family attending here every Sunday! I can scarcely bear to think about it.'

It was, thought Gabriel, the strongest expression of sorrow and regret he had yet heard on the subject. But even as the thought came to him, something niggled at the back of his memory and then, before he could grasp it and bring it to the light of day, eluded him.

'I did not think Lord Dunning was a devout church-goer,' he said instead.

'No, no, only now and again. Such a busy man, but his family: Lady Dunning and Miss Dunning every Sunday regular as clockwork; and the governess and the dear little children, so sweet and dutiful. And charmed, like all the children in my flock, by Millie the Mouse.'

Gabriel snuffled a little but restrained himself from saying that he could not see Master Percival Dunning ever being charmed by Millie the Mouse.

'That book,' said Vernon-Osbert, diverted by the thought of it, 'the good it has done! The truths that children learn from it. Lady Brown was saying only yesterday—'

'Lady Brown?' said Gabriel.

'Yes indeed,' said Vernon-Osbert, beaming. 'Dear Lady Brown, one of our most generous benefactors, as well of course as the most devoted friend of St Saviour's Orphanage. Always there with kindness and support, even after the orphanage has sent the girls off into the world. And they are devoted to her. She is to be a helper at Sunday School. The numbers have grown, you know, since we have become known as the home of *Millie the Temple Church Mouse*. I need not ask if you have read it, Sir Gabriel, since you have read everything, have you not?'

'I hope not,' he said, 'or I should feel there was nothing left to live for. But as to *Millie the Mouse*, I have read it, for professional reasons. There has been a little difficulty for the publisher.'

'I am sorry to hear that.' Vernon-Osbert's cherubic face crumpled with concern. 'Mr Herbert Moore is also one of my congregation, and very grateful to him we all are for the good the book has done. What a wonderful woman Miss Cadamy must be. So truly inspired in her ability to educate young children. Families are coming in legions to the Temple Church nowadays. It is a great joy to me. But I digress. How may I help you?'

'You attended the Treasurer's Little Dinner on the night Lord Dunning died?'

'Yes indeed.' Vernon-Osbert, guileless himself, saw only the honour of the invitation and the happiness of the occasion. Had he been told that behind his inclusion must have lain manipulation, he would have been astonished.

'I was much gratified to be consulted over a little – plan, shall we say? – of the Treasurer's. Or perhaps I should rather say a *big* plan? Such a happy occasion… never have I tasted such a good egg custard as Mrs Bugg produces.'

'Lord Justice Wilson told us there was a little – er – tension,' said Gabriel. 'Between Lord Justice Brown and the Lord Chief Justice?'

Vernon-Osbert looked unhappy. 'Oh, it was really nothing, Sir Gabriel, just a little thoughtlessness on the Lord Chief's part. And an unexpectedly irritable, shall we say, reaction by dear Lord Justice Brown. Really, it was nothing. A *happy* occasion,' he repeated firmly.

'What was the purpose of the occasion?' asked Gabriel.

'Now that I could not possibly divulge. Dear me, no. You know our dear Sir William. So ambitious for the Inner Temple. I must not reveal his dream. More than my life is worth!'

His words fell into a sudden silence and he blushed furiously.

'Oh, forgive me, how insensitive. It is merely an expression…
oh, dear, I meant only that you should ask the Treasurer…'

'Yes, yes,' said Gabriel hastily, attempting to divert Vernon-
Osbert from his own tactlessness. 'And what time did you leave?'

'Oh, with Sir Vivian Barton, at about ten o'clock. Yes, ten.
I distinctly recall glancing at the clock as we left.'

'And I believe you went to the church that night?' Attempting
to hurry through what was so palpably to him a formality,
Gabriel did what he would never have done in court and asked
the leading question without thought. He was surprised to see
Vernon-Osbert's suddenly peevish expression.

'How can you possibly know that?' he exclaimed; and if it
were possible for so saintly a man to sound huffy, Gabriel would
have suspected him of irritation. He looked at the vicar in some
surprise.

'One of the judges mentioned it. To pick up some papers, I
believe?'

Vernon-Osbert recovered himself. It seemed to Gabriel that
he visibly relaxed.

'Oh, Sir Vivian accompanied me, yes indeed, to fetch the
papers – and I never lose an opportunity to show off my church.
Sir Vivian is not a very regular attender. It was a glorious night
and the church in the moonlight, the Knights Templar lying
there at peace, the great weight of history – it can be very salu-
tary for those of us who may *doubt*.'

So Barton, too, was a straying sheep whom Vernon-Osbert
wished to gather in. Perhaps that was all that had lain behind
that little display of – what? Embarrassment? Temper?

'And then?'

'Why, we retrieved my papers from this office, strolled around
the church, and then we parted: he for Fleet Street, I for my
home across the churchyard.'

As the two men made their way out of the church, Vernon-Osbert pottering along behind them, something scuffed across the stone flags against Wright's heavy boot. He bent down to look and gave a sudden exclamation of disgust. Lying there were the remains of a fish, the intact head and tail bookending the central spine from which the flesh had gone.

There was an astonished silence.

'A fish?' said Wright blankly. 'In a church?'

'And where is the loaf?' said Gabriel, never able to resist word association.

'But how clever of you, Sir Gabriel!' Vernon-Osbert's voice held an odd note of almost hysterical relief. 'The parable of the loaves and fishes! The best way to teach the choirboys is by a little practical demonstration of the miracle wrought by Our Lord when he fed the multitude. And I am afraid the laundress has not been diligent.'

He ushered them firmly out into the sunshine.

'Well!' said Wright, when they were alone. 'Reverend gentleman he may be, but I don't believe that story, sir.'

'No,' said Gabriel. 'I put the idea of the parable into his head. And mighty relieved he was when I did. I am afraid I am an inept detective. But what the deuce can the real story be?'

'He was very anxious about his visit to the church on the night of the Little Dinner too.'

'Precisely,' said Gabriel. 'And I wonder why that should be?'

Wright hesitated. 'One thing has occurred to me, sir. Could they all be in some sort of society? Like Freemasons?'

Gabriel blinked in astonishment. 'Good heavens, Constable Wright, what do you mean? Many of the judiciary are Freemasons and, as you will be aware, so is a large proportion of the senior police force. The Freemasons could not be more respectable. What on earth makes you think of them?'

'Well, not the Freemasons, sir, but something like that. It was the bare feet, sir. These societies have rituals, like, don't they? I think we should check what they were all wearing on their feet, sir.'

'I cannot really see the Treasurer of the Inner Temple, two of His Majesty's most senior judges, an eminent KC and a vicar of the Church of England, wandering about the Temple in the middle of the night with no shoes on.'

'No, sir,' said Wright. 'But the Lord Chief Justice of England seems to have done so.'

Gabriel chuckled. 'Touché, Constable Wright. We will go to see the porters and we will remember to enquire into the footwear of all those entering and leaving the Temple on the night in question. It is, if I may say so, an ingenious theory.'

Constable Wright went rather pink once more. The two men, lost in individual thought, made their way across the Temple to the Gatehouse.

Suddenly, Wright said, 'I've just realised what sort of fish it was, sir. My mother cooks them as a treat for Saturday tea. It was a herring.'

Gabriel snuffled. 'So all we need to know now—'

'—is whether it was a red one?' The two men spoke together, smiled at each other and walked on, each with a sense of increasing camaraderie.

13

Day in, day out, winter and summer, three hundred and sixty-five days of the year, the Temple porters guarded the Inn from the outside world and all its wickednesses and manifestations, as set out in the Regulations. Ensconced in their small gatehouse a short way down the lane from the Great Gate, or strolling around the precincts of the Temple, their vigilance disguised by an elaborate show of deference, the porters reigned supreme.

Accordingly, no street music was ever allowed to play there. The muffin man could not ply his trade within the Temple gates, welcome though his wares may have been on cold winter Sundays. No pedestrian might stray there without a purpose nor horse clatter over the cobbles without leave of the porters. All idle wanderers and suspicious persons must be barred from entrance and all unknown women must be excluded after six o'clock in the evening. The enforcement of the Temple's sacrosanct peace prevailed over all other demands.

But that morning something had changed; the Great Gate stood half-closed and a pair of porters stood, vigilant, on either side. A large notice bearing the Inner Temple Pegasus emblem was attached to one gate. Outside in Fleet Street, before the gates, metal barriers had been installed, behind which a number of newspaper reporters had set up camp. One, recognising Gabriel, shouted across hopefully: 'Can you confirm it is murder, Sir Gabriel?' And another, more aggressive, yelled: 'Why won't you lot let the City Police in?' And another, yet more emboldened, 'Yes, what has the Inner Temple got to hide?' Simmonds, the head porter, glared at them.

'They can sit there shouting as long as they likes,' he said morosely to Gabriel. 'We have put up a notice, as Sir William ordered, confirming that the Lord Chief Justice has been found dead and that we are investigating before handing the matter over to the police. Still they sits there, shouting silly questions at all who goes in and out. And not above trying to sneak in neither. Into the Temple! The cheek of it! What with protecting those within from horrible danger and keeping them lot of vultures out, we don't know which way to turn.' He ushered Gabriel into the gatehouse, beckoning one of the other porters to follow him.

Simmonds and the accompanying under-porter, Wray, had it seemed been the two on duty on the night of Lord Dunning's death.

Simmonds was an old and trusted member of the close-knit group that constituted the servants of the Inn: loyal, fiercely proprietorial, servile to Inner Temple members, bulldogs to those identified as unsuitable to be permitted within its privileged confines. Wray, though a relative newcomer, through worshipful emulation of Simmonds was fast learning the demeanour, combining deference and authority, of a Temple porter.

Simmonds was a snob to his very backbone. He thought that every man had his place, and that it was the job of the porters to recognise that place at a glance and to ensure that no person stepped outside it. Within it, they might all do as they pleased.

There were some things a gentleman did and some he did not. That was not to say that everything gentlemen did was acceptable; no, it was more subtle than that. Some things the gentlemen barristers did, particularly the young gentlemen, made Simmonds very cross indeed. Paddling in the fountain, for instance; or skylarking on the immaculate lawns of the Inner Temple garden; or rising to the dangerous challenge of climbing up the outside of the Inner Temple library clock-tower. Or sometimes even less forgivable transgressions: smuggling a young woman no better than she ought to be into the exclusively male residential chambers; becoming inebriated at a Temple dinner; even the very occasional bout of fisticuffs.

All of these were completely unacceptable, but the unacceptability was always tempered in Simmonds' eyes by the fact that he regarded them as sins appropriate to the social position of the men who committed them. They would be dealt with internally, by admonishment. Repeat offenders would find themselves reported to the Treasurer. Simmonds worshipped the Treasurer. Any of the gentlemen who were reported to the Treasurer – my word, Simmonds said, they would catch it then!

As for the others, the outsiders, they too were judged by their position in Simmonds' social hierarchy and treated accordingly. Solicitors and clients 'and such', as Simmonds always referred to them, he accepted as a necessary evil of his masters' world, since only through them could a barrister earn a living; they were tolerated as they went about their daily business. Anybody else seeking entrance to the Inn by day was 'the public'; they were permitted to enter with a good enough reason, but once inside, they could never do anything right.

And by night all outsiders, of whatever category, were firmly excluded by the simple expedient of locking all the gates leading into the Inn.

The truth was that the centuries-old Regulations, so rigidly adhered to, were merely rituals, and such protection as they afforded purely notional. At the heart of the Temple had always lain not fear, but arrogance. Individuals were excluded on the grounds of status, not because anyone seriously believed they might cause harm to those who lived and worked there. But now danger lurked within and the porters' complacency was shaken to the core.

The death of the Lord Chief Justice by foul means in the heart of Simmonds' domain was an event for which he had no point of reference and so he had ruminated on the details rather than the unimaginable crime. The combination of bare feet and evening dress had caused Simmonds considerable distress. The use of one of the Inn's prized pieces of silver to stab Lord Dunning to death was deemed an insult. The crime itself seemed almost secondary to the outrage of the event taking place after one of the Treasurer's Little Dinners. Simmonds was inclined to take umbrage over the whole event. He glowered at Constable Wright and began to parrot his orders.

'No policemen,' he said. 'The Inner Temple is to take responsibility for the investigation of Lord Dunning's death until such time as the Treasurer instructs otherwise.'

'Yes, yes,' said Gabriel soothingly. 'Constable Wright is here merely as my guest, and with the express permission of the Treasurer.'

Simmonds thawed a little.

'This is a very bad business, Sir Gabriel,' he said. 'Murder in the Temple? Never did I hear of such a thing. And the Lord Chief Justice! Always the perfect gentleman, he was. Asked regular after my family, always lifted his hat of a morning. Just what a gentleman should be.'

Both Gabriel and Wright reflected in their different ways that this was a somewhat limited assessment of the qualities of a gentleman.

'I hope you will forgive me, Simmonds,' said Gabriel, 'if I ask you a few questions on behalf of the Treasurer about events in the Temple that night.'

'There were no events, sir, just a quiet, ordinary evening. Me and Wray here were on all the time. Walker was with us earlier but he went at eleven o'clock.'

'And where did Walker go?'

'He left the gatehouse into Fleet Street and turned right to go and see his friend at the Cock,' said Simmonds. His face softened a little. 'He was going for a drink and then coming back to walk that Meg of his back home when she finished in the kitchen. She's a good girl, is Meg.'

'I had gained that impression,' said Gabriel. 'What time did she arrive at the porters' lodge on the night of Lord Dunning's death?'

Simmonds shook his head. 'I didn't really take no notice. I know she waited around a good old while. I was in the gatehouse for most of it and then her father came for her. I suppose that must have been just a few minutes before we locked the gates. All the gates except these are locked by six o'clock in the evening. After that everyone uses this entrance. Midnight sharp, these gates are locked too. Now and again gentlemen come home later and knock to come in, but not on that night. No one came in until we opened up in the morning. And no one went out neither.'

'Could anyone have got in before these gates were locked, without being seen by you, Walker or Wray?' Constable Wright asked.

'No,' said Simmonds firmly. 'No,' echoed the subservient Wray, who until that moment had stood silent next to him.

Wright doggedly persisted with his questions. 'And those entering the Inner Temple during the evening before you locked up – can we see your log?'

Simmonds glowered at him. '*Log?* We don't have no log here. This is a gentlemen's residence. They come and go as they please; we don't nosy about taking notes of their movements. We are the Temple porters. We aren't policemen, I thank God, nor we aren't common watchmen. We are here to keep the Temple safe and to keep our gentlemen comfortable.'

'But when they was coming and going, prior to the gates being locked, who came and went?' continued Wright patiently.

'I told you, we don't take no note,' said Simmonds witheringly. 'A number of the gentlemen who live here came in and a few went out, and quite a number of gentlemen barristers who live elsewhere left their working chambers late to go home. The staff went in and out. Just the usual. The Treasurer had one of his Little Dinners; Lord Justices Wilson and Brown, they came in from the Royal Courts of Justice across the road at around seven-thirty in the evening.'

'Together?'

Simmonds paused a moment to consider. 'No, as I recall on their own, maybe ten minutes apart. Lord Dunning arrived last by hansom cab, tipped his hat to me, asked after the family like the gentl—'

'Yes,' interrupted Wright rather testily, 'we know he was a gentleman, we know they are all gentlemen, what could never do no wrong, but what I want to know is, other than the servants, how do you tell who is allowed in and who isn't?'

'Some we know personally,' said Simmonds, his exaggerated patience making it clear that his dignity had been seriously affronted, 'and some we know because we recognise a barrister and a gentleman when we see one.'

'Yes, but how?' persisted Wright.

Gabriel intervened. 'I think what Simmonds is trying to convey, Constable,' he said, 'is that, by general demeanour and appearance, it is not hard to differentiate between those who have business being in the Inn in the evening and those who do not. By the by, Simmonds, talking of appearance — one question

I wished to ask was whether you noticed anything odd about anyone's footwear?'

'No,' said Simmonds uncompromisingly.

Wray, clearly wishing to be helpful, broke in.

'Actually, sir, we don't really see people's feet, because of the little wall.' He gestured to the stone edging of the narrow lane that led into the gateway; it was true that it would impede a porter's observation, cutting the passer-by off from view just above the knee.

'And the servants? Which of them would have been on duty that evening?' persisted Wright.

'A few of the laundresses from various chambers.' Simmonds ticked them off on his finger. 'Violet, Walker's wife, who does Fig Tree Court; Mary who does Tanners Court, Lucy who does Lamb Buildings, your Annie, Sir Gabriel. Then Mrs Bugg, later, when she'd finished in the kitchen. And then Meg.'

'Annie?' said Gabriel. 'Annie comes and cleans One Crown Office Row during the day.'

'Yes, sir, and she does somewhere in Paper Buildings, down by the garden, at night,' said Wray.

'Anyone come in by coach or cab?' Wright was taking notes.

'One messenger boy come in with a parcel for a barrister who lives in the Middle Temple; and Lady Wilson came in by carriage to pick up Lord Justice Wilson from the Treasurer's Little Dinner. She and Lord Justice Wilson left together about eleven o'clock. I recall Lord Justice Brown walking alongside their carriage.'

Simmonds seemed to have something more to say. He cleared his throat anxiously. 'When you speak to the Treasurer, Sir Gabriel, I hope you will tell him no one came in here who shouldn't have and the gates were locked at midnight. I pride myself it never varies.'

'Yes,' added Wray staunchly, 'midnight, never varies. And once the gates is locked, they are all that heavy, and the bolts so big and stiff, that even the postern takes a minute or so to open. Many a gentleman I've seen running up the lane to get out in the minute before we close 'em: "Are you after a train?" I says. "No," they says. "Just want to slip out or I'll be waiting half the night for you to open up again."'

'Did such an event occur on the night in question?' Gabriel enquired.

'Not running, so to speak, though one gentleman barrister put on a little bit of speed, as I recall,' said Simmonds.

'Who was it?'

Simmonds shook his head. 'One of the barristers, sir. Little Meg had just gone off with her father. Then he came up the lane at quite a pace. "You're the last one out, sir," I said. "Goodnight, Simmonds," he said. Out he went, and then I began to close the gate. And that was it for the night, sir.'

14

Back at Old Jewry, Police Constable Wright stood nervously in front of Detective Inspector Hughes' desk. Until two days ago he would have said that Inspector Hughes was his hero. But now he had met Sir Gabriel Ward KC, he was not quite so sure.

Detective Inspector Hughes listened without comment to his report. But when he reached his account of Lady Dunning's suspicions of Broadbent, the ex-convict, he interrupted with some enthusiasm. 'Broadbent?' he said. 'That man is a bad lot and a nuisance. He has been hanging around Fleet Street ever since he came out of prison a year or so ago.'

'I know, sir,' said Constable Wright apologetically. 'He sleeps in the outside area of Moore's Bookshop. Mr Moore has too kind a heart to move him on. I – I'm not sure what the present position is with the Inner Temple – sir. Should I investigate Broadbent?'

The inspector slammed down his hand on the desk.

'This has been mismanaged from the very outset,' he exclaimed. 'A dangerous maniac on the loose and we are not heading the search! The Commissioner,' he said, rage overtaking the discretion normally adopted when talking to a junior member of the force, 'seems to be a bit too chummy with a few other toffs he meets at City dinners, and I have these ludicrous instructions to allow the Temple to investigate its members before we do. Well, I hope they do not live, or perhaps I should say die, to regret it! All this nonsense about their autonomy, and being a so-called Ancient Liberty and the police not allowed in without their say-so! Anyone would think it was 1850. And this uncertainty is the result!'

'I am sorry, sir,' said Wright, hanging his head.

'No call for you to be sorry,' said Hughes gruffly. He had developed a soft spot for young Wright. 'Anyway, Broadbent is not one of their precious members, nor he isn't in the environs of their precious Ancient Liberty. You go and find him as soon as possible and then I suspect the case will quickly be closed.'

Wright looked hesitant. 'Sir Gabriel Ward expressed considerable doubt that Broadbent could have been in the Temple at night. As you know, sir, it is surrounded by buildings on three sides and by the Embankment railings and the river on the fourth; the gateways are manned by porters, and all the gates are locked by midnight. After that, exit and entrance to the Temple can only be gained by those who ring for a porter to let them in, and then only by the Great Gate that leads in from Fleet Street. Of course, it is important to find Broadbent, sir, now Lady Dunning has told us he nursed a grudge against her husband, but Sir Gabriel is of the view that it will only be to eliminate him from our enquiries.'

Hughes snorted. 'And I'd like to know what Sir Gabriel Ward knows about modern policing?'

The question, Wright knew, was rhetorical but nonetheless he gathered his courage to answer it. 'Quite a lot, sir. He is the most extraordinary man, and it seems there is not much he doesn't know. All about bloodstains and the importance of not moving the body, sir, and – and – Latin – and – sherry – and – and all kinds about books, sir. And a way with him when he asks questions that I cannot describe. You feel they must be answered, sir.'

'That is the result of thirty years of cross-examining,' retorted Hughes, who had not infrequently been on the sharp end of this process. 'Never trust a barrister, my boy. Slippery as eels they are – say what suits them, change sides from one day to the next, always for hire… just like whores. Don't you get taken in by Sir Gabriel Ward. You steer clear of barristers. And whores, come to that.'

Wright looked unhappy. Gabriel had not seemed to him any of those things and his loyalties felt divided.

'Well,' said Hughes more kindly, seeing his crestfallen expression, 'have you and Sir Gabriel discovered anyone with a motive except for Broadbent?'

'Not really,' said Wright. 'It seems the Lord Chief Justice was a popular man, sir, no close friends but no enemies either. Yet his family do not seem to be as distraught as you'd expect, and…' he hesitated before he added '…the men who attended the dinner on the night he died, they strike me as being a bit rum about it all. No one will say why they were there, and the judges got quite upset when asked to account for their movements; then the vicar seemed edgy. Me and Sir Gabriel – ' he liked the sound of that ' – we just cannot put our fingers on it. Then there is the matter of the bare feet, sir, that is so peculiar.'

Hughes snorted again, though this time it was a reasonably tolerant-sounding snort.

'Nothing very peculiar that I can see. Broadbent is a vagrant, isn't he? And one with a known grudge. Stabbed the Lord Chief Justice and pinched his shoes. All you need to know is how he got in and you are home and dry.'

'But then why were Lord Dunning's feet dusty?'

'Perhaps he hadn't washed them before he came out. Perhaps a lot of things. You mark my words, my lad, Broadbent will be our man.'

'And then there is the bloody handmark what I took a picture of—'

'Not much we can do with that,' the inspector said briskly, 'without anyone to match it to. Remember, you are not living in a detective novel, lad. And never you mind what Sir Gabriel Ward has to say. You go and find Broadbent. That is an order from me. *Then* you will have done a job worth doing.'

Constable Wright, returning to tread his beat that afternoon, did it as dutifully and conscientiously as he did everything, with earnest attention to detail and mindful always of the regulations that bound him, covering his designated patch at the required two and a half miles an hour, not loitering or gossiping, ensuring the security of all buildings, removing from the street proscribed items such as orange peel on which pedestrians might slip and being always on the ready to halt runaway horses. He regularly, as was required of him, arrested beggars and drunks, moved on inharmonious street musicians and restored lost children.

But underpinning Constable Wright's attention to these mundane duties there lurked always in his mind the regulation of the greatest interest to him: a requirement to keep a close observation on all persons passing, lest any should be recognised from the *Police Gazette* as being sought for apprehension. For Constable Wright's dream, despite his youth, his humble background and basic schooling, was a transfer to the Detective Division; and, given those disadvantages, he knew that such an opportunity would only arise in the event of his apprehending a felon in the commission of a serious crime.

He was too decent a man to regard the death of the Lord Chief Justice so close to his beat as a matter for celebration; but the fact was that it had led to this one glorious, if bewildering, week with Sir Gabriel Ward KC, and his chance to behave as though he were a proper detective. And who knew what might be the result? His mother had been quite right: 'You just do your duty,' she had said, 'and work hard and mind your betters.'

And so he had; and now, at last, he was actually treading his beat with a view to interviewing a man who might prove to be a murderer.

He proceeded slowly in his large boots down the perilously narrow steps that led to the basement area of Moore's Bookshop. In front of him was the basement door and to the right of it a small paved area some eight feet square. Wright peered hopefully at the basement walls as he descended. If, now, he could only find a bloody handprint that seemed to match the one outside 1 Crown Office Row, how impressed Sir Gabriel would be! If he could only return to the station and tell Inspector Hughes that he had caught the murderer – well – red-handed! But the walls revealed nothing but stone, blackened by centuries of London filth.

On the paving in the basement and taking up most of the space was a makeshift bed comprised of old blankets. Beside the bed was an ancient kettle, a tin plate bearing the remains of what appeared, through the blue furry mould adorning it, to be a piece of bread, and a pot of black paint with a brush sticking out. Propped against the wall was a large placard with the painted legend: 'What are judges for.' The artist had apparently yet to conclude it with a question mark, and the space left underneath the words suggested that he had also intended to provide an answer to his own query.

As Constable Wright surveyed this scene, the basement door opened and a clerk appeared bearing a dustbin. He jumped and then, at the sight of the policeman's uniform, relaxed.

'Can I help you, Constable?' he asked. 'Has Broadbent been up to something he shouldn't?'

'Not so far as I know, sir,' said Wright stolidly. 'This is where he sleeps, is it?'

'It is. Mr Moore is a very good-hearted gentleman. "What harm does Broadbent do?" he says to me. "You leave him be if he's no trouble." And he isn't and so we do.' He looked around.

'Though it's not like him to leave it like this; rolls up his bits in his blankets every morning when I arrive and brings them back every evening to sleep, and we don't usually know he's even been. As far as I know, he spends his day outside the Royal Courts of Justice.'

'When did you last see him?' asked Wright.

The clerk scratched his head. 'I don't really pay much attention, I'm that used to seeing him of a morning when I'm tidying up down here. But not for a day or two, now I come to consider it.'

'Well, when he comes back,' said Wright, 'you might send word to the station, quietly, like, and we will come and have a word with him before he can scarper.'

The clerk nodded, his interest diminished by the apparently unsensational nature of the policeman's enquiry, and turned his attention to the dustbins.

Up again at pavement level in Fleet Street, Wright continued his ponderous way down the street, looking into every basement and alley and shop doorway until he reached the great façade of the Law Courts, stretching along the road in an orgy of turrets and twiddles, and culminating in the shallow steps that led to its massive Gothic doorway. On the steps, the usual smattering of people had congregated: clerks waiting for their barristers, bearing their wigs and gowns; preoccupied solicitors waiting for clients; journalists waiting for sensation; but there was no sign of Mr Broadbent.

Methodically, Constable Wright retraced his steps down Fleet Street past Moore's Bookshop and explored the other way, down the narrow alleyways and glancing inside the churches and churchyards all the way to St Paul's Cathedral. Two hours of fruitless searching later, he returned with his usual dogged determination to Moore's Bookshop.

'When Broadbent has the money for it, where does he go to drink?' he asked the clerk he had spoken to previously.

'The Old Bell.'

And so Wright crossed the street and made his way back towards St Paul's. Since the sixteen hundreds the Old Bell had snuggled between Fleet Street and St Bride's Avenue. In the cool dim interior, the early-evening sunlight filtered through the stained-glass windows and across the bar, so that the publican was polishing green and red and gold tankards with blue hands. There was only one customer sitting by the empty fireside – a surly-looking man accompanied by an equally surly-looking dog. Both were small-eyed and thick-necked and heavily built. The man was marking up the *Daily Racing Form* with a stub of pencil. The dog was gnawing meaningfully at a fresh bloody bone.

'Yes,' said the publican, 'Broadbent drinks here when he can and props his placards up on my bar and yarns away to anyone who will listen about the evils of them down the road.' He jerked his head towards the Temple and the Royal Courts of Justice. 'Always has a bit of gossip about them so-called gentlemen lawyers and there are plenty who want to hear it.'

Wright looked enquiring.

'The newspaper men,' elaborated the publican. 'They all drink here, and many a time I've seen them slip Broadbent a free drink in exchange for a little story about Mr Justice Whoever.'

'When did you last see him?'

'Yesterday midday. Blind drunk he was, and the last I see he rolled off down the road with the Barkers.'

'Who are the Barkers when they're at home?'

'Fred Barker and his dog. In here every day. Over there.'

He lowered his voice as Wright made to move. 'You want to watch Fred Barker. He is rather fond of looking around other people's houses, so to speak. The dog acts as lookout. The dog is called Barker too. And they can both get ugly. Truth to tell, I was worried for Broadbent. He's just a harmless old man with a bee in his bonnet. Punching above his weight with the Barkers and no mistake.'

Wright nodded his thanks. On his approach, the human Barker looked sideways at his uniform, and the canine Barker growled menacingly.

'We haven't done nothing,' said the human Barker.

'I never said you had,' said Wright amiably. 'I only want a little bit of information. Where's Broadbent?'

Barker shook his head. Wright got out his notebook.

'You went off with him. Yesterday. Where did you go?'

'On a binge,' said Barker sullenly. 'Bloke from the *Evening News* gave us a few bob. Is it a crime?'

'But where?'

Barker shrugged. 'Cheshire Cheese, George, down the Strand, ended up in St James'. Then I met a pal and we went off.'

'What time was that?'

'I dunno. Early evening?'

'And Broadbent?'

'As I remember, we left him passed out in a flowerbed in St James' Park. Too drunk to be any use to anyone.'

'Any use?'

Barker shrugged again.

Wright thought about asking which flowerbed, but it seemed a question too far. Barker got up and jerked the dog lead.

'Is Broadbent still there?' asked Wright, more to delay the man's departure than because he expected a helpful answer.

'He'll probably be dead if he is,' Barker observed, callously. 'No one can't stand more than a day or two unconscious in a flowerbed without copping it. Is that my fault? I've had enough of this.'

Wright watched them go. Two years' experience of drunk and disorderlies had taught him the truth of Fred Barker's statement. Broadbent might indeed be dead and with him his knowledge, innocent or guilty, of the murder of Lord Dunning. Or he might still be there in the flowerbed, lying at death's door. Or the whole story might be a cover-up. And Sir Gabriel Ward KC and Detective Inspector Hughes were relying on him to find out. The responsibility felt a heavy one.

15

The prospect of an unsolicited visit to Miss Susan Hatchings was one that would have filled Herbert Moore with horror, had it not been for one circumstance. Indeed, his first reaction to the suggestion, made by his loving and supportive wife on the evening of his depressing consultation with Sir Gabriel Ward, had been a very firm 'No'. He had no idea whether such an approach to the opposing side in litigation – the enemy, his nemesis – was permissible. It might even be illegal. It would certainly be uncomfortable.

Herbert's wife, though in many ways unworldly, was nonetheless a consummate diplomat and loved him dearly. Having elicited from him the unwilling admission that no one had told him not to, and that he had no pressing engagements in the next two days, she delivered what she knew to be an almost irresistible enticement.

'You have not yet travelled on the new train service to Edinburgh, have you, my dear? The Flying Scotsman has been quite refurbished, you know. The carriages are linked by corridors and now there is no need to stop in York for luncheon or –' she hesitated delicately ' – any other personal need. For all is now provided on board and, believe it or not, you arrive there in eight hours and thirteen minutes.'

Ever since he was a small boy, Herbert Moore had loved trains. He had been known to catch one bound for a random destination merely for the sound of the steam being expelled on departure and the excitement of the rhythmic chuntering rattle of the wheels on the track; for the slackening speed and the groaning brakes that heralded a danger sign; for the shrill whistles and the shouting porters at the bustling stations. Just for the sheer joy of a form of travel as near as any human being could come to flying.

Mrs Moore, observing his expression, knew the battle was won.

'I will pack your Gladstone bag, my love,' she said fondly. 'And you will see – Miss Hatchings will explain how this all came about and all will be well, I promise you, my dear one.'

And so, on the morning that Gabriel and Wright were travelling to Kensington, Herbert was already rattling through Grantham, and the therapeutic effect of his mode of travel had made him begin to believe that his wife's prediction really could be true. By the afternoon, with York left behind and Newcastle still to come, full of boiled cod and egg sauce followed by steamed honey pudding, both cooked at King's Cross Station and heated up for service in the new first-class dining car, he had relaxed. His head began to nod in unconscious time with the dribble of oil oscillating from side to side in the lamp swaying above him, and he had gently fallen asleep.

Optimism upheld him throughout his arrival at Edinburgh Waverley station, a comfortable night spent in the George Hotel, his breakfast kipper, and during his walk through the streets of Edinburgh right to the door of The Laurels, Sinclair Road.

He looked curiously at the house. It was trim and conventional, of the newly built terraced type, with a square bay window and a small porch.

Feeling that he had reached his journey's end in more ways than one, that behind this door lay a happy resolution for both parties, perhaps even a fruitful partnership for the future, he rang the bell. There was no response.

Herbert peered through the bay window into a sunny room. Hanging on the wall directly facing the window was a simple cross above a carefully posed studio photograph of a very old lady smiling into the camera. Below the picture on a finely polished table stood a vibrant display of anemones in a blue bowl. Herbert's buoyant spirits rose higher; there was something very satisfying about the little tableau against the cream wall. And the old lady was really very like his imaginary Miss Harriet Cadamy. Perhaps after all…

The door opened suddenly.

'Miss Hatchings?'

'Yes!'

She was not at all what he had been expecting. The woman who greeted him with a radiant smile was, he guessed, in her late thirties. Her dark hair, cut in a fringe, curled rather appealingly around her face and she had wide-apart blue eyes. Her pale skin was of the translucent type that blushes easily and she was blushing now with what appeared to be not shyness but enthusiasm. She was smartly dressed but Herbert knew instinctively that his wife would have said she was not quite a lady. Her expression as she looked at him was certainly not that of a lady, though it was one that Herbert, a handsome man, encountered not infrequently. It could best be described as expectant.

He raised his hat and smiled in return. Herbert was well aware of the effect of his smile.

Miss Hatchings came close to a simper. 'Come in,' she fluted in a high-pitched, self-consciously genteel voice and, even as she spoke, flitted back into the shadowy hall and disappeared through the door of the bay-windowed room that led off it. A stickler for social etiquette, Herbert hesitated, hat in hand, on the doorstep, uncertain if she was coming back or he was expected to follow.

'Come in, come in,' trilled the voice. And so he made his way into her house.

The room was as neat, decorous and conspicuously clean as his glimpse through the window had suggested. An upright piano stood against the wall opposite the window. Around the cast-iron fireplace was the conventional arrangement of an armchair to either side and a sofa facing it. No book or magazine or knitting defaced the surface of any of the profusion of small tables placed around the room.

On the chair facing the door through which Herbert now tentatively entered sat an enormous doll, with dark curly hair and deep blue eyes.

From across the room, through the open doorway on the other side, the hospitable chirrup continued.

'You have come a long way, I believe, and God is treating us to such a sunny day, isn't He? There is lemonade or perhaps you prefer coffee?' she enquired. 'Don't gentlemen sometimes prefer coffee?'

Susan Hatchings emerged from the other doorway and followed the direction of his gaze.

'Oh, you are admiring Dolly,' she said. She crossed to the chair and ran her hands lovingly through the doll's curls, proprietorial as a proud mother. 'Dear Dolly,' she said. 'Do you think she is a little like me?'

'I— yes,' he stammered, now utterly at sea. 'The eyes...' he trailed off, swamped by Susan Hatchings' delight.

'Yes!' she cried. 'And the dark curls! My dear mother gave her to me, as a last gift. I was never blessed with a sister, you see, and oh, how I wanted one! And my mother knew she was leaving me. So now Dolly comes everywhere with me. To the shops and to church! And she has her own dear little perambulator! The

Reverend Blair says it is so charming! Don't you think that it is charming?'

Herbert bowed rather helplessly, overcome with an odd sense of unease.

'And the children who come all love to play with her.' Her elation diminished; she looked earnestly at Herbert. 'It is important, when teaching children music, to have constant diversions for them. A little prayer when they arrive, then fifteen minutes practising scales, I say to them, and then fifteen minutes with Dolly, as a reward. That is the way to teach children.' And with a swing back to her earlier euphoria, 'And then we are all happy. Oh, so happy! Children and music!'

'You teach music to children?' said Herbert, grabbing with relief at the lifeline of normality.

'Yes indeed. I was a governess for some years with such a lovely family. Oh, how I enjoyed it, looking after little Emilia and oh, Harold, the little scamp, such dear children! Out and about every day! Such fun! But then…' She hesitated and looked rather coyly at him from beneath her fringe. 'Oh, well,' she said, with an odd smile, 'Mamas can get a little bit jealous, can they not? If the little ones come to love the governess. And, dare I say it, perhaps they even get a little bit jealous in relation to Papa too?' She put her hand to her mouth in a burlesque of embarrassment. 'Oh, no, how naughty of me. I should not say that.'

Herbert began to find this arch discourse rather uncomfortable. Could this woman really be the author of a book of the calibre of *Millie the Temple Church Mouse?* Unheeding, Susan Hatchings prattled on.

'And then, anyway, my mother was ill and I thought, Susan, you may love this little family but your own mama needs you more, and so I left to care for her.' She gestured reverentially towards the picture on the wall. 'But, oh, the isolation of it, in my mother's remote little cottage by the sea, miles from anywhere!

For me, who loves people! But now I teach little children in my own home, and I have Dolly and the church and Reverend Blair, and I do believe God has arranged for happiness to come peeping around the corner again. Dear Reverend Blair,' she continued, misty-eyed. 'So understanding! With such a holy vision for his church! I was very lonely when I moved here, but Reverend Blair came to see me and invited me to join his congregation. I will always remember his own special saying: "God is here. Come and meet Him." And so I did and God welcomed me.'

And then, briskly, with one of the sudden changes of mood that Herbert was already beginning to recognise as characteristic of her, 'Now, would you like to try it out?'

'T-Try it out?'

'The piano! It must be collected by next Tuesday, you know, as the new one arrives on Wednesday and this is not a large house.' She trilled with laughter. 'What should I do with two pianos?'

The whole situation seemed to be getting out of hand. Herbert drew a resolute breath. 'Miss Hatchings, I am afraid you are under a misapprehension. I have not come about the piano. I am Herbert Moore, the publisher—'

Susan Hatchings went first very white and then very red. The perpetually gesticulating little hands were suddenly still, balled into fists at her sides, all the frivolity quite gone. The trill was noticeably absent from the voice in which she said, 'Go away at once.' It had been replaced by something Herbert could not place. Was it anger? Or fear?

'Miss Hatchings,' he said, 'I have not come to upset you or make trouble. I hoped that away from all the lawyers you and I might be able to – to help each other reach a resolution that makes us both happy.'

'How *dare* you?' she exclaimed, and her fury was now unmistakable. 'I do not want a resolution. There is nothing to resolve. It is my book. Millie is my mouse. You stole my book.'

'Of course,' began Herbert hesitantly, 'if you did indeed write the book—'

He got no further.

'If?' shrieked Susan Hatchings. '*If?*' She seemed transformed, unrecognisable, her voice rising to a crescendo of indignation.

'Thief,' she shrieked, 'fraudster! Coming to my house, pretending you wanted to buy my piano, calling me a liar…'

She seized the bowl of anemones.

'Please,' Herbert protested. 'If we may just talk—'

The bowl of anemones flew through the air towards him, missing by an inch and smashing against the door jamb. Herbert fled. The front door slammed behind him. He stood ruefully in the porch, put on his hat and removed an anemone from his left shoulder.

Gathering all his courage, he rang the bell again.

'Go away.' The voice sounded so unnervingly close that Herbert leaped back from the door onto the tessellated path that led to it before realising that Miss Hatchings had not materialised beside him but that the voice emanated from the open letterbox. He bent down to the same level.

'Miss Hatchings, I beg of you, may we not talk? Surely it is in both our interests that we at least have a sensible conversation?'

'You are a devil,' observed the disembodied voice. 'I will not have you over my threshold. You should not be here.'

Uncomfortably aware that this last observation was probably correct, Herbert's voice trembled with sincerity. 'Miss Hatchings,' he said, 'I intended only to say that I have been proud to publish the book and it is a great achievement for its author.'

There was a silence.

Emboldened, he continued. 'It has brought pleasure to children everywhere…'

The letterbox closed, and the door opened an inch.

'I did it for God,' hissed Susan Hatchings through the crack.

'…not to mention instilled into them the principles of Christianity,' said Herbert hastily. 'But the book's commercial success, also, has been remarkable.'

'Commercial success!' The voice was rising higher and higher. 'You have cheapened Millie! Millie toys, and books in America! I do not want to make money—'

'In that case,' said Herbert reasonably, 'why are you suing me?'

'I want to stop your wicked profiteering! I want the world to know it is my book! I want it back! It is mine! You have stole my mouse!'

And the door slammed again, this time with unequivocal finality.

16

S o great was his concern at the outcome of the interview that Herbert had walked hurriedly away from Susan Hatchings' front door for quite five minutes before realising that, in his haste, he had walked off in a different direction to that from which he had arrived. He was now in an unknown street. It was one o'clock. The happily consumed kipper seemed to have been in another life. In front of him was a respectable if uninspiring public house advertising a saloon bar, and he made his way towards it. And then, as if indeed God had taken him by the hand, he saw that the public house was situated next door to a church, and that emblazoned on the noticeboard outside was a greeting. 'GOD IS HERE,' it said. 'COME AND MEET HIM.'

Surely, surely it could not be coincidence? Herbert hovered indecisively. Should he investigate? What if he was accused of spying upon Miss Hatchings? Or interfering with the course of litigation? Caution prevailed. He made his way into the public house and ordered himself a glass of beer and a chop.

Sitting at the bar, he reflected on the extraordinary interview. The neat house, Dolly, the flirtatious confidences, the desperate gaiety and sudden, staggering venom of Miss Susan Hatchings. The elusive sensation, almost palpable in that immaculate little room. What had it been? He had not been able to place it. But he could now. It had been loneliness.

'Visiting from London?' said the amiable publican, eyeing Herbert's smart overcoat and hat.

'Yes,' said Herbert unexpansively.

'Here for long?'

'Just overnight.'

The publican was not to be put off. 'Come up on the Flying Scotsman? What did you think of her, then? My word, isn't she a beauty? Seven coaches now, isn't it, which means two hundred and sixty-five tons for the boilers to service; only time will tell if they can draw that weight in the long term.'

Herbert started; he drew closer to the bar; his eyes met those of the publican; and with a thrill of joy the two men recognised in each other the burning flame of a common passion.

Half an hour passed; a half-hour of boiler capacity and the future possibilities for diesel; of pistons and wagons and valve gear and blast pipes; of favourite trains and favourite rail routes and the case for nationalisation.

'My friends call me Jim,' confided the publican.

'And I am Herbert Moore,' said Herbert enthusiastically; but even as he introduced himself cold reality rushed in. He was Herbert Moore, the distinguished legal publisher, and the next train he caught would not take him on a glorious, steaming, puffing flight to freedom, but back to a grim battle for his reputation and livelihood. He put down his glass.

His new friend Jim eyed him anxiously. 'You suddenly seem troubled, man. Can I help at all?'

Herbert leaned further over the bar. 'Jim, the church next door – do you know anything about it?'

Jim snorted. 'The Reverend Blair's outfit? Come and meet God and all that? He is no friend of mine. A Temperance man – no wine or song for him. Not so sure the same can be said of women.'

'Is he particularly fond of them?'

'They are certainly fond of him,' said Jim. 'Famous, his church is getting; something about him, apparently. Can't think what myself, mind, but they come in shoals to hear him preach and end up worshipping the preacher. A congregation of them, rich and poor, old and young. Which one is going to lead him to the altar is the joke around here.'

'He is a bachelor?'

'Aye, so he says,' said Jim cryptically. 'Did you come to see him? He's in the church. I saw him arrive just before you did.'

It was fate. Herbert gathered his hat and his courage in his hands, bade his new friend farewell, promised to look him up some day, and made his way next door.

The church was cold, cavernous and empty. Herbert hovered and while he did so, a door opened at the back and a clergyman emerged, carrying a pile of hymn books. He paused enquiringly. 'Have you come to meet God?'

Nonplussed, Herbert stared at him helplessly. Despite the dog collar, the Reverend Blair looked to him like a bounder; but he could see that the tall frame and theatrical air, the rather too long leonine mane of hair, the penetrating, overly intimate gaze, might indeed seem glamorous to the less discerning.

'He is here,' said the clergyman.

Herbert looked round rather hastily. The conversation seemed to have taken an unnerving turn.

'Do you wish to meet Him? My next service is at eleven o'clock tomorrow morning.'

'Thank you,' said Herbert collecting himself at last, 'but I am only a visitor in Edinburgh. I wonder, may I ask, is Miss Susan Hatchings a member of your congregation?'

The cleric beamed. 'Indeed, yes.' His voice, Herbert would have been forced to admit, was striking: deep, persuasive, almost hypnotic in its power.

'I visited Miss Hatchings this morning and she mentioned your name.' This at least, he thought to himself, was the absolute truth.

The Reverend Blair inclined his head benignly. 'Yes indeed, one of my ladies. So devoted, so truly spiritual. A relative newcomer to my fold and a very welcome one.'

'A newcomer?'

'Oh, well, in the last few months, arriving from Mull, and always accompanied by dear Dolly! We should be allowed our little eccentricities, should we not? Particularly those of us blessed with other desirable qualities.' The Reverend Blair was inclined to expand on his theme. 'The creative mind, you know, and the wealth it carries with it! Wealth of the spirit, I mean, of course. Every lamb that our Holy Shepherd gathers in, I as His instrument on earth am glad to welcome. And I understand, prior to caring for her dear mother, she had a job in London. A sophisticated and well-travelled lamb, you might say. Or perhaps,' he added with a meaningful smile, 'mouse would be more apt?'

'Mouse?'

'Yes indeed, truly astonishing, and such a wonderful boon to my church. So modest and so discreet!'

'Mouse?' said Herbert again.

The Reverend Blair leaned confidingly towards him and lowered the deep, soft voice until he seemed almost to vibrate.

'Miss Hatchings,' he said, 'I discover, to my astonishment, is the author of the children's book that has been so extraordinarily successful, *Millie the Temple Church Mouse*. Quite incognito. No one else here knows, but she confided in me so touchingly, so frankly. She was exploited by a wicked publisher, but with justice and God's help, is soon to reclaim her rightful ownership in the English courts. And, of course, one hopes she can then benefit the church.'

'The Temple Church?'

'No.' Here Reverend Blair looked a little self-conscious. 'The book was written while Sus— Miss Hatchings resided in

London, but *we* are now her church. Such a romantic little lady; quite taken during her sojourn with the Temple Church and the story of the Knight Crusaders who built it, but she knows she is in her true home now.' Once started, there seemed no stopping his confidences.

'So precious to me… yes indeed. And who knows? Such a fervent soul, and what riches… spiritually speaking,' he added hastily.

Such was his self-absorption that he appeared not to notice Herbert's lack of contribution to these observations. Now Blair held out his hand.

'I am delighted to have met you. Any friend of Miss Hatchings must always be welcome. I am so glad you saw fit to visit my church. God is always here and as Sus— Miss Hatchings will tell you, so too am I.'

Dazed, Herbert found himself shepherded out onto the steps and down into the busy afternoon street. It was pouring with rain. He waved to a passing hackney carriage and asked for the George Hotel. There would be no Flying Scotsman service until the next morning.

Staring out of the window at wet, grey streets, Herbert wondered for the first time why he had really come to Edinburgh at all. Mr Dawson was after all responsible for verifying the facts of Miss Hatchings' case. Had it been, as his wife had suggested, to appeal to Miss Hatchings' better nature? Or had it been to prove to himself that she really existed? That there was a real person who had written the book that had been the centre of his world for the preceding four years? Not his dream Miss Cadamy, but quite another sort of individual.

If so, he told himself, he had fulfilled the purpose of his journey. 'His' Miss Cadamy was gone forever. He realised now, with something like a blush, that he had lost an imaginary friend who had become important to him. If this really was Miss Cadamy, she was not a genteel old lady with a richly creative mind living in a remote village. She was a relatively young, overly smart, distinctly peculiar urban dweller with a fervent devotion to her God and possibly to her equally peculiar and slightly unsavoury vicar. Why, then, did he feel such a lingering sense of doubt?

He thought back to the very beginning of it all and to the fresh joy of little Elsie's discovery, ultimately echoed by children everywhere: the bitter pill of the legacy of stern Victorian religious instruction for children had been sweetened into something they could understand and respond to. But its real genius had lain, he now saw, in retaining, along with its appeal to children, enough of a moral imperative to persuade the adults in their lives that reading this book would also promote proper religious development. That was the special combination that had led to the book's phenomenal success.

Could that subtle, engaging message, written in deceptively simple, lucid language, really have come from a woman whose speech, as she became more excited, had strayed a little into the ungrammatical? 'You have stole my mouse,' she had shrieked in her final fury. Could that clever adaptation of mid-Victorian moral values to suit the modern child really have been created by a woman in her thirties? Could the woman who had now joined a distinctly alternative church with a new brand of Christianity have been the same person who had been able to convey the grave worship of the Temple Church, deeply rooted in the traditions of formal Anglicanism?

Herbert might have confined his talents to a narrow field, but he was still a publisher to his core, with a publisher's nose for potential. All his instincts throughout that uncomfortable day had made him feel there was something wrong here. But what? If the book she was laying claim to was not written by Miss Hatchings, how could she have known enough of its history to feel herself safe in making such a claim? She would have to explain all the thought and inspiration behind it and all the details of how it had fetched up at Moore's; above all she would have to know that the real author would not come forward to challenge her claim. The thing was unfathomable.

The more he thought about it, the more his instinct told him that Susan Hatchings was not the author of the universally loved *Millie the Temple Church Mouse*. What, then, was her motive in claiming that she was? He knew now that he was not up against the hard-nosed commercialism of a cynical copyright claim, but against something far more alarming: a zealot with a cause. Was it sex or religion? Or both? It did not matter. The woman who was suing him was doing so for mysterious reasons of her own; offers of money, it seemed, would be of no avail. She wanted her day in court and nothing was going to stop her having it. Could a sufficiently clever cross-examination break Miss Susan Hatchings?

The cab jolted. Herbert started from his reverie. He rapped on the glass partition. 'Stop at the next post office,' he cried.

And three hours later, back in London, Anthony Dawson, senior partner of Dawson, Dawson & Dawson, about to drop into his club for dinner, opened a telegram that read: *Very real doubt about authorial authenticity stop Back in London tomorrow stop Tell Sir Gabriel Ward KC stop Moore*

17

On the morning after the interviews he had conducted with Wright, Gabriel made the short journey from his own chambers to those of Sir Vivian Barton KC in Fig Tree Court. The two buildings were divided only by the narrow passage running between 1 Crown Office Row and the kitchen before it opened into the quaint old courtyard in which no fig tree had ever grown.

Gabriel felt no need of an ally to accompany him to this interview. Barton was an old friend and professional foe, soon to be his opponent in the up-and-coming trial of *Cadamy v Moore*. It was fortunate that both men were happily unaware of the unauthorised and ill-advised encounter taking place that very morning in Edinburgh between their respective clients.

Barton was that most dangerous of barristers: a thoroughly fair, very clever, personable and amiable man. He did not grovel to judges any more than the ritualised procedures and hierarchical traditions of the law absolutely required, yet judges liked him. He was tough and competitive but he did not take unfair advantages or make cheap points. So his opponents liked him too. He was kindly and professional with his clients and solicitors, and they also liked him.

His cases against Gabriel had become legendary, two intellectual gladiators locked together in forensic battles over decades at the Bar: 'Ward and Barton are against each other in Court Six,' pupil masters would say to their pupils. 'Cut across the road to the Law Courts and learn how it is done.'

Each had their critics and their followers but Vivian Barton was generally thought to be the safer pair of hands and as a result was certainly the more successful financially. Few clients wanted their barrister to be a genius, with all the overtones that that word carried, except occasionally when the odds of winning were low and the stakes high, when the facts were unprecedented and the law impenetrable. Then there was only one man who might, just might, pull it off, solicitors told their clients: and that was Sir Gabriel Ward KC.

Barton was clearly visible at his desk through the ground-floor window of his chambers in Fig Tree Court. When Gabriel rapped unceremoniously on it, he threw it open.

'Morning, Ward. The answer is no,' he said genially.

Gabriel looked blank, though he knew very well what Barton meant.

'That is,' said Barton, 'if you have come to negotiate a settlement in Cadamy and Moore.'

'Certainly not,' said Gabriel. 'I am going to win the case.'

'That's funny, so am I.'

They both chuckled; this ritualised conversation took place before every case in which they were to confront each other.

'I would, however, welcome a chat,' said Gabriel. 'It is a beautiful morning. Would you care to take a stroll around the garden?'

The two men made their way down the alleyway to the Terrace, and so to the garden steps.

'Clockwise, please,' said Gabriel firmly, when they reached the path that circumnavigated the garden. Barton changed his intended course without comment. He knew Gabriel of old.

'It is about the Lord Chief Justice's death,' Gabriel began.

Barton's genial expression faded.

'Dreadful business. Poor chap. I dined with him that night, you know. Quite unbelievable. And bare feet, they say.'

It was odd, Gabriel reflected, how that one bizarre detail dominated the others; all over the Temple, the same refrain was being repeated. And the detail had lost nothing in the retelling: the Lord Chief Justice's feet had been muddy or bloody or mutilated, it was whispered, when in fact they had been none of those things, but merely the dusty, pink, bare, nicely manicured feet of a man of the professional middle classes. Just the sort of feet that, had one thought about it at all, one would expect the Lord Chief Justice of England to have.

'I have been asked by the Treasurer to investigate on behalf of the Inner Temple.'

Barton roared with laughter.

'By what Machiavellian means did he persuade you to take on that thankless task? And now you want to know where I was on the night of the crime? Well, my dear and most unlikely sleuth, I attended the Treasurer's Little Dinner, I helped to entertain the Lord Chief who was on sparkling good form and, by the way, conventionally shod. I listened to the Treasurer's usual fatuous plotting, which was wasted on the Lord Chief who was unreceptive, to say the least. I drank the best port I have ever had, and I went home to the family.'

Barton was a famously devoted father, ever anxious to relate the latest antics of his seven beloved children, but Gabriel was not to be diverted.

'What was the fatuous plotting about?'

Barton twinkled. 'That, dear boy, you must ask the Treasurer to reveal.'

'And at what time did you leave?' Gabriel persisted doggedly.

'I left early, around ten o'clock. Vernon-Osbert decided to leave with me. It really was the most glorious warm night, the Temple at its beautiful best. We walked through to the church. Vernon-Osbert wanted to pick up some papers he had left there earlier in the evening. Then I went up to Fleet Street and hailed a hansom cab. My wife can tell you I arrived home at just before eleven. I suppose you will be talking to my fellow guests?'

'Barton,' said Gabriel, 'confidentially, what do you think of Brown and Wilson? I never knew them well at the Bar.'

'Both jolly clever chaps. Brown is a reserved sort of man, as you know. That is why his little outburst at the dinner was so surprising. Said to be devoted to his wife. She is very religious. No children. He is steeped in the law; his father was a very distinguished judge, too, who retired surprisingly young. Don't know what happened to him. Wilson is a bit of a pompous ass. Knows a lot about roses. Couple of sons. Wife a bit of a tartar. Both men all right really. Shouldn't think any of that's much help, dear boy.'

'Tell me about the outburst. Wilson mentioned it. Vernon-Osbert seemed anxious to skate over it. Brown himself denied there'd been any outburst, but he sounded pretty unconvincing. So what happened?'

Sir Vivian Barton absently pitched his cigar stub into the nearest border. 'Brown has always been teetotal, you know. There is no secret about it. Frightful waste of the Treasurer's Château Lafite. The Lord Chief chaffed him about it and Brown lost his rag. God knows why.'

'Chaffed him?'

'Yes, you know… how could Brown resist the Treasurer's best vintage? And then some slightly schoolboyish hectoring about couldn't he trust himself not to be found drunk in a gutter? Can't think why Brown bothered to react.'

'What did he say?'

'He said, believe it or not, "Why the devil don't you mind your own business?"'

'Good heavens!' said Gabriel. This, at any formal dinner, would be unacceptable enough. Directed at the Lord Chief Justice of England, accustomed to grovelling deference and respect, it must have been incredible.

'How on earth did the Lord Chief react?' he asked curiously.

'Well, he was very taken aback. Then he tried to laugh it off. You know he was always a pretty amiable chap. He slapped Brown on the back and said, "Well, no offence, old boy. You're a damned good judge. Chip off the old block, eh?" And Brown seemed to get more and more furious. Looked at the LCJ as though he could have killed him.' Barton caught himself up. 'Sorry. Figure of speech. Anyway, then there was a rather embarrassing silence. No one could imagine what Brown was so upset about. And then dear old VO passed it off with a rather hasty remark about the worthiness of the Temperance Movement, and the moment passed. Brown was pretty quiet for the rest of the evening, though. Odd,' he concluded cheerfully.

'Very,' said Gabriel thoughtfully.

'Have you seen the Dunning family?' asked Barton.

'Yesterday.'

'Was the sister there?' enquired Barton. 'What has become of her?'

'Do you know her?'

'Know her? Good God, no. Only of her.'

'The Treasurer described her as eccentric,' said Gabriel.

'That is certainly one word for her. Surely you remember hearing about the scandal?'

Gabriel shook his head. 'She did not strike me as a woman who would be mired in scandal.'

'Not that sort of scandal. Must have been well over thirty years ago… Theodora Dunning is a couple of years older than her brother. He and I were still up at Oxford. My father was practising here then. She wrote to his chambers, applying for admission to train as a barrister. My God, the furore! Family didn't know she had done it, of course; Old Man Dunning was on the Bench then. You know what the Dunnings are like. They say she finished the old boy off; he couldn't stand the shame.

Massive heart attack felled him one morning while he was in court.'

'What happened to Miss Dunning's application?' asked Gabriel.

'They wrote a letter to her after a meeting of the senior barristers in which the unanimous decision was made that they should politely decline the application, for obvious reasons.'

'They have never seemed obvious to me. In all my reading I have never seen anything that convinced me of a correlation between gender and intellect; though certainly it is the case that, by convention, education and expectation, we do our best to make such a correlation.'

'True enough,' said Barton with his easy tolerance. 'Jolly bad luck on the ladies, but there it is. Mind you,' he added pensively, 'you never can tell. Violet, for instance, our laundress, I found her reading that Stoker chap's horror novel. Can't remember the name.'

'*Dracula*.'

'That's it. She was completely engrossed. Just goes to show. There are always exceptions. Anyway, Theodora was certainly of your view. She didn't leave it there – oh, no, she appealed right up to the House of Lords. Represented herself and, legend has it, made a damn' good job of it. My father represented the Bar. Apparently, power to admit to the Bar is not given to the barristers anyway but delegated to the judges. And there are no rules expressly banning women from becoming barristers.'

'That is correct,' said Gabriel. 'All set out in *Origines juridiciales* in the 1600s. No reference to gender. Many references therein to "persons who wish to become barristers".'

'Exactly,' said Barton. 'But the judges refused to exercise their power to admit her; all terminology that purported to be neutral as to gender they ruled, was to be read as referring to the male owing to "inveterate usage".'

'Inveterate usage,' said Gabriel with a snort, 'what crimes are committed in thy name!'

Barton looked at him curiously. 'It sounds as though you took to her,' he said. 'What is she like? I heard she never married. God and crochet and good works, like all spinsters?'

'I have no idea of her religious views,' said Gabriel, 'nor of her pastimes. As for "taking to her", a deplorable expression from one of your customary purity of speech, she was distinctly hostile towards me. Despite that, I felt sorry for her. She seemed to me to be a – ' he struggled for the correct expression ' – a light extinguished.'

'How frightfully poetic,' said Barton cheerfully. They were nearing the completion of their circuit of the garden. 'By the way, old boy,' he added in a histrionically casual tone, 'while we are talking, what about Cadamy and Moore?'

'What about it?'

'Devilishly difficult case on the law, don't you think?'

Gabriel was not to be drawn. 'My pupil master always told me: get the facts straight first, worry about fitting them to the law later.'

'My dear chap, my client is a devout and innocent spinster who inadvertently dropped her manuscript in Fleet Street. The next thing she knows about it is that her pseudonym has been, if not forged, certainly used unauthorised, her book has been published without her consent, and as if that were not bad enough, shamelessly exploited by means to which she would have expressed abhorrence, had anyone bothered to ask her. I am not too worried about getting the facts straight.'

'And my client,' said Gabriel imperturbably, 'is a highly professional publisher of unblemished reputation who says he came by the manuscript, may I point out, not by picking it up in Fleet Street, as you appear to suggest, but because it was found on the doorstep of what was, after all, a publishing company. He tried to find the writer by reasonable means; he signed contracts not in your client's name but in a name to which she is no more entitled than he is; he then exerted very considerable commercial skills that led to the book's success. And furthermore, four years have passed and the proceeds are inextricably entwined with the overall finances of his business.'

Barton's usual geniality seemed a little ruffled by the vigour of this defence. They had reached the garden steps.

'Very well, if that is your attitude, we will see you in court,' he said abruptly and, with an airy wave of his hand, briskly ascended before Gabriel could respond.

'I think I shall take another turn,' Gabriel was left saying to thin air. He retraced his footsteps (clockwise) round the garden and halted by a large camellia.

'Come out, if you please,' he said, not too severely.

There was silence, then a frantic floundering.

Gabriel sighed and parted the foliage. There in the flowerbed sat Meg the scullery maid, dirty and woebegone. Somewhat to his own surprise, Gabriel silently held out his hand; and just as much to his surprise, Meg took it and clambered out onto the gravel path. Her small hand, the palm heavily scored from hard work, yet delicately boned, felt curiously vulnerable. If there was one characteristic Gabriel found particularly difficult in others, it was vulnerability. He dropped the hand hastily, and steered Meg instead by a less emotionally communicative bony elbow to a bench.

'If you wish to cry undetected in a flowerbed, you must learn not to sniffle and wriggle,' he said. 'Now tell me: what is the matter?'

Meg lifted a corner of her dirty apron and blew her nose.

Gabriel could be accused of intellectual snobbery, but he was not remotely concerned by the social divide. He sat on the bench beside her with complete indifference to the astonished sidelong glances of those of his fellow members of the Bar who were enjoying a mid-morning stroll around the Inner Temple garden, none of whom would have contemplated being seen sitting with a scullery maid. It never entered Gabriel's head, as he placed his top hat beside him on the bench and handed Meg his immaculate white linen handkerchief, that there was anything singular about the picture they made. Equally, it never occurred to him to speak to her any differently than he would to a colleague at the Bar.

'May I suggest,' he said in his formal, courteous way, 'that you refrain from crying? Unless you communicate in a way that is intelligible to me, how can I alleviate your distress?'

Meg was sobbing too hard to unravel this, but she understood the kindly intent and the practical aid of the beautiful handkerchief in which she buried her nose and blew luxuriantly. And having done so, answered him quite clearly, if rather surprisingly.

'I am going to hell.'

Gabriel blinked. 'I am sorry to hear it. May one ask why?'

'I stole something and I told a lie,' declared Meg uncompromisingly.

'Well,' said Gabriel, 'one should always examine these things carefully. In confessing to crime, one often finds that a lack of accuracy leads to error. The theft, now: did you take something that you absolutely knew belonged to someone else?'

'Yes.'

'Did you perhaps think you might be able to return it later?'

'No.'

Gabriel sighed. 'Like most of my clients, you do not make it easy to defend you, Meg. Let us look at it another way. Did you think you were doing a wrong and dishonest thing?'

Meg shook her head vigorously. 'I thought Mrs Bugg would think it was right.'

'Come, that is better. If you were not dishonest, it was not theft, Meg.'

'Truly?' She looked up hopefully.

'Truly. Now: the lie?'

She hung her head. 'I lied to you, sir. I did not go straight to meet my father on the night the Lord Chief Justice was murdered. I did something first.'

'I assume that at some point that night you did meet your father?' said Gabriel.

'Yes, sir.' Meg looked bewildered.

'In that case, you told me no lie; you merely omitted something that you are now going to tell me,' said Gabriel. 'And far from going to hell, you are now going to be very helpful. Shall we begin again?' And he smiled at her. Although a little tremulously, Meg smiled back.

'What was the – er – thing you didn't mention when we spoke earlier?' Gabriel asked delicately.

'Four slices of bread and two thick slices of the beef what came up from the gentlemen's dinner and some of the dripping. I made it into a sandwich,' said Meg miserably.

'And for whom was the sandwich destined?'

She drew a deep breath, as one about to plunge into an unknown river with the outcome uncertain.

'It was for Mr Broadbent, sir. Oh, please, sir, do not get poor Mr Broadbent into trouble!'

Gabriel's face was grave. 'Mr Broadbent the tramp?'

Meg, now committed, unburdened her heart all in a rush and with obvious relief.

'He lives on Fleet Street, you know, sir. I sees him in the morning when I comes in to work, sir, and I feel that sorry for him. He gets hungry, sir, if no one gives him money, and if he begs he gets arrested; and he has a chesty cough, even though it is May. And that day, he looked quite bad and I thought he might be ill, sir.' She faltered and then continued bravely, 'I just wanted him to be sheltered for the night while he was coughing so, sir, and

I thought of the church…' At Gabriel's look of consternation, she trailed off.

'Meg, what are you telling me? Are you telling me Mr Broadbent was actually *inside* the Temple that night?'

Meg nodded miserably.

'But how did you get him in past the porters?'

'I told you,' she whispered. 'My father is one of the porters. I went down to the gate at about ten o'clock when the pudding went up to Master Treasurer's Little Dinner. I have a break then. So I went to the gate and had a joke with my father, and while I did, Mr Broadbent slipped in and hid and then I took him to the church. And then I went back to work. And then when I had finished work, I went back to the church with the sandwich. It was on my way. It only took me a few minutes. And then I went and met my father like I told you.'

'And Mr Broadbent?'

'He said I was very kind and he was grateful, and that he would slip out in the morning. I never saw him no more,' she wailed.

'Meg, you must know that no one but the barristers and their guests and the servants are permitted inside the Temple at night. What made you think Mrs Bugg would have approved of such conduct?'

'Every time the Treasurer has a Little Dinner, we throws away good beef afterwards, sir. Every day there is bread goes in the bin, and Mr Broadbent and his like arrested and put in the cells if they beg in Fleet Street. Mrs Bugg says the waste in the Temple is a crying shame. I heard her tell the Treasurer so.'

Gabriel blinked and, just for a moment, his safe world seemed to shift.

'*Did* she?' he said. He could not imagine anyone telling Sir William Waring that anything was a crying shame. 'What on earth did the Treasurer say?'

'He told her not to forget her place,' said Meg.

Gabriel snuffled a little. That particularly fatuous expression certainly had the ring of truth.

'And then he said, or she soon wouldn't have one to forget. And then he slammed the kitchen door.'

That, too, had the ring of truth.

'You won't get Mrs Bugg into trouble, will you, sir?' said Meg anxiously. 'Mr Bugg has been sick, you know, and Mrs Bugg's Ruby's Fred has lost his job and Ruby has another mouth to feed soon and no help from Fred, Mrs Bugg says.'

Gabriel's little world shifted again.

'I will not get Mrs Bugg into trouble,' he said. 'Or you, Meg.' It felt like a promise. One he thought it might be hard to keep.

18

The concentration required and adrenaline engendered by the prospect of a looming trial was the breath of life to Gabriel. Free from the emotional demands made on other men and with neither need nor desire to venture out of the Temple, or to manage a domestic life, the intellectual gymnastics of the next case were all that mattered to him.

Over the last few days, dominated by the timetable imposed upon him by Sir William, he had had to erode his usually carefully choreographed preparations for trial. But *Cadamy v Moore* had been listed to begin in six days, the day after Sir William Waring's deadline of a week was up. The laborious preparation process could wait no longer.

Not the death of the Lord Chief Justice, nor the threat to his home, nor his unaccustomed role as an amateur detective could override Gabriel's compulsion to prepare his case. He would delegate to no junior and those notionally assigned to his cases earned fat fees with no work required. The fact that they also learned, through listening to a master, consummate skills in advocacy made junior barrister to Sir Gabriel Ward a popular position.

Gabriel did the work. *Had* to do it. *Himself*. He had to analyse and mark up the pleadings and correspondence and to compile chronologies and determine tactics, all eventualities covered. Trials, unpredictable by their nature, must somehow be shaped by him into his own kind of certainty, achieved by the ordering of the papers and the margin notes in his immaculate small copperplate handwriting in coloured inks. The law must be researched and analysed and checked and rechecked and noted and cross-referenced to indicate its applicability to the facts of the individual case. In every spare moment, now, Gabriel applied himself to the preparations without which no trial could be conducted by him.

It was on the Saturday, two days before the Treasurer's deadline, when, emerging from just such a concentrated morning of work, he donned his Panama hat, his only sartorial concession to the fact that it was not a weekday, and made his way across the Temple to the gardens for his clockwise daily walk. On his way he encountered, to his surprise, Herbert Moore hurrying across in the other direction towards the gates to Fleet Street.

The meeting seemed to Gabriel opportune, a chance to have a word with his client without the inhibiting presence of Mr Dawson of Dawson, Dawson & Dawson. Such a word, contrary to all the rules of professional conduct that prohibited conversations between barrister and client in the absence of the solicitor, could, he felt, be justified if such a conversation occurred merely by chance in a social setting.

He had, after all, nothing to hide from Mr Dawson; it was merely that he had felt that Herbert Moore might be more forthcoming in relation to his mysterious telegram from Edinburgh if his solicitor were not there expressing his trenchant views on the undesirability of clients who undertook their own investigations, accompanied by his constant apocalyptic warnings about the cost of litigation.

Accordingly, Gabriel fell into step beside his client.

'This is well met, Mr Moore,' he said. 'I am in the very midst of preparations for your case. But what brings you to the Temple on a Saturday?'

Herbert grimaced. 'Like you, work, I am afraid, Sir Gabriel. I must go to my office and catch up after three days playing truant.' He looked sheepishly at Gabriel. 'I think you may have heard…?'

'Mr Dawson conveyed the content of your telegram and an account of the personal investigations that led to it,' said Gabriel disapprovingly. 'But it was accompanied by his own strong view that you were, not to put too fine a point on it, grasping at straws. Miss Hatchings' past and credentials have all now been followed up by him in a rather more orthodox manner than that used by you. He has checked her places of birth and of employment and of residence. All seem unimpeachable. Her life, it appears to Mr Dawson, is an open book. Mr Dawson is a senior and experienced solicitor. The damage to your reputation, should you pursue the line that Miss Hatchings is an imposter and be unable to prove it, would be extensive. And,' he snuffled, the wordplay irresistible, 'with the substitution of one letter in that word, would also ruin you in another sense. Mr Dawson feels you should be saved from yourself, Mr Moore, and I am inclined to agree with him. But I would like to know why you reached the conclusion you did?'

The younger man stopped in the middle of the path.

'Sir Gabriel, I have been anxious to see you – I felt you might understand – it is so nebulous, an instinct only – but so strong, so – so *certain* to me. You of all people should understand… You are a book lover, I believe?'

'I am.'

'Then you will know, Sir Gabriel, that if someone were to give to you a work by Mr Dickens that was unfamiliar to you, you would not mistake it for a work by Mr Trollope, would you?'

'No,' said Gabriel. 'I like to think I would have recognised the differences in the styles of writing. But that is rather a different case. Both are prolific writers and I have become familiar with the style of each.'

'Very well then, this new author Miss Beatrix Potter who has just privately published *The Tale of Peter Rabbit*, say, and our well-loved Lewis Carroll. No one could mistake that one work is written by a woman and one by a man; that one is contemporary and one now begins to seem a little dated.'

'I will grant you that too,' said Gabriel. 'But these examples all involve a comparator; in this case, we have one book, written by one person and nothing with which to compare it. And one person claiming, apparently credibly, to have written it.'

'But that is just my point!' cried Herbert, almost stammering in his eagerness. 'It is *not* credible, Sir Gabriel. I have met this woman and talked to her. I have studied that book. I *know* books. For all its sentimentality, *Millie the Mouse* was written by a clever, sophisticated mind, not by – by – a nincompoop.'

'Did you know,' said Gabriel, diverted, 'that that word, according to no lesser authority than Dr Johnson's *Dictionary*, is a derivation of the legal concept of *non compos mentis*?'

'No, really?' Herbert was also momentarily diverted. 'Well, perhaps in that case I do her an injustice. I suppose I have no real reason to call into question her sanity. She undoubtedly loves children and she is clearly religious. It must be acknowledged that she has a fertile imagination. But the kind of imagination that lies behind *Millie the Temple Church Mouse*? Never, Sir Gabriel! If Miss Hatchings had created Millie the Mouse, she – she would have been quite a different sort of mouse.'

Gabriel looked enquiring.

'Oh,' said Herbert impatiently, 'she would have been a great deal *more* sentimental. And coy. And she would have worn a frilly frock, not plain grey fur.'

Gabriel snuffled and Herbert grinned rather sheepishly. 'You know what I mean. In the last analysis, Miss Hatchings was *silly*. She was arch and fluttery and flirtatious. All giggles and hints about her employer and her own irresistible charms. *Millie the Temple Church Mouse* was not written by someone so silly.'

'No,' said Gabriel slowly, 'but that is not evidence. I cannot say that to a judge, Mr Moore.'

'Sir Gabriel, you are the most famous cross-examiner in London. You must question her inspiration, her thought processes, her imagination; you must *expose* her as a woman who could not have written this book.'

Gabriel shook his head.

'You flatter me, I fear, and you overestimate the subtlety of the judicial process. A court is not a forum for literary criticism. It deals in facts, not in ideas. It seeks certainty, not nuance. Furthermore, cross-examination requires material and you have nothing but a personal instinct.'

'And I also have no choice,' said Herbert. 'That woman wants blood, Sir Gabriel, as she made all too clear to me. She wants her day in court and she wants the verdict to state that she wrote the book.'

'If that is indeed the case, then there is nothing we can do to prevent her pursuit of the claim,' was Gabriel's sober reply. 'She is, come what may, entitled to her day in court.'

They had reached the gates to Fleet Street and the sun had gone in.

'I ask you only,' said Herbert earnestly, 'to do your best for me.'

Gabriel offered his hand; there seemed nothing left to say.

'I will do my best, Mr Moore.'

As the two men shook hands it occurred to Gabriel that his promises were mounting up.

19

On Sunday, as was expected of residents of the Temple, Gabriel attended the Temple Church. The morning service was about to begin. Drawn into the large congregation hastening towards it, he too entered under the great Norman arch.

As the organ's swelling sound reverberated around him, he slipped into the Inner Temple pews on the south side of the church. The pews were set sideways on to the pulpit and faced across the nave to the Middle Temple pews on the north side, in comradeship or confrontation, depending on one's point of view.

Surrounding Gabriel were his colleagues at the Bench and Bar. Sir Vivian Barton, he noted, despite his reputation for irregular attendance, was amongst them. With him was Lady Barton, a nursemaid and his seven children ranged in a row in their pew, a squirming entity of barely suppressed energy. The two smallest were engaged in an unseemly struggle for a furry, dilapidated Millie the Mouse and the two eldest in an even more regrettable fight over a prayer book. The three in the middle were helpless with unexplained giggles. Sir Vivian looked on indulgently.

Lord Justice Brown was there, accompanied by his wife whose face was upturned with rapt attention to the altar as she prayed for the guidance to support her through her forthcoming role as the wife of the new Lord Chief Justice. The couple sat close together. Gabriel's gaze rested on Lord Justice Brown's pale, ascetic profile. What had occupied the man between his leaving the Little Dinner and arriving home at half-past two in the morning? A mistress? But he was famously devoted to his wife. Insomnia? But why hadn't he said so? Worry? And if so, what was he worrying about? Sneaking back to the Temple to murder the Lord Chief Justice? The very idea caused Gabriel to emit a small snuffle. He could not think of a man less likely to kill. But he recalled uneasily Brown's uncharacteristic rudeness and anger towards Norman Dunning. That, too, had been unlikely. But nonetheless it had happened, and Brown had been evasive about it.

His gaze passed on to Lord Justice Wilson and Gabriel smiled to himself. Perhaps he could think of one man less likely. Lord Justice Wilson sat, smug and conventional, an exquisite *Rosa* 'Alba' in his buttonhole, apparently utterly satisfied with his lot in life. He also was accompanied – in his case, by two stolid boys and his wife. She too was looking straight at the altar while she calculated in her head how many lobster patties she would require for her next At Home. The lobster patties would mark the onset of her pre-eminence as a glittering hostess, a role which awaited her as the wife of the new Lord Chief Justice.

To Gabriel's left, the body of the great church was packed with families inspired by Millie the Mouse to worship here. Amongst the pews crowded with mamas and papas and governesses and children clutching toy Millies, he noticed Herbert Moore with his wife and daughter Elsie. And then Theodora Dunning, accompanied by a tall, thin, drably attired woman with drooping garments and a drooping head who appeared to be in charge of Seraphina, Percival and little Claud, all of whom were dressed in deep mourning.

He glimpsed Meg, standing with her father and mother. He vaguely recognised the latter as the laundress from Vivian

Barton's Chambers. They stood at the back of the church, almost obscured by one of its great pillars; and, in front of them, poured into the straining satin of her Sunday best, was Mrs Bugg, the Inner Temple cook, accompanied by a large husband, an adolescent son no less large and her sister Annie, still as pale and red-eyed as when Gabriel had last seen her, escorted from his Chambers by Chapman after her traumatic discovery of the body of the Lord Chief Justice.

The sermon was one of Vernon-Osbert's best. *Media vita in morte sumus*: in the midst of life we are in death. He did not shirk mention of the tragedy that had rocked the Temple, but in his devout hands it became a manageable grief. The will of God obscured to the fallible human eye; the intervention of evil that was the inevitable result of mankind's control over his destiny; the ultimate triumph of God over that evil, revealed in the legacy of the loving family Lord Dunning had left behind, and of his contributions to England's judicial system. The judgments he had made would be enshrined forever, batons handed on in the great intellectual relay race of the common law.

After the service, the congregation crowded outside into the leafy sunshine of the churchyard and Gabriel found himself in the porch at the same time as the Barton family. He raised his hat, as did Sir Vivian. 'Morning, Ward,' he said cheerfully, 'I am trying to instil some spirituality into my little rapscallions – an uphill task, I fear.' And he was swept on, his children tumbling after, so that he looked like a portly, prosperous Pied Piper of Hamelin.

Behind him came the Dunning family. Those around them had fallen back a little, as people will when confronted too closely by tragedy, as though they feared infection, leaving them an isolated little group in black. Overwhelmed, little Seraphina Dunning pressed closer to her aunt's coat. As the family drew level with Gabriel, he saw Theodora Dunning, with strikingly softened face, bend to comfort the child.

'If you were to go and look, Seraphina,' she said, 'I do believe that you might see Millie in the church. I distinctly saw her tail as we left our pew.'

Seraphina smiled uncertainly and then turned back.

'Millie is a pretend mouse.'

Gabriel did not have to look to identify that precise little voice; he lingered, wondering how Miss Dunning would handle this betrayal. She did so with impressive speed.

'Do not be spiteful, Percival,' she said. 'Millie is not a pretend mouse. A lawyer would tell you that she is Seraphina's truth. You too may have a truth and, if you wish, it can be a different truth; but it is no more nor less true than hers.'

'Bravo,' said Gabriel involuntarily.

Theodora Dunning bowed to him and gave him a thin smile, acknowledging the tribute.

'Good morning, Sir Gabriel. We are here as usual, you see. *Media vita in morte sumus.*

'Yes indeed,' said Gabriel. 'Lady Dunning is not with you?'

'She is prostrate,' said Percival.

Theodora ignored him.

'I should introduce the children's governess,' she said, gesturing towards the drooping figure who embodied the drab, downtrodden governess of popular fiction and who now murmured something unintelligible.

'She is my third,' said Percival proudly.

'That is a matter for shame and not self-congratulation,' said Theodora reprovingly. 'Kindly take Miss Murray and Claud with you and wait by the tree.'

And as Percival showed signs of lingering, the drooping figure of Miss Murray suddenly asserted herself.

'Percival,' she said, in tones that, though quiet, brooked no argument, 'now.'

Percival went. It occurred to Gabriel as he watched them depart that crushing Master Percival Dunning, even momentarily, indicated an unexpectedly impressive personality.

Theodora looked thoughtfully after them. 'I fear Miss Murray may go the way of her predecessor,' she said, half to herself. 'And this time it will not be Percival's fault. I appointed her because she seemed to me remarkably well read and I felt that would be most helpful to the children's education. She is clearly intelligent, but I fear she is an uninspiring teacher and half the time she seems to be thinking about something else.' She turned her attention to Gabriel.

'How does your detection proceed, Sir Gabriel?'

'It is kind of you to dignify it with that name,' he said, 'but it scarcely deserves it. Merely some gentle enquiries for form's sake. I did not anticipate making any Holmesian discoveries.'

Theodora did not disappoint; she acknowledged the literary allusion with her thin smile.

'But did you nonetheless make any?'

In the midst of his automatic denial Gabriel paused.

'I suppose,' he said slowly, having only just himself thought of it, 'I have learned that each of us has places in the heart where we do not wish others to trample.'

She raised her eyebrows. 'Then you are a late learner, Sir Gabriel. Hadn't a lifetime at the Bar already taught you that?'

'Ah, that is different; there I am licensed to trample. I have not before had occasion to do so without rights or purpose. I have discovered many sensitivities in people's experience of that night, which I believe to be irrelevant to your brother's death, and so I hesitate to intrude. I hesitate now, but may I ask you one thing?'

'You may, though I make no undertaking to answer it, truly or at all.'

'Not truly; but perhaps with your own truth?'

She laughed then. It was transforming. 'Touché. But that was a glib answer to a child. I am not sure I could have carried the logic through. It is fortunate that Percival did not pursue it with his customary rigour. Now what is your question, Sir Gabriel?'

'In fact, it concerns Percival. The child told us his mama had forbidden him to say where his father was on the night of the murder. We know where he was, of course, but the purpose of the Treasurer's Little Dinner seems somewhat shrouded in mystery. Is it a matter you can assist me with?'

Theodora shrugged contemptuously.

'I know very little, since I took no interest. I believe it concerned the plans for the Inn's celebrations for the forthcoming coronation; Sir William Waring wishes to arrange a lavish affair, thereby stealing a march on the Middle Temple and indeed the rest of London. I believe he had some very special plan and wanted to enlist my brother's aid. I can tell you my sister-in-law was beside herself with excitement at the prospect of an event that would necessitate her buying yet another dress from Paris. But I really do not know what was required of my brother. In general, he was extremely cautious about involving himself in anything new. Consciousness of his own elevated status precluded any genuine collegiate spirit, his inherent laziness discouraged him from taking on unnecessary duties, and his deep snobbery made him reluctant to commit to a voluntary role lest there should be something even grander to do just around the corner.'

Gabriel blinked at this incisive criticism.

'And Percival?'

'Oh, we were all sworn to secrecy, including Percival who was discovered to have eavesdropped on a parental conversation on this subject. None should know, lest the world should steal the Treasurer's ideas and the Inner Temple lose its rightful place as leader of that world.' Her tone was ironic.

The words also held the ring of truth. So much, thought Gabriel, almost wistfully, for Constable Wright's exotic theories of barefoot cults and rituals with the Treasurer as a masked Grand Vizier.

From the corner of his eye, he now saw the Treasurer himself bearing down on them. Over by the tree, Miss Murray was standing alone watching Percival and Claud playing with the other children, newly released from church. As he watched they were joined by Seraphina. On impulse Gabriel said, 'Miss Dunning, would you object if I had a quick word with your governess?'

Theodora looked quizzical. 'More detecting, Sir Gabriel? I have no objection.'

'Thank you,' he said to her and made his bow. As he did so, she caught his arm.

'One more thing, Sir Gabriel. What of Mr Broadbent?'

'He is certainly a suspect, but has, I fear, disappeared.'

She let him go, but not before he noticed an expression of unmistakable relief pass across her face.

It was, thought Gabriel, just one more puzzling, seemingly irrelevant little thing; one more person who reacted in a way that was not wholly as he had expected. But then who was he to make judgements about human behaviour? He who had shunned company for so long in favour of his own absorbing interior life?

He crossed Church Yard to join the governess. On closer inspection he saw that under the long fringe was an unusual face. Nanny would have called her a Miss Plain, but Gabriel was struck by the singular bone structure and a pair of remarkably astute grey eyes, lively with intelligence, which met his with composure. He saw that she was holding Seraphina's toy Millie the Mouse and, as a way of breaking the ice, he gestured to it.

'Millie the Mouse seems to be everywhere. I lost count of the number in church this morning.'

She looked a little wary and said nothing.

'Do you find as a governess it helps the children in their religious education?' Gabriel persevered.

'It is invaluable. If only because it keeps the little ones quiet in church.' The tone of her voice was repressive. He began to see why Percival did as he was told. He gave up on preliminary pleasantries.

'Miss Murray, you may be aware that I am conducting some questioning about the death of Lord Dunning on behalf of the Inner Temple. May I enquire as to one matter you may be able to help me with?'

'I know nothing about it,' she said. 'Or the Inner Temple. I look after the children, that's all.'

'On the morning that the news of Lord Dunning's death was broken to the family, I believe you had already been out?'

'Yes,' she said.

'To St Saviour's?'

'I do not know how you know that.'

'There is no secret about how I know,' he said in his gentle way. 'Lady Brown told her husband and he mentioned it to me. I gathered that the visit was not an expected one. Would it be impertinent to ask why you made it?'

'Yes,' she said.

Gabriel looked at her in pure astonishment. Although he would have said he neither expected nor noticed it, the truth was that he was accustomed to the deference usually accorded to those who benefited most from the social divide.

He felt for a moment sharply offended and opened his mouth to utter a blistering rebuke. But then, quite suddenly, snuffled instead.

'Well, Miss Murray, I asked the question when I had no real right to do so and so I suppose you may say I cannot complain about the answer.'

She thawed a little. 'It was a personal matter. It had nothing to do with Lord Dunning's death.'

'May I be the best judge of that?'

'No,' she said.

This time Gabriel gave a real chuckle. 'I can see, Miss Murray, that rhetorical questions are ill advised when conversing with you.'

She gave what might have been the beginnings of a smile and then quite deliberately raised her voice. 'Come, children,' she called. The moment for private conversation was over.

His week was so nearly up. And what had he learned? Little that could possibly be said to matter. What did it matter that Lady Dunning was a frivolous woman who was not particularly grieved by her husband's death? Or that the victim's sister Theodora was a thwarted lawyer who had little time for anyone, save perhaps the children, in the household in which she lived? What did it matter if the Treasurer's grandiose dreams had been met by the Lord Chief Justice with a certain lack of enthusiasm? What did it matter that Lord Justice Wilson was defensive and disagreeable? And that Lord Justice Brown had been rude to the Lord Chief Justice and had taken a long time walking home? Or that both these gentlemen harboured ambitions to step into the Lord Chief Justice's shoes? (Oh, dear, thought Gabriel, now *I* am doing it; how apt that phrase is and how unfortunate in the circumstances.) Or that the Reverend

Vernon-Osbert was a little cagey about his movements on the night in question? Gabriel could not seriously think that behind any of these small mysteries could lie a motive, direct or indirect, for plunging the Inner Temple's best carving knife into the heart of the Lord Chief Justice.

Surely there was only one suspect with a real case to answer, and that was Broadbent? Where else did logic lead one? Broadbent, who had nursed a long, very publicly expressed grudge; Broadbent, who was destitute (and very possibly down to shoes with no soles) with nothing to lose except his life, which probably held little joy for him. Broadbent, who would never have been allowed through the gates of the Temple at any time of the day or night. Broadbent, who had nevertheless spent the night in the Temple Church.

And yet somehow Gabriel did not think Broadbent was the murderer either. It did not feel to him like the savage crime of a vengeful ex-convict, that fine, elegant knife so neatly inserted into that fine, elegant body. Not prolonged hacking due to bloody hate but the execution of a cold judgement.

Really, Gabriel chided himself, you are behaving like the worst kind of juror; never mind what you think, unless the evidence supports it. And in his heart, he knew why he was so anxious that Broadbent should not prove to be the murderer; it was because of the blame that would inevitably fall upon Meg.

Gabriel's scholarly little world, so carefully protected, into which no messy emotion had ever intruded and in which relationships with his fellow men and women were courteous and detached, now faced what he dimly recognised as a true moral dilemma, created not by the demands of his profession but by a fifteen-year-old scullery maid whom he scarcely knew.

There had been something about Meg – her love and trust in the security of the Temple, her valiant recognition of the lifetime of hard work that faced her, her kindness to Broadbent – which had touched a heart Gabriel had forgotten he had. He knew that the girl's escapade that night played into the Treasurer's hands. If the crime had to have happened at all, then the discovery it had been committed by an ex-convict with a known grudge would be a welcome result. A wicked man who was nothing to do with the Temple and who had invaded its hallowed precincts undetected was an extremely unfortunate occurrence, but the reputation of the Inner Temple and those who lived and worked there would remain unblemished. If it were known that this situation had been brought about by the intervention of one of the servants, and the lowliest kitchen maid at that, it would provide a very convenient scapegoat for the obvious deficiencies in security. Meg would be shamed and disgraced, and she and her father and mother would be dismissed without references.

As far as Gabriel knew, Meg had told no one but him what she had done; and he had not yet told Wright. Upon promising her he would see no harm came to her, he had recognised immediately the dilemma that might result. Then the appalling difficulties of the looming *Cadamy v Moore* court case and a propensity to ignore the intrusion of inconvenient practical demands had intervened. And after all, Gabriel comforted himself, concealing the information that Broadbent had been in the Temple on the night of the murder scarcely mattered, since the man seemed to have disappeared.

But now he acknowledged that at some time he was duty-bound to pass on this information to the Treasurer and to the police. And this would result in Meg's dismissal, regardless of whether Broadbent was found and whether he was the murderer.

Had Gabriel been able to pace his room in 4 King's Bench Walk, he would have done so, but the piles of books impeded this activity, and so he sat instead in his customary wing chair and agonised over the problem. It was not precisely a dilemma since he had no doubt as to where his duty lay.

It was the consequences of this duty with which he was grappling. Meg and her family with no income, reduced to the life of destitution lived by those who 'lost their place', eking out an existence, if they were lucky, in the network of slums spread like a malign web behind Fleet Street. Destined, if they were unlucky, for one of the workhouses hidden from genteel view in the East End.

Gabriel was a lawyer with a most distinguished reputation. Such men usually had large houses and wives and servants. They wielded influence and supported charitable works. They would have had no difficulty, should the need arise, in finding a suitable place for Meg and her parents.

Gabriel looked around his room, his world. He was conscious of the deep sense of insecurity that was present whenever he thought of Sir William's power over his right to live here. And on top of that was this unaccustomed tug on his emotions as he thought of Meg's probable fate, her looming homelessness so much worse than his could ever be. He crossed to the window by his desk; the sun was streaming in and he drew down the Holland blind against the glare and against the outside world. As he grasped the edge of the blind, his thumb folded into his palm and he knew that from then on it must always be the way he drew down the blind, absolutely exactly like this time: right hand only, thumb folded into his palm. A little insurance against the horrible risk of loss.

In the gently filtered light, he felt suddenly for the first time that his room was very small; but even as he thought it, he knew the thought was incorrect. It was in fact brimming with the learning of centuries, filled with thought on a vast array of subjects; filled, most importantly of all, with legal learning, with casebooks containing centuries of decisions of judges, their ideas expressed and polished and adjusted by them over the years, developed to fit the infinite variety of circumstance in which people turned to the law for resolution. Hundreds and hundreds of leather-bound books containing that strange, shape-shifting, nebulous entity called common law. The people of England had been guided and governed by it from time immemorial. In it, somewhere, must be the means to help Meg. And he realised to his own astonishment that he would set aside his work for the remainder of the day if, by so doing, he could help her.

He grasped the mahogany rail of his library steps and gingerly began his ascent up the dusty mountain of books, lingering for a while in the foothills of decisions by the lowlier, long-forgotten judges, and then mounting higher and higher into the rarefied air of the great summits of intellectual thought.

Four hours later he descended, washed his by now filthy hands, ate the cold supper left for him on Sundays when Hall was closed, snoozed over the *Annual Register*, and went slowly and contentedly to bed.

20

'Will it look bad if I go?'

'What on earth does it matter how it looks?'

'There is no need to snap, Theodora.'

Miss Dunning looked at her sister-in-law with exasperation. 'I beg your pardon, Charlotte, but really! Surely the question is whether it feels bad to you, not how it looks.'

'Well, I think I should go,' said Lady Dunning, who had every intention of going regardless. 'After all it is work for charity, not a social occasion. Perhaps you would come with me? That would look better.'

'My dear Charlotte, it does not take twenty ladies and coffee and cakes for two hours to decide upon the distribution of a few items of clothing to the poor. It is a social occasion and we are in mourning. If you think it will look bad, how would it look better if I came with you? Surely it would look twice as bad.'

But this logic was beyond Charlotte Dunning. She pouted and flounced.

'Well, I shall go,' she said.

'No one is preventing you,' said Theodora. 'You may make your own decisions, as I shall. I shall not accompany you.'

'I think Norman would wish me to face the future with courage and optimism.'

'I am sure that he would. He might be a little surprised, however, to know that you had turned your mind to it with quite such resolution within a week of his death,' said Theodora drily.

Following a sulky silence, Charlotte Dunning ordered the carriage, gave the coachman an address in Bloomsbury Square, and settled down for the short drive with pleasurable anticipation and only a slightly uneasy twinge of conscience. It was the monthly meeting of the Reverend Vernon-Osbert's 'Ladies in Law and Charity'.

The membership, save for the founder Vernon-Osbert himself, consisted of the wives and widows of the barristers and judges of the day. It had seemed to Vernon-Osbert as a young clergyman that the ladies who attended the Temple Church by virtue of their husbands' occupations did not have quite enough to do. Their dear children, he told himself, were the very centre of their lives and they were assiduous supporters of their husbands' careers. But he could not help but notice that the dear children had all practical needs provided by the phalanxes of nannies and nursemaids who accompanied them everywhere, and that many of the husbands seemed to regard long hours of work alone in the Temple as the most effective route to the success they sought. The ladies, thought Vernon-Osbert in his kindly way, would benefit from a sense of purpose in matters unrelated to the home. And so he had evolved the scheme that had now run successfully for many years.

Although many who lived and worked within the privileged environment of the Temple contrived to ignore the world that clamoured at its gates, Vernon-Osbert was not among them. On the contrary, he saw clearly the filth and destitution on their doorstep, in the tenements that had grown up in the dark alleys and courts to the north of Fleet Street and the south of St Paul's Cathedral, where neither the sunshine by day nor the feeble gaslight by night ever reached. To the depths of his charitable soul, he yearned to help, and so he had evolved a plan.

By the door of the Temple Church he left a large hamper, and every Sunday he invited his wealthy congregation to deposit in it any item of utilitarian clothing for which their own servants had no further use and which might assist some of the impoverished families living locally. Once a month the hamper was then conveyed to the house of one of the ladies who volunteered to host a Monday morning At Home. Vernon-Osbert (who was very fond of cake) attended with a list of those in need, and the ladies rummaged through the hamper and decided on the distribution of each item. It took, as Theodora had observed, very much less time than that allocated to the chitchat about families and fashion and vicarious gossip concerning the state of the legal profession and those who worked in it. On this latter subject, the 'Ladies in Law and Charity' usually became rather less than charitable.

On this occasion, the hostess was Maud Rentoul, whose philanthropy was motivated by the social opportunities it presented rather than any desire to help the poor, a sector of society she regarded with a barely suppressed indignation. The poor poor could not help it, of course, but really! Maud's life had been cushioned, literally and metaphorically, since the day she was born and she could understand no other. The pretty, pampered daughter of rich parents and then the equally pampered wife of a wealthy barrister, she was now a prosperous widow with an exquisite house, a loving son, a devoted daughter-in-law and two enchanting grandchildren. She lived in a welter of pot-pourri and hothouse lilies, of tasteful chintz and *papier-mâché* bibelots and silver frames containing watercolour portraits of her highly satisfactory family. She was still a very pretty woman. Her hair was artfully golden, her porcelain complexion carefully tended, if now just a little crumpled around the edges, and her dress sense, fuelled by a happy combination of perfect taste and wild extravagance, was generally agreed to be unrivalled.

But still she did not have the one thing that she felt would have made her happy. Her late husband, of great independent wealth, had been amiable, kind and unambitious. These characteristics are inimical to success at the Bar. He had not needed the money and he lacked the cutting competitive edge of his opponents. He was never appointed to the senior honour of King's Counsel and he never became a judge and so was not awarded the knighthood that went automatically with these honours. He had remained an ignominious 'Mr' and Maud plain Mrs Rentoul.

'All my friends are ladies,' she had reproached him endlessly.

'So I should hope, my dear,' he had chuckled imperturbably.

'You know what I mean!' she had wailed.

But there was simply nothing to be done about it. And although plain Mr Rentoul was long dead, it still rankled, and Maud's natural tendency to spitefulness had become her predominant characteristic.

Amusing and vivacious, she had a never-ending store of gossip which she distributed, while gleaming with malice, amongst her friends. It was a tribute to her charm, and perhaps a little to the lavish nature of her entertaining, that she had a lot of these, despite her reputation for spite. One of the closest and oldest of those friends was first to arrive for the meeting.

'*Lady* Wilson,' announced the butler. In fact, the overemphasis lay only in Maud's imagination, but she gritted her teeth at the reminder even as she oozed welcome.

The two ladies sat in Maud's charming drawing room, and while awaiting the others indulged in a positive orgy of speculation as to whether poor Charlotte Dunning would attend or not.

'Of course,' said Lady Wilson, 'dreadful though it is, one cannot expect her to be heartbroken. She is years younger than he was, and it was an odd marriage. They say her mother pushed her into it. She was only eighteen, he took a fancy to her, and naturally everyone has known forever he was going to become a distinguished judge, just as the Dunnings have always done.

Certainly not a love match. And then she has had years of that ghastly sister of his living with them.'

'Enough to drive anyone mad. If she had been the one to be murdered it would have been far less surprising,' said Mrs Rentoul. 'Mind you, of course, insofar as poor Lord Dunning is concerned, you and Frederick have the best of motives for murder! When are you expecting the announcement of your husband's elevation?'

'We do not know. And you should not make jokes about murder, Maud,' said Lady Wilson nervously.

'My dear, I was forgetting... it happened the very night that you had supper with me, did it not? Weren't you intending to go home via the Temple and take Frederick home with you? Did you see anything odd there?'

'I did go and Frederick came home with me in the carriage.' Lady Wilson looked a little self-conscious as she added, 'You will remember that I left you at about a quarter to eleven.'

'No, my dear, earlier than that. About ten, I'm sure.' Maud was distracted, checking that the maid had remembered the coffee spoons.

'Oh, no, Maud,' said Lady Wilson with fatal emphasis. 'It was definitely not one minute earlier than a quarter to eleven.'

Maud Rentoul was no fool. Her eyes at once sharpened and then rounded with interest.

'My dear! What *can* you mean? What were you doing?'

'I was not doing anything,' said Lady Wilson, red with vexation and confusion.

The butler entered.

'*Lady* Dunning,' he said. And Maud gritted her teeth once more.

Charlotte entered to a flurry of embraces and condolences, and after her the other ladies, and then the Reverend Vernon-Osbert and the hamper. Lady Wilson's angry flush died down, but she knew she had made a bad mistake – one that Maud would not forget.

Their hostess was her usual charming and welcoming self. But as she tucked away her friend's strange behaviour for later dissemination, she pondered the reasons for it. Could she have been deceiving Frederick? If so, one could not blame her. Such a pompous ass. But Louisa, a lover? Surely not? Or could she and Frederick possibly have been implicated in——? But no, no, that really was quite impossible. She checked the attendees. Lady Brown was missing.

'Are we expecting her?' she said. 'I never remember which is the wretched orphans' day.'

'Not wretched, surely?' said Lady Wilson, glancing anxiously at Vernon-Osbert.

'Oh, well, you know what I mean,' said Maud airily. 'They cannot help it, of course,' she added without conviction. 'But Maria could help being *quite* such a saint, don't you feel? One cannot but think that there are more entertaining things to do than telling stories to a bunch of unfortunate little persons; or if she must, she need not bore the rest of us with anecdotes about the adorable things they say.' She looked sideways and maliciously at Lady Wilson. 'Of course, I suppose it is *just* possible that she, too, may be wondering if she is about to assume a new role?'

Louisa Wilson looked at her with a complete lack of comprehension, and then, as the meaning of this remark dawned upon her, a whole series of transparent emotions crossed her face: astonishment that there was any conceivable rival to her Frederick, consummate rage, and lastly a look of the most steely determination.

None of these were missed by Maud. Her cheerful flow of spite continued until it was interrupted by the apologetic arrival of Maria Brown and the business of the morning began.

The hamper was gratifyingly full that month. A coachman's overcoat with only a very little moth would continue to keep a pauper warm for many years. There were several patched but still serviceable woollen shirts, no less than five woollen waistcoats, some thick leather men's gloves, six pairs of finely darned woollen stockings, a dozen handkerchiefs, two maid's frocks; and, at the bottom of the hamper, a large cook's apron.

'How kind people are,' said Vernon-Osbert happily, his faith in human nature confirmed. He extracted the apron from the bottom. 'And I think that is all,' he said, shaking it out. 'Now it is just the question of alloc—'

His voice trailed away as he peered at Maud Rentoul's exquisite Aubusson rug. Lying upon it, after being shaken from the last item in the hamper, was a pair of gentlemen's black silk evening socks.

'It was quite electrifying,' Maud Rentoul recounted, describing the scene to a friend later on. 'We were all *transfixed*, my dear. They just *lay* there. And somehow one thought that, although they had no feet in them, at any moment they were *simply* going to dance around my drawing room all on their own! And dear old VO just *gawped*, my dear, and then he said, "How kind, though I don't quite think—" As if someone had seriously donated silk evening socks to the Poor Hamper! And of course, we were all *paralysed*, for everyone knows Norman Dunning was found barefoot! And then there was this most fearful shriek and I *nearly* leaped out of my *skin*…'

It was Charlotte Dunning who shrieked: 'Norman!' And nineteen ladies and one elderly vicar all jumped as one and as one stared wildly, as though expecting the Lord Chief Justice of England to be resurrected before their very eyes.

'Those are Norman's socks!' screamed Charlotte.

'Charlotte,' said Maud briskly, 'how can you possibly know? They are just evening socks.'

Charlotte picked one up in trembling fingers and pointed to a discreet monogram: 'ND', embroidered into a tiny circle at the ankle. 'We had a dozen pairs embroidered in Venice,' she wailed.

After a shaken Charlotte Dunning had been escorted to her carriage, there was plenty to be said by the remaining ladies and even by Vernon-Osbert, shaken from his usual policy of abstaining from Temple gossip. Speculation was rife, questions were numerous, answers unhelpful. Who could have come into the church? Anybody whom the porters did not deem unsuitable could come to visit and to worship during the day. Who would be able to put an article in the Poor Hamper? Anybody could do so at any time, quite easily and unobserved.

'This must be reported,' said Maud Rentoul at last.

'The Treasurer does not wish the police to be involved at present,' responded Vernon-Osbert unhappily. 'He has asked Sir Gabriel Ward to do a little – a little exploration on behalf of the Inner Temple.'

'Oh, Sir Gabriel Ward! He is such a dear, funny, reclusive old person,' trilled Maud who was some ten years older. 'I do assure you he positively *hides* when he sees me on the horizon. I suspect he has a soft spot for me.'

It was quite correct that Gabriel hid; he would have been truly astonished at the interpretation put upon it.

'I shall certainly go and *ferret him out* in his burrow where there can be no escape,' she continued, thrilled with the anticipation of active involvement in this most sensational of events. So saying, she scooped up the socks that lay like two black question marks on the rug, and tucked them in her reticule. 'In fact, I shall come back to the Temple immediately with you, dear Vicar.'

There was no denying her; and so, while the unknowing Gabriel pored over the statements in the now imminent case of *Cadamy v Moore*, she was trundling her way to the Temple in a hansom cab accompanied by Vernon-Osbert and the now empty Poor Hamper.

Gabriel's fierce concentration had been broken once that morning already. A bashful Wright had arrived to report on his search for Broadbent and had recounted the story of his visit to the Old Bell and where it had led him. It seemed that the budding delphiniums and lupins in the St James' Park flower-beds had suffered greatly under Constable Wright's heavy boots, as had the fresh foliage on the shrubs pulled apart by his large pink hands, but there was no sign there of Broadbent, dead or alive. Wright had turned then to the mortuary lists but nowhere upon them did Albert Broadbent's name appear. He had checked the basement of Moore's Bookshop twice daily, but it had remained as Broadbent had left it. In despair Wright had mingled with the poverty-stricken families eking out their survival in the hovels surrounding the Fleet Street alleyways, asking for leads. But nobody knew anything. Broadbent had simply disappeared.

When Wright had been consoled for his lack of success and had at last left, Gabriel had bent determinedly to his work once again. Tomorrow was Tuesday. His week of investigation was up and tomorrow afternoon held the dreaded prospect of an interview with the Treasurer.

His consternation, as Chapman ushered in Maud Rentoul, was not well hidden.

'*Goodness!*' Maud exclaimed without any other greeting, her eyes fixed on his desk. 'You must have a great many godchildren, Sir Gabriel.'

Gabriel looked blankly at her, and then, following her gaze, saw what had drawn it: the fifteen copies of *Millie the Temple Church Mouse*, delivered by the solicitors in case of need during the forthcoming trial — twelve for the jurors, one for the judge, one for the witness and one for Gabriel himself.

'They are for a case.' His tone was intended to discourage further enquiry. 'How may I help you, Mrs Rentoul?'

'A case?' exclaimed Maud, momentarily diverted by this new source of gossip. 'But how *exciting*, Sir Gabriel! Who is your client? Can it be that you have met Miss Cadamy? What an interesting old lady she must be. And what a shame she is so retired from society. I should very much like to meet her. I hold literary luncheons and she would be such a catch!'

'I cannot discuss my work. How may I help you?'

But Maud was in full swing. 'Do you know,' she said confidentially, 'I have often thought that Miss Cadamy must know the Temple well. Not just the church, but the people who attend worship. Many of her descriptions are really most *astute*. In fact, one or two made me simply laugh aloud.'

Unwilling though Gabriel was to encourage her speculation, he was also only too conscious of the looming cross-examination of Miss Susan Hatchings and the paucity of the material for it that he had at his disposal; it was this latter concern that won.

'Really?' he said, not too repressively.

'Yes indeed. For instance, the character she so amusingly calls "The Lady in the Hat": the hat she wears is an almost exact description of one worn by Lady Barton — *feathery*, you know, and rather *too much*! And the one she calls "The Fat Judge" is Lord Justice Bradley to a T! And I could give you any number of other examples, were I to be so unkind.'

This was disappointing. The world in Gabriel's eyes was too full of ladies in horrid hats and fat judges to attach undue significance to them.

'I think you may find,' he said, 'that they are mere literary stereotypes. Now, if you will forgive me, Mrs Rentoul, I am very busy. How may I help you?'

'Oh!' she cried. 'Silly me. I had quite forgotten the grave nature of my errand!'

She fished from her reticule the silk socks and flung them on top of the pile of books, then leaned across the desk, her bosom perilously close to the inkwell. Gabriel backed against his bookshelves.

'They belonged to the Lord Chief Justice,' she hissed like an actress in a melodrama, confiding to her audience across the footlights. 'His monogram is embroidered on them, you see.'

'Where did you find them?'

'In the Temple Church Poor Hamper!'

Gabriel blinked. 'Now that surprises me very much,' he said, obscurely and half to himself.

'Discovered by the "Ladies in Law and Charity", and recognised by poor Lady Dunning herself. You may imagine the embarrassment! And the dear vicar said to tell you that the hamper has been there a month and simply anyone could have *popped* in a pair of socks and no one the wiser, since no one looks in it between one meeting of the "Ladies" and the next.'

Gabriel picked up the socks, retrieved an envelope from his desk drawer and placed them carefully in it.

'Thank you,' he said, in a tone clearly intended to bring the interview to an end.

But Maud was not deterred. 'You cannot keep me in suspense, Sir Gabriel! What do you intend to do next?'

'I intend,' he said deliberately, 'to inform the Treasurer that the socks have been found.'

Still Maud lingered. 'Your investigations must be so *fascinating*. All the funny little secrets you must be discovering! And people's memories are never completely reliable, are they? We all know that the most unexpected people make mistakes. And of course it does not *necessarily* mean they are not telling the truth or have something to hide, does it?' She waited hopefully to be asked what she meant.

But Gabriel merely held open his door with infinite courtesy and bowed. Maud was left with no option but to pass through. Standing outside his chambers her sense of thwarted drama was strong. She thought for a few moments and then, with determination and a new feeling of purpose, made her way to the Royal Courts of Justice.

21

Before his interview with the Treasurer, Gabriel felt he had to see Meg. He went the next morning. The meeting was as distressing as he had feared it would be. The girl, summoned from her inner scullery, stood at bay by the vast kitchen table, tears restrained as best she could.

'I will lose my place,' she said. 'And so will my parents.'

'Meg,' said Gabriel gently, 'I will not conceal from you that this is a possibility; but I believe I have found a way through and must ask you to trust me. I think you know there can be no alternative but to tell the truth. A man has died; someone deliberately cut short his life. Don't you think that whoever did that must be found, whatever the cost?'

'I don't believe it was Mr Broadbent, sir. I know he hates judges but it – it was just a bit of a joke to him, sir. He didn't have much left and it gave him something to do every day, painting his signs and sitting outside the Law Courts with them. I don't believe he meant any harm, sir. And I don't believe he did any.'

'As it happens,' said Gabriel, 'neither do I. But if he is innocent then I think you will find that will become apparent, Meg.' He looked doubtfully at her. 'Do you understand me when I say that real innocence has a habit of making itself clear and bright?'

She nodded. 'Yes, sir,' she said simply. 'Like children.'

'Yes,' said Gabriel, 'that is exactly what I meant.'

'But whether Mr Broadbent murdered the Lord Chief Justice or not, Sir William will say I should never have let him in.'

'I fear that he will. And you know you should not have done so,' said Gabriel. 'But I am going to do my best with Sir William.' He smiled at her. 'Nanny, who looked after me when I was a little boy, always said: "Cross the bridges as you come to them." Shall we do that?'

She nodded, respectful and unconvinced.

Gabriel hesitated. 'You know, Meg, we are aware of the time of the Lord Chief Justice's death. Your account of that evening may prove to be important. You told me that you left the kitchen at a quarter to midnight. Are you sure of that?'

She nodded again. 'I am certain.'

'And you then made your — er — quick visit to the church before you went to wait by the gate?'

'Yes, I was only in the church for five minutes, sir. Oh, sir, what will happen to me?'

Gabriel looked rather helplessly at her. How little he knew of these other lives that made his own comfortable. What did this child wish her life to be?

'Do you want to be here forever?' he asked her.

'My mother says she wishes she was more than a Temple laundress. She would have liked me to have more book learning. Always on at me to read stories like she does, but I know what I want to do. One day I want to be the Temple cook. When Mrs Bugg lets me help make the egg custards, the gentlemen cannot tell the difference. And now I am in sole charge of sending the puddings up in the service lift. Mrs Bugg says, go on like this and there is no knowing what she will let me do.'

Gabriel rose from the kitchen chair to make his departure and as he did so she put her hand on his sleeve. 'I could not bear to leave the Temple, sir.'

'No,' said Gabriel. 'Neither could I.'

Sir William Waring ushered Gabriel into his room and thrust him into a visitor's chair. One week since their last meeting, the sun was a little higher in the sky and dazzling through the window. Roses were beginning to appear under the sill.

'Say nothing,' said Sir William to Gabriel, who had said nothing, 'until you peruse my note.' And he handed over a neatly type-written page, which read:

7.30 onwards: arrival of guests for Little Dinner which commenced at 8.00 p.m.

10.00: departure of Sir Vivian Barton and the Reverend Vernon-Osbert

10.45: departure of Lord Chief Justice

11.00: departure of Lord Justice Wilson with Lady Wilson, followed after a few minutes by Lord Justice Brown

'Now does that accord with the information you have been given by others?'

'Yes,' said Gabriel when he had digested it. 'It does. You are the only person I have not yet heard from.'

William Waring immediately looked irritated. 'Really, Ward, do you imagine I murdered the Lord Chief Justice?'

'You asked me to investigate, Sir William.'

Something in the steady reply caused the Treasurer to collect himself.

'Quite right, quite right. Justice must be served. Well, Sir Gabriel, I sat quietly at the table and finished my port. I snuffed out the table candles myself as I always do when my guests have departed, and then I made my way to my bedroom by the little back staircase. As you know, I have my own room near the Dining Hall for those evenings when I am too late to return to the family home in Greenwich. It is most convenient for me.'

Gabriel bowed politely. Despite his unworldliness he was well aware of the rumours as to the uses to which that room and the little back staircase were sometimes put. It was none of his business.

'And the Little Dinner?' he said.

'Was uneventful,' said Sir William in a final tone.

'Could you elaborate a little on uneventful?'

'Really, Ward, there is nothing to say. It was just a dinner. I chose the wines myself and they were quite excellent. Mrs Bugg was a little off form, I thought. The duck was not pink enough and the pudding was not quite as hot as I would have liked. One of the maids sent it up to the servery far too early.'

'I did not quite mean that,' said Gabriel politely. 'All your guests, Sir William, showed reticence in relation to the purpose of the occasion. I gather you had requested secrecy?'

'I had,' said the Treasurer shortly. 'And I do not propose to divulge that purpose now. It is, as I believe I informed you before, of no relevance to the Lord Chief Justice's death.'

'It concerned some kind of coronation celebrations?'

Sir William flushed almost purple.

'I do not know from whom you heard that. Our dear Queen has been dead only four months. I regard any gossip on such a subject as grossly inappropriate.'

With a sinking heart Gabriel abandoned the subject and turned instead to Meg's story. As he had anticipated, Sir William was much mollified by the prospect of a scapegoat in relation to the embarrassment of Lord Dunning's murder. He leaped upon it with alacrity, his purple face dying down to its normal, slightly florid, hue.

'You have been very helpful. The clear suspect is not a member of this institution and the reputations of its senior members are untarnished. The girl and her parents will be dismissed, of course, and the police can continue the search for this wicked murderer.'

'He is not yet proven to be a murderer, Sir William – '

'Of course he is the murderer!'

' – and you will not dismiss Meg and her parents,' continued Gabriel serenely. 'Meg made a mistake. She is aware of it. She will not do it again.'

'A mistake! She clandestinely allowed a murderer—'

'Not a proven murderer.'

'Oh, very well,' said Sir William who was, for all his failings, still a lawyer. 'Not proven. It is wholly immaterial. She let a vagrant into the Inner Temple and I shall dismiss her for it.'

'You must not dismiss Meg,' said Gabriel. 'She has known the Temple all her life and she loves it, Sir William, as much – as much – as you do.'

'As *I* do? She is a kitchen maid!'

'She has intelligence and kindness; she saw a fellow human being in want and brought him to somewhere she regarded as a place of safety.'

'Nonsense! She will be dismissed forthwith.'

Gabriel made his last appeal. 'She is just a vulnerable child, Sir William.'

'You may wish to remind yourself that there may be areas in which you are a little vulnerable yourself,' said Sir William nastily; and looked meaningfully out of his window towards 4 King's Bench Walk.

Gabriel drew in his breath and knew that his moment had come. He heard his own dry, precise voice say: 'You cannot dismiss her, Sir William, for giving a beggar sanctuary.'

'Sanctuary? *Sanctuary?* Have you run mad, Ward? Every law student knows that the law of sanctuary was abolished in 1624!'

'Not in the Temple,' said Gabriel steadily. 'The Temple is believed to be one of the so-called Ancient Liberties. The church is a Peculiar, a self-governing autonomy in all ecclesiastical matters. All fascinatingly complex, in legal terms. But one thing is clear: since the days of the Knights Templar in the twelfth century, the entire area of the Temple has had the privilege of sanctuary. That privilege was confirmed once again in 1608 in the royal charter granting the land to the lawyers. When the law of sanctuary was abolished in England in 1624, the abolition was never acknowledged within the Temple; it carried on, and I find there are cases where it was successfully claimed up until the 1700s. When I was researching the point last night, Sir William, I stumbled upon it in a volume of 1732. Do you know what it was called then? The law of mercy.'

'Nonsense!' said Sir William again. 'By your own admission, such a claim has not been made for nearly two hundred years! You would lose such an argument in any court of law.'

'Very possibly,' said Gabriel equably. 'But not in the court of public opinion, Sir William. And not, I think, in the Temple. Meg is a popular little person here, I find. May I suggest that you give the matter some thought and await the outcome of investigations into Broadbent's whereabouts?'

'Certainly not! It is a ridiculous contention.'

'I do not think the newspapers will regard it as ridiculous. I think they would be very interested to know that the Inner Temple, a society of distinguished lawyers, had dismissed a servant for allowing sanctuary to a beggar.'

'Can you possibly be threatening me, Ward?'

'I am merely observing that it is a very interesting legal point, Master Treasurer.'

'Ha! It is unarguable.'

'Nothing is unarguable to a good lawyer.'

Sir William's eyes narrowed in fury. 'I think that this discussion must now be concluded,' he said. 'I wish to hear no more about the law of sanctuary, Ward, and if you pursue this argument you may find that your own – er – sanctuary in King's Bench Walk is not quite the safe haven you like to think it is.'

Gabriel's heart beat faster and his hand gripped the edge of his chair while, unseen, and very carefully, he traced upon it a little familiar reassuring pattern with his finger. But his voice remained quite steady. 'I cannot think, Sir William, that you would contemplate terminating a barrister's right to live in the Inn because of the legal arguments he proposed to advance on behalf of a client. All are entitled to representation, Sir William – even the kitchen maid.'

And then, quite suddenly and miraculously, his hand relaxed on the edge of the chair and he felt in control of the interview. By some curious process, the balance of power seemed to have shifted. He knew that the Treasurer felt it too.

Gabriel rose from his seat, and as he did so, something occurred to him.

'By the way,' he said, 'I propose to ask the gardener if he can find a position for Mrs Bugg's Ruby's Fred. I trust you have no objection?'

'Who the devil is Mrs Bugg's Fred's – what you just said?'

'Mrs Bugg's daughter Ruby is married to Fred and there will be another mouth to feed soon.' It was his parting shot.

'In Heaven's name!' said Sir William to his cronies in the Garrick Club when recounting this conversation that evening. 'The kitchen maid! The cook's son-in-law! I could scarcely believe my ears. Do you suppose the fellow is turning into some kind of revolutionary? You know, like those Russian chaps who are beginning to cause such frightful trouble?'

There was a roar of laughter; no one could quite see Sir Gabriel Ward as a revolutionary.

In fact the nascent revolutionary had walked slowly back to 4 King's Bench Walk. Although he was a small man, he felt unaccountably taller. And his usual care to avoid the cracks in the pavement was today perhaps just a little less assiduous.

22

Meanwhile Lord Justice Wilson had been suffering. Despite his conviction that he was to succeed Dunning as the next Lord Chief Justice, and despite the fact he could see no near rival for the post, he was becoming a little nervous not to have received notice of the appointment from the Lord Chancellor. He was in the middle of trying a complex appeal. It required the immense attention to detail for which he was justly renowned. Perhaps, he had comforted himself, the Lord Chancellor was waiting until the case was completed for fear of distracting him. That was perfectly plausible; he seemed to recall there had been a short lapse between Dunning's predecessor, that old fool Grant, and Dunning himself.

All the same it was becoming a little odd, and what made it even more distressing was the mounting speculation amongst his colleagues as to the identity of the next incumbent. Lord Justice Wilson – though he did not say so, for fear of attracting derision from them – did not think that there was any speculation needed; it seemed to him, as it did to his wife, a foregone conclusion. Then, too, his wife was an additional trial to him. The fierceness of her ambition on his behalf was becoming alarming. Every evening, as he entered the drawing room after a hard day in court, Lady Louisa Wilson greeted her husband with one word: 'Well?'

He found it increasingly stressful to meet her expectant eye, and to pretend he thought the question was a mere query as to the nature of his day.

On top of that, his roses – his pride and joy, his hobby, his consolation – always responsive in a way that Louisa sometimes was not, should now be at their very prime. Instead of which they appeared to have developed powdery mildew and were not giving him quite the satisfaction this May that he had come to anticipate annually with keen enjoyment.

Really, all in all, it was too much. After a particularly grumpy day in court, in which counsel seemed to him to be deliberately goading him past endurance ('What the devil is the matter with the old bastard?' they were in fact saying to each other in the robing room), he thought that his situation could not be much worse.

Taking off his robes in his private room at the end of the court day, he could not face going home to another 'Well?' As he was thinking this, the clerk put his head around the door to announce a most surprising visitor.

'You had better bring her in,' said Lord Justice Wilson. In she came, and turned his world upside down.

———

It was Gabriel, exhausted from his week and from all the little routines he had exercised to give him the confidence to triumph over Sir William, who spotted the judge wandering in the Temple in the gathering twilight. Judges frequently had cause to visit the Temple: meetings and dinners and appointments of one kind or another; it was the wandering that seemed a little odd. Few judges had time for aimless strolls at the end of the working day; most were hurrying, purposeful figures, walking directly across the Terrace. And of all purposeful strides, that of Lord Justice Wilson was usually the most determined. But now he appeared to be criss-crossing between one set of barristers' chambers and the next, peering at the painted names above the lintels of the doors, hovering as though looking for someone;

occasionally stopping altogether and gazing apparently unseeingly across the gardens to the river. He even, thought Gabriel, peering out of the window of 4 King's Bench Walk, seemed to be wobbling a little. Surely, surely, a judge of His Majesty's High Court could not be drunk in the early evening within the precincts of the Temple.

Then it occurred to him that the man might be ill. Hastening to his door, in too much of a hurry to worry that he was in his shirtsleeves and braces, but not in too much of a hurry to close his door and to press it three times, nor, once he was outside, to avoid the lines between paving stones, Gabriel hurried over to the figure now leaning heavily with one hand on the wall of the library. He seemed somehow diminished, his portly form shrunken, even the rose in his buttonhole wilting.

'Good evening, Judge,' said Gabriel. 'May I help you? I fear you are feeling unwell.'

Lord Justice Wilson lifted a ravaged face and put one hand to his forehead. He peered and then recognised Gabriel.

'Ward?' he said. 'I – I am a little upset.' And Gabriel, looking with horror at the face he had seen dozens of times in court – pompous, powerful, unruffled, faintly disagreeable – saw that he had red eyes and tearstains on his cheeks.

He put his hand under the judge's elbow, doing his best to ignore his own shrinking embarrassment. This was worse than Annie on the day of the murder, worse than Meg in the flowerbed. The trite sayings of Nanny, the offer of a clean handkerchief, were of no use here with another man, a social equal, a contemporary. The only resonance from early experience would be 'I say, don't blub'; hardly appropriate in the circumstances.

Privacy seemed to be urgently required. And so Gabriel, his short, slight stature almost comical beside the solid figure of Lord Justice Wilson, tightened his grip on his elbow, steered him back into 4 King's Bench Walk, up the stairs and into his rooms. Lord Justice Wilson looked around in a daze. Gabriel, having removed from a chair several volumes of Montesquieu's philosophical tract *The Spirit of the Laws*, almost pushed him into it. Weaving his way through the banks of books to a cupboard, he retrieved from it a brandy decanter and a sturdy eighteenth-century rummer, poured into it a generous measure, and thrust it into Lord Justice Wilson's hand.

There was silence. The grandfather clock ticked gently. Outside in the garden rooks cawed. The natural light fading in the unlit room was soothing. The books seemed to wrap the occupants in the learning of centuries. Lord Justice Wilson, like the few others privileged to enter Gabriel's sanctuary, began to feel a little better.

At last he muttered, 'I am sorry.'

'There is nothing to be sorry for,' said Gabriel. 'And no need to feel you must say anything further. I am pleased to have been able to offer you a – a moment's respite.'

The judge looked distractedly at the pile of books displaced to give him a seat.

'I fear I am disturbing your work.' His voice was husky.

'No, no,' said Gabriel, 'I assure you, the merest diversion. I am very fond of the legal philosophy of Montesquieu and often browse through his thoughts on the law when I need to relax my mind a little. Written in the mid-eighteenth century and yet so contemporary, don't you think? I stumbled upon his views on criminal punishment this evening and was much struck by his advocation of merciful proportionality when sentencing. We have still so far to go in this matter, have we not? I have always been deeply opposed to capital punishment, though whether we shall ever see its abolition—'

To Gabriel's horror, in his random attempt to divert, he seemed to have said something disastrous. Tears began to trickle slowly down the judge's cheeks once again; abandoning the glass on the nearest pile of books, he buried his face despairingly in his hands.

'Oh, God. The horror of it, Ward. During my time on the Bench, I have had to sentence two men to death. I realised I had never seen real fear until I saw those men in the dock, their faces as the sentence was passed – and now, oh, God, might I have to experience it closer to home?'

Gabriel looked uneasily at him: what event could have possibly triggered this horror of the noose, a fact of professional life for a lawyer?

'You seem very distressed,' he said at last. 'Would it help you to discuss it?'

Lord Justice Wilson took a deep breath. 'Do you know Maud Rentoul?'

Gabriel blinked; among the many things he had expected, this was not one of them.

'Yes,' he said cautiously. 'Not well, though. I became acquainted with her through her husband – who is dead now, of course. I had not seen her for a good while until yesterday when she had occasion to visit me in my chambers.'

'What was the purpose of her visit?' the judge demanded, his face tight with anxiety.

Gabriel hesitated, but he saw no reason why he should not say.

'There has been a curious incident involving the Lord Chief Justice's socks—' He got no further.

'His socks!' It was almost a wail. 'Oh, no, Ward, no! How did Mrs Rentoul come by the Lord Chief Justice's socks? What did she tell you? What terrible story is she spreading? Where did she get them from? Did – did she say who gave them to her?'

'No story at all,' said Gabriel. 'It was merely that the socks Lord Dunning was wearing on the night of his death had turned up in the Temple Church Poor Hamper.'

'She did not mention Louisa?'

'Louisa?'

'My wife.'

'May I say, Judge, that this story is becoming a little confused?' Gabriel told him politely. 'I suggest that we begin again and you elucidate a little.'

The judge managed a watery smile. 'It is usually me saying that to barristers.'

Gabriel smiled back encouragingly, and though Nanny's phrase 'Come, that is better' came to mind, he did not say it.

'My wife would describe Maud Rentoul as her best friend,' the judge said, 'though why, I cannot imagine. Maud is a cat.'

'And?'

'Yesterday afternoon she came to see me in my room in the Royal Courts. That was unprecedented. I feared Louisa had met with an accident. But Maud had come to tell me – to tell me – I scarcely know what she had come to tell me. She insinuated and hinted and smirked until it was past bearing. I understood her at last to be telling me that – that Louisa had asked her to lie for her.'

'To lie for her?'

'Yes, to cover up for her. As I told you when you came to question me, on the night Dunning died Louisa had been to supper with Maud in Bloomsbury, and had said she would ask the coachman to return via the Temple so that in the event the Treasurer's Little Dinner had concluded, I could go home with her. Maud told me that Louisa left her house to come and collect me at just before ten o'clock. Louisa afterwards asked her to say that she had left some three-quarters of an hour later, closer to eleven.'

'Yes,' said Gabriel slowly, 'I see.'

'It is only ten minutes' drive from Bloomsbury to the Temple at that time of night. Louisa sent the coachman in at eleven to say she was waiting outside. I know that what Maud said was the truth, Ward, because this morning on the way to work our coachman, who is the most dreadful old moaner, was complaining that Lady Wilson had gone off, leaving him waiting for the best part of an hour in the Temple on the evening of the Little Dinner. He is prone to exaggeration; I dismissed it without another thought. But now it all ties in,' he concluded miserably, and took a large gulp of his brandy. 'That dreadful Rentoul woman seemed to be suggesting that – that – Louisa had some sort of – of – romantic liaison in the Temple that night.'

He gripped the arms of his chair. 'I cannot believe it, Ward! I studied the names above the doors in the Temple this evening! All are known to me. All are decent men. But then – then – I thought…'

'What did you think?' prompted Gabriel softly.

'I can hardly think it, let alone say it. Where was she, Ward? The Lord Chief Justice died shortly after we dined together. He had left the dinner before Louisa arrived to pick me up.' Wilson paused for breath. 'She is ambitious for me. But there is no harm in that. She – she— No, I cannot bear to contemplate it.'

'Judge,' said Gabriel in his deliberate, quiet voice, 'are you telling me you are afraid your wife stabbed the Lord Chief Justice to death with the Inner Temple carving knife?'

'No! I am afraid of nothing of the sort. It is an outrageous, preposterous suggestion! How dare you?' cried Lord Justice Wilson, somewhat inconsistently. 'But where was she? For an hour, late at night in the Inner Temple? Where on earth *was* she?'

Gabriel shook his head. 'I do not know, Judge. I am sorry. It is not for me to advise you as to how to approach this matter. If you fear a – a – romantic liaison, you could, I suppose, ask your wife—'

The judge leaped to his feet. 'No. Good God, no! That is not the sort of conversation— Good God, a liaison! That would be worse than— No, I do not mean that. Of course I do not mean that! Oh, I do not know what I mean. I must think. *Think*.' He repeated the word with a vehemence that somehow suggested that he thought Gabriel was preventing him.

Gabriel rose politely to his feet.

Lord Justice Wilson seemed suddenly to realise that some sort of courtesy was required of him.

'You have been very kind. I should not have— I beg you will respect my confidence. I-I must *think*.' And, grabbing his hat, he fled.

Gabriel sighed. He was quite exhausted. And *Cadamy v Moore* was to begin the next day.

23

At this moment the only thing that mattered was the battle ahead. Only the sweating hands and knotted stomach, the feverish rehearsal of argument and counter-argument running through the head. The sharpening of the words that served as weapons, the cut and thrust of question and answer, the scent of vulnerability and fear, and the battle tactics that would determine victory or defeat.

Gabriel, encircled by the halo of his own concentration, sat in court immobile, in the row reserved for leading counsel. His notebook was carefully aligned in front of him so that the middle stitch in the spine was level with his gold pencil lying beside it, and his jug of water placed so that the handle of the jug pointed exactly towards the left-hand corner of the inkstand.

In the same row some feet away, in a happy disarray of papers and pens and illicit toffees, a dust of ash down his gown from the last cigar in the robing room, chatting happily to his instructing solicitor, sat Sir Vivian Barton KC, Gabriel's opponent.

Behind each barrister sat their juniors (in the case of Gabriel's, wholly redundant) and instructing solicitors. All were surrounded by piles of paper underneath which the real star of the case, Millie the Temple Church Mouse herself, peeped out from the front cover of copies of the book.

The public gallery of Court Number Two in the Royal Courts of Justice was packed with spectators, the press seats were filled with newspaper reporters, and the gentlemen of the jury sat expectantly in the jury box. The case of the plaintiff Miss Susan

Hatchings (suing as Miss Harriet Cadamy) versus the defendant Mr Herbert Moore (publisher) was about to begin.

All eyes were focused on the curtains that shrouded the doors leading to the judge's room. Just as the anticipation in the courtroom seemed to be becoming unbearable, a clerk appeared from between them, stepped onto the bench and declaimed the unnecessary exhortations that always marked the beginning of the court day.

'Silence!' he bellowed into the breathless silence. 'Be upstanding!' he instructed the already-standing occupants.

Mr Justice Anderson, a judge of great experience and little patience, entered, and looked characteristically at the clock in order to convey that not a moment of court time was to be wasted. After each of the twelve jurymen had taken the oath, Barton, clutching a formidable, if untidy, wodge of notes, rose to open the case.

'Gentlemen of the jury.' His voice resounded around the courtroom, deep and kindly. 'There cannot be many people in England who have not heard of Millie the Mouse and her adventures in the Temple Church, that ancient place of worship so close to this courtroom and to the hearts of Londoners. Every father and uncle and godfather amongst you must have heard about Millie or read her story to your little ones. Most of you will have experienced the joy of the old message of Christianity heard by little children through the tale of that mouse. The book was, as you all know, written by Miss Harriet Cadamy.'

He shifted his burly, reassuring bulk, half turning to the seats behind him and making a sweeping gesture towards Miss Hatchings who sat there meekly, clad in a neat blue costume and unostentatious hat.

'Members of the jury,' he said, 'here is Miss Harriet Cadamy. Her real name is Miss Susan Hatchings. She is the author of *Millie the Temple Church Mouse*. I am proud to represent her.'

He had struck exactly the right note. The jury all looked at Miss Hatchings and seemed to purr collectively. Barton continued, his eloquence buoyed by the approval of his audience, and in his expert hands his client's story came to life.

'It seems so very sad, does it not, that here we gather in a court of law to argue about a book that has given such joy to children everywhere, and even sadder to reduce to pounds, shillings and pence the value of that joy? But that, gentlemen of the jury, is the world of publishing for you. That is why Miss Hatchings wants none of it, but only an acknowledgement that she is indeed the author of *Millie the Temple Church Mouse*—'

Gabriel shifted in his seat and tapped his fingers gently on the table in front of him. Barton, catching the movement from the corner of his eye and knowing very well what it signified, backtracked hastily. He was aware that Miss Hatchings had to have a properly constituted reason in law for her litigation, and that simple desire for recognition was not such a reason.

'That is not to say,' he recovered smoothly, 'that my client is not entitled to benefit from the considerable financial gains that have resulted from the success of her book, and so of course I shall submit on her behalf. But the most important verdict that I ask of each of you is the finding that she did indeed write this book, and that she alone has control over the words she has written. My client wants her book to resound to the glory of God. She wants the profits from her words to benefit her own church as she thinks fit. She does not want associated toys and other such nonsense to be manufactured in order to earn bigger and bigger profits.' Sir Vivian Barton dropped his voice an octave to emphasise the terrible fate that threatened Miss Cadamy. 'She certainly does not want her book to be published in the *United States of America!*'

The jury seemed to swell approvingly with collective patriotic insularity.

For the next hour, Barton outlined to the jury the story that ultimately would be fleshed out by his client in the witness box. The writing of the book; Miss Hatchings' use of a pseudonym, testimony to her shyness about her first attempt at authorship; her visit to the Temple Church with the manuscript in her shopping bag; and the terrible moment when she realised she must have dropped it in Fleet Street. And then, all that time later, the discovery that the book had become, so to speak, public property.

Sir Vivian Barton had learned his brief well and he delivered the climax with consummate style: 'Gentlemen of the jury, she wants her mouse back.'

Then he called his first witness.

Mrs Mary Mundy was the very pattern of respectability, a witness who had plainly resolved to tell the truth, the whole truth and nothing but the truth, and to do so lucidly and pleasantly.

She lived near Kensington Gardens, she told the jury, and her husband was the Reverend Giles Mundy, a canon of Westminster Abbey. They had two children: Harold, now aged eleven, and Emilia, now nine. About six years earlier, when Harold was five and Emilia three, Miss Hatchings had come to reside with them as the children's first governess. She had been a great success in those early days; the children liked her and so did Canon and Mrs Mundy.

Gabriel, silent and watchful, made a short note. *In those early days*, he wrote, and underlined it.

The teaching, Mary Mundy continued, had been of the kind suitable for small children, simple reading and sums, and of course religious education. Mrs Mundy remembered particularly that Miss Hatchings had liked to make up little stories for the children; indeed, Canon Mundy had given her his old type-writing machine to facilitate this hobby, and she had kept it upon leaving their employ. No, Mrs Mundy was not surprised to learn the typewriter had ultimately been discarded by Miss Hatchings. It had been so very old.

Most days after lessons, Miss Hatchings, along with many other governesses from the neighbourhood who had charges of similar age, took the children to Kensington Gardens so that they could play together. Harold had been fond of the model yachts on the Round Pond and Emilia liked to feed the swans. It was a little far for her to walk, but she still had her perambulator. Miss Hatchings simply loved to push Emilia in her perambulator. She said nothing made her feel so proud as walking through the gardens pushing it. Mrs Mundy said she had found that very touching. Otherwise, Miss Hatchings had seemed quite a solitary young lady, devoted to her two little pupils and with none of the giddiness that (in Mrs Mundy's opinion) characterised many young women today.

The family usually worshipped at Westminster Abbey, but on occasion they went to the Temple Church; Mrs Mundy's papa had been a barrister and she liked sometimes to go to the church of her childhood. They had introduced Miss Hatchings to the Temple and to the church with the round nave, and she had been very taken with the romantic tale of the crusading knights who had built it. Mrs Mundy recalled that Miss Hatchings had eagerly asked questions about her childhood memories of the place.

'Were you aware that Miss Hatchings was planning to write or was writing a book?' asked Barton.

'Oh, no, we had no idea. Miss Hatchings left us, you know, after about four years—'

'Yes indeed,' Barton intervened smoothly. 'In order, as we know, to care for her sick mother.'

Gabriel's antennae twitched; it was not like Barton to interrupt his witness unless he had some reason for wishing to steer the questions away from a sensitive area. He made another note.

'Yes,' continued Mrs Mundy. 'And we heard occasionally from her with cards for the children and such like but then we really lost touch; never did we dream that the children had been fortunate enough to have a governess who was to become a famous author. To think that one day Harold and Emilia will be able to tell their own children that they were cared for by Miss Harriet Cadamy!'

Barton sat down. He looked smug.

'Do you wish to cross-examine, Sir Gabriel?' Mr Justice Anderson's tone conveyed that he felt this course to be a wholly unnecessary waste of time.

Undeterred, Gabriel rose to his feet, a slight figure in a battered silk gown and a yellowing wig, both of which were a little too large for him. There was a pause while he fumbled for his gold-rimmed half-spectacles and put them on his nose. He looked carefully at the witness for a minute that seemed interminable in the silent court, and then he began his cross-examination.

It was the first time the jury had heard his voice. It was very quiet and precise with none of the oratorical flourish that even the most sophisticated juror rather enjoyed. The truth was that when people heard Gabriel's first few words in court, they were sometimes a little disappointed. But quickly they became aware of an indefinable, compelling quality.

'Mrs Mundy, I should like to ask you a little about the circumstances in which Miss Hatchings came to leave your employ. Did she tell you she wished to leave to care for her mother?'

Mary Mundy hesitated. 'We knew that her mother had not been well,' she said.

'That is not quite what I asked you.'

'Miss Hatchings was devoted to her, you know. It was very natural that she would wish to return home to be with her.'

'That is not what I asked you,' said Gabriel again, his voice very gentle. I repeat, did Miss Hatchings tell you she wished to leave to care for her mother?'

'Not precisely that,' said Mary Mundy.

'Then tell us precisely what she said, if you please.'

Mary Mundy shifted uneasily in the witness box and her gloved hands gripped the rail in front of her. 'Well – well – the truth is that we – my husband and I – felt that – that – perhaps it would be best.'

'Best for Miss Hatchings to leave?'

'Well, yes – perhaps.'

'Why was it best?'

'Well,' said Mary Mundy desperately, transferring her hands from the rail to cling to the small handbag in her lap, 'happier for her, perhaps.'

'Why happier?'

'We felt that – that perhaps she was – becoming a little too – too '

'Yes, Mrs Mundy? Too?'

The pressure might be gentle, but it was inexorable.

Mary Mundy dropped her handbag on the floor, fumblingly retrieved it and then gave up. Blushing a little, she tumbled into a tangled explanation.

'A little too fond of Canon Mundy. And not just that. She became very – well, almost *too* religious and a little bit odd, and my husband felt – that it was in some way connected to him. Oh, dear, I am not explaining it very well. It was all rather embarrassing and, well – a little bit *silly*.'

'Thank you, Mrs Mundy,' said Gabriel, and he sat down.

———

During the luncheon adjournment, Herbert Moore was jubilant in the face of Gabriel's reserve.

'It is just as I said!' he exulted.

But Gabriel shook his head. 'Mr Moore, it may indeed be just as you said. But the fact that the evidence indicates Miss

Hatchings is a silly woman who falls in love with vicars does not mean that she did not write *Millie the Temple Church Mouse*. Indeed, were I Sir Vivian Barton, I would be working hard with the material I have myself brought to light to paint the picture of a devout young lady stricken by a hopeless love who, thwarted in her desire for children of her own, turned to the comfort of writing for them.'

'Oh.' Herbert was nonplussed. 'Do you believe that to be the case?'

'Mr Moore,' said Gabriel patiently, 'what I believe is not the issue. The question is simply whether it can be made believable. It is not your surmise or mine that matters but what the jury can be persuaded to adopt as fact. I am trying to demonstrate to you that we are a very long way from establishing our case.'

Herbert sighed. It seemed to him that he was back once more on the switchback railway that lawyers seemed to delight in.

24

At two o'clock Vivian Barton resumed his case.

Self-consciously basking in the attention of those present, the Reverend Blair of the New Church of God, Edinburgh entered the witness box.

Miss Hatchings, he told the jury in answer to Barton's questions, was a member of his congregation and had become a valued friend into whose confidence he was flattered to be admitted. He had learned of her years as a governess, and of her devotion to her mother; but only recently, to his utter astonishment, had she told him at last, so shyly and touchingly, that she was the author of *Millie the Temple Church Mouse*.

Gabriel immediately rose to his feet.

'My lord,' he said in his quiet, diffident way, 'neither my learned friend nor your lordship requires from me a lecture on the basic rules of evidence. Reverend Blair's testimony that Miss Hatchings told him that she wrote this book is not evidence of the issue of authorship. It is hearsay. The Reverend Blair, by his own account, met Miss Hatchings some considerable time after the book in question was published. His statement as to the authorship of *Millie the Temple Church Mouse* is not therefore material to the issue that the jury has to determine.'

'I am bound to say,' said the judge, looking over his spectacles, 'that there is some force in that. Sir Vivian, what is the status of your witness?'

'He is a character witness,' said Barton smoothly.

'In that case,' said the judge, 'he should confine himself to evidence relating to Miss Hatchings' character.'

The remainder of the Reverend Blair's evidence was a fervent tribute to Susan Hatchings. He spoke of her love for little children and her rapport with them; of her charmingly imaginative approach to life; and of her devotion to God and to the reverend's own church.

Gabriel began his cross-examination with questions as to the contrasting nature of the solemn services so beautifully described by Miss Harriet Cadamy in *Millie the Temple Church Mouse*, and those apparently espoused by Miss Susan Hatchings, now worshipping at Reverend Blair's low-church populist services. It was quickly apparent that this was not a fruitful line of enquiry.

'Miss Hatchings has grown in faith since she wrote the book,' the Reverend Blair intoned unctuously. 'At my New Church of God she has seen the light.'

'Tell us about your New Church,' said Gabriel, changing tack. 'You have sought a different way of conveying the Christian message, have you not, but in an old church building?'

The Reverend Blair beamed. 'Yes indeed, you put it so well, Sir Gabriel. An old and dilapidated building, in which God has found a new home.'

'Dilapidated?' pursued Gabriel, his tone sympathetic. 'Is that not a great worry for you?'

'Oh, but not for much longer. My own church will be rebuilt, and we want to bring other old churches back to life too, offering a new way to meet God.' He looked over towards the jury, his expression pious. 'I hope that more and more preachers will adopt my personal message and people will come to meet God in towns all over the United Kingdom.'

'And the practical support necessary to implement these ambitious plans?' said Gabriel delicately.

The Reverend Blair waved his hand dismissively. 'God will provide, Sir Gabriel. My own little congregation will be the first instruments of His provision. Indeed, the many ladies who have met God through me have revealed they are anxious to help; in minor ways, perhaps, but the widow's mite, you know, Sir Gabriel, the widow's mite.'

'But will the widow's mite be enough, Reverend Blair?' asked Gabriel, and his tone was still solicitous.

'I say to my ladies we must begin in small ways.'

'That is the second reference you have made to your ladies. Do no gentlemen attend your church?'

'The widower's mite is just as welcome,' said the Reverend Blair smoothly, 'but it is a sad fact of life that there are fewer widowers.'

Gabriel privately gave him credit for a certain dexterity and metaphorically honed his own rapier in response.

'In any event, to put it plainly, you rely on your congregation to fund your ambitions?'

'I guide my congregation in worship and worship engenders a zeal to spread the word to the world,' parried Reverend Blair.

By looking down at his papers, as though seeking inspiration, Gabriel quite deliberately gave the jury the impression that he felt he was not getting anywhere. Looking up again, he saw that his quarry had relaxed and was looking a little smug.

Gabriel resumed, as though on a new topic. 'Tell the jury about your plans,' he said encouragingly.

And the Reverend Blair, unable to resist the invitation, did so. Two more churches in Edinburgh, drawings of the buildings already sketched out, and then other Scottish towns, and then – then London. All was ready, it needed only a sizeable injection of capital. He looked forward with fervour and reverence to spreading His message. All would hear. God would be there. They would come and meet Him.

'This is very impressive indeed,' said Gabriel. Reverend Blair preened himself. 'Do you never feel any doubt, as to whether this huge ambition can be achieved?'

By now, as Gabriel had intended, Reverend Blair had completely dropped his guard.

'When I ask for help, God sends it. On one occasion I shared with my congregation a little moment of uncertainty as to our future viability. And dear Miss Hatchings stayed behind after the service and, purely to divert and cheer me, told me about her secret authorship and the riches her book might bring her.'

Gabriel pounced.

'And so you encouraged Miss Hatchings to bring these proceedings?'

'No, no, it was quite — all her own — I simply expressed a wish that the world should know of her great talent. Sus— Miss Hatchings, I said, it is for you to decide whether you claim the riches to which you are entitled, but we are here for you, and I shall of course esteem your support of my church, and indeed of me personally, should you find the courage to take on this world of commerce and greed.'

'And when she found the courage to support your church, what form did your personal esteem take?'

The Reverend Blair's eyes narrowed.

'Are you suggesting something dishonourable, Sir Gabriel? I think I should tell you that last night Miss Hatchings did me the great honour of agreeing to become my wife.'

The jury looked gratified. Susan Hatchings glowed.

Mr Justice Anderson sighed. 'I am not sure,' he said, 'where this evidence is taking us, but it is four o'clock, gentlemen of the jury, so we shall adjourn until tomorrow and hope that, with a new day and with the assistance of counsel, some clarity will be vouchsafed to us.'

Outside the courtroom Herbert Moore's optimism was restored.

'You see,' he crowed once more, 'it is just as I told you! That dreadful man is a Svengali. He incited her to bring this case and he is marrying her to benefit from the money he believes she will receive. You have done a wonderful job, Sir Gabriel!'

Gabriel shook his head. 'He is indeed an unsavoury man, Mr Moore,' he said. 'And like you, I have little doubt that he encouraged Miss Hatchings to bring these proceedings and hopes to gain from them. But that does not mean that Miss Hatchings invented her authorship to ensnare him. We need much more. At present, were I Sir Vivian Barton, I should feel reasonably happy with the progress of the case. Indeed, the jury may well have gone away with the happy notion that Miss Hatchings not only wrote the book but has found her vicar, and they should now live happily ever after on the book's profits.'

'Oh,' cried Moore, exasperated by this continuing display of objectivity, 'how is it, Sir Gabriel, that you constantly seem to take the other side? And make it sound so convincing?'

Gabriel snuffled. 'That is the nature of my profession, Mr Moore,' he said, 'and the only way to win a case. I fear that any prospect of success lies firmly with Miss Hatchings' performance in the witness box tomorrow. Believe me, I will not endear our side to the judge and jury by suggesting, however subtly, that Miss Hatchings has a fixation on vicars, or, even worse, that the Reverend Blair is after her money. I can only try to instil some doubt as to her authorship, via an exposure of her personality; it will then be for you to try and explain in your evidence why that particular personality could not have written that particular book.'

'Then we must follow that plan!' cried Herbert. But even this optimistic exclamation contained a note of desperation.

25

Removing his wig and gown in the robing room, Gabriel felt the full weight of his concerns. They still oppressed him as he left the Law Courts and headed to his chambers with an aching head. Annie was back, he noticed, sitting on a stool, assiduously polishing the brass doorplates in the hall. He paused dutifully and she leaped up in some confusion, bobbing her knees and tumbling into apology.

'There is no need,' said Gabriel. 'It must be a relief to find a job you can do sitting down. I work sitting down, after all.'

She gave a little smile but he was nonetheless shocked by her ravaged expression, the heavy eyes and white, woebegone face.

'You work very long hours,' he said gently. 'It must be hard on the feet.'

She bobbed again and put down her rag.

'Yes, sir,' she said simply. 'All my working life I've suffered badly with my feet, so I sits on the stool when I can, sir.'

'I am pleased to see you are returned to us, Annie.'

'Thank you, sir,' she whispered, and then, 'I am sorry, sir, to have been – to have been so upset before.'

'There is no need to apologise,' he said again. 'It was a dreadful shock for you.'

'Do you know who done it, sir? Mr Chapman says you were asked by Master Treasurer to find out.'

'Well, not quite that, Annie. Just to ask a few questions. No, no one knows as yet, I fear.' And then, as she continued to gaze tremulously at him, 'I am sure the police will identify the culprit in the end.'

'I do hope so, sir.' She picked up her rag again. 'It was a wicked person that did such a thing to him.'

From the clerks' room came the familiar sounds of Chapman berating the youngest member of chambers, an almost weekly occurrence and, in consequence, going in one ear and out the other of the Honourable Cecil Haynes, who had no real desire to be a barrister anyway.

'It's not good enough, sir.' (Chapman always began like that.) 'It is just one thing after another. This is the third time the judge has complained you were late for court. Do you know, I am now obliged to ensure that the clerks' room clock is running fast in order that there is at least some chance of you arriving in time to robe and be in court before the judge? Do you know that Sir Gabriel has twice this quarter been obliged to pay to the Inn your portion of the chambers rent? Now a solicitor complains that you were impertinent to him! And not just any solicitor! One of Sir Gabriel's most valued—'

His diatribe was cut off as Gabriel closed his door with a sigh. There was no doubt that young Haynes was now becoming something of a liability and that a confrontation with Gabriel, as the most senior member of chambers, was on the way. But not, he hoped, this afternoon, after a hard day in court. Walking to his window and gazing out over the sunlit garden, on an impulse he put his hat back on and retraced his steps. As he emerged from 1 Crown Office Row, he saw the unmistakable figure of Miss Theodora Dunning emerging from an archway, almost as tall and thin and angular in the flesh as the shadow she cast on the cobblestones. Behind her followed her coachman, bearing a leather bag.

Gabriel paused and bowed, as did Theodora.

'Good afternoon, Sir Gabriel. I have been collecting my brother's effects from the Law Courts.' And then, seeing he was still wearing the wing collar and stiff linen bands of his court dress, she added with a touch of wistfulness, 'You have been there yourself, I see.'

'Yes,' said Gabriel, 'in a very hard case, and am now seeking inspiration in the garden.' He hesitated. 'Would you care to walk round with me? I should value your opinion.'

'Are you patronising me, Sir Gabriel?' was the sharp reply.

'No,' he said in his considered way, 'and I should be sorry if you thought I was. I merely sought a fresh mind, and yours was available.'

'Well, that is frank at least.' She nodded dismissal to the coachman, who proceeded to the waiting carriage with his burden. Theodora watched him go. 'It is a curious thing to see a man's life reduced to the contents of a bag,' she said. 'I wonder why it is that, once a man is dead, we speak of his effects?'

'Because,' said Gabriel, 'he cannot have belongings. There is no one left to whom they may belong.'

'Of course,' she said with her thin smile, 'I should have worked that out for myself, should I not? Are you aware that I once wished to become a lawyer?'

'I am aware,' said Gabriel. He said no more, but he hoped his neutral tone somehow conveyed sympathy. He fell into step beside her, and together they turned into the garden.

'My legal problem concerns the book *Millie the Temple Church Mouse*,' he began. 'You will know it?'

'Yes indeed. I bought one of the first copies for Seraphina as soon as it appeared in Mr Moore's bookshop window.'

'Not for Percival?'

They both smiled.

'Percival is not an objectionable child really, you know,' she said. 'It is simply that he is extremely clever, with a passion for facts and no imagination. Have you ever noticed, Sir Gabriel, that the one quality we demand in all children is imagination?

We allow for differences in interest and aptitude and ability, but we cannot tolerate the lack of imagination in any child. Percival simply has none. There is no point in trying to foster it when it is not there to be fostered. I am very much saddened to say that he has trouble enough with understanding God without adding imaginary mice into the equation.'

'And the other two children?'

'Claud is still merely a pink unformed baby,' she said dispassionately, 'but Seraphina is blessed with a vivid imagination. Millie the Mouse is as real to her as I am and through the book my niece is learning true spirituality. So tell me, what has brought Millie into the Royal Courts of Justice?'

As they walked the gravelled paths (clockwise), in and out of the dappled shadows of the great trees overhead, brushing between the lush herbaceous borders and releasing their heady scent, Gabriel told Theodora Dunning the story of Miss Susan Hatchings' claim to authorship and of Herbert Moore's strong, though as yet unsubstantiated, doubts about that claim.

'The case is difficult on so many levels,' he concluded, 'that I confess to being unable just at present to see my way through it. The first question of course is whether she wrote it at all. My instincts and those of my client Mr Moore suggest to me she did not. But I fear that the jury may think otherwise; she has not yet been in the witness box, but the omens are poor for Mr Moore.'

'She must surely be closely connected with the author to risk such a claim, if it is indeed false, without fearing exposure. Who on earth is she? What do you know of her?' asked Theodora Dunning.

Gabriel shook his head. 'Nothing that leads to any other obvious claimant to authorship. But if she is not, then someone else is. We do not know if that someone also used Harriet Cadamy as a pseudonym or if there is a real Harriet Cadamy. But whoever she is, Mr Moore had no contract with the author, nor agreement from her as to his use of the book. But then there is also the issue of Mr Moore's expertise: he has undoubtedly made Millie the mouse she is.'

'But if Miss Susan Hatchings is the author, as I understand from what you have told me, that is just what she is objecting to.'

'Yes,' said Gabriel, 'that, too, is an irony. The whole case is a dreadful muddle.'

'Isn't it a question of "money which ought not in justice to be kept"?'

Gabriel stopped. 'That is a striking quotation, Miss Dunning. And I confess that I cannot recall who said it.'

'It was the great eighteenth-century judge Lord Mansfield – one of my brother's predecessors as Lord Chief Justice. In a case in 1756 in which a man had come by money entirely accidentally, the person to whom the money really belonged had no legal cause of action in contract. There was no contract or indebtedness between the parties. There had been no promises nor representations made. Consequently, he had no way of recovering it in law. Yet the judge held it should nonetheless be returned to him.'

'Yes,' said Gabriel slowly, 'I recall.'

'Lord Chief Justice Mansfield said that there were occasions when courts should dispense with all legal considerations and act *ex aequo et bono*, simply to the right and good.'

'Good heavens!' exclaimed Gabriel. 'That was certainly progressive. I thank you for reminding me of it; it gives me food for thought. It also confirms my view that Mr Moore's only real hope is to prove that Miss Hatchings did not write the book. If she can establish to the court's satisfaction that she is the author, as she claims, I have always thought, as it seems you do too, the judge would endeavour to find a way through to a remedy for her. I could not precisely see how. The case you have described may well provide that way. Although a true lawyer might describe Lord Mansfield's ruling in the absence of any legal cause of action as mere well-meaning sloppiness of thought.'

Theodora offered an ironical smile. 'It depends, I suppose, Sir Gabriel, on whether you think the law is there to achieve true justice between opposing parties or merely to apply the existing rules. I myself am a believer in the application of creativity to achieve a just result.'

And insofar as Sir Gabriel Ward ever felt intellectually put in his place, he felt it then – combined, he confessed to himself, with a great deal of respect for the elegance of Miss Dunning's argument.

In the cut and thrust of debate, he found his headache had quite gone.

'I wonder,' she said now, tentatively, 'whether perhaps – if I have been a little helpful – I might come and watch the trial tomorrow?'

'Why, of course,' said Gabriel. 'It may well be, if Miss Hatchings is indeed found to be the author, that we will tomorrow reach the very legal arguments we have been discussing. I will ask Chapman to reserve you a place.'

He escorted her back to the carriage waiting for her and watched it roll up Middle Temple Lane and swing out to the right into Fleet Street. Standing there, he recalled his conversation with Vivian Barton, and his own description of Theodora Dunning as a light extinguished.

How apt that phrase had been, he thought sadly, and how bitterly unfair that that incisive mind, with all the qualities of a lawyer, that precision of thought and language, that detachment, above all that questioning intellect, had been born into a body that human beings had decided, through 'inveterate usage', was the wrong body to be a lawyer. While Norman, her brother, not very clever, conventional in thought, impoverished in imagination, had been enriched and ennobled by the same 'inveterate usage'. Gabriel wondered how much Theodora Dunning minded.

And Theodora, meanwhile, looked out of the window of the carriage at the little world that she had wanted so much to be her world. That rigid, impenetrable club with its high walls of tradition and, tucked away within them, available only to those whom it regarded as entitled, all its camaraderie and fun and, above all, its intellectual stimulus. As a wave of impotent bitterness washed over her, somehow exacerbated by her interchange with Gabriel in which she had so triumphantly held her own, she minded very much indeed.

26

On that same afternoon, and for much the same reasons as Gabriel, Herbert Moore also suffered from a headache brought on by his day of concentration in the courtroom. It was an oppressive environment. The only natural light filtered through the skylight some forty feet above the judge's bench, which was raised high as though to ensure the cricked necks of all those sitting in the well of the court. The oak seats and tables, reminiscent of the schoolroom, were too narrow for the purposes intended. It all served, in addition to impressing the courtroom's occupants with the majesty of the law, to make them physically very uncomfortable.

It was with relief that he emerged into fresh air and sunlight to walk the couple of hundred yards back to his office, and with relief that he settled himself at his desk, his back to the portrait of Millie the Mouse, and his mind turned to the reassuringly routine demands of legal publishing. During the days leading up to trial his post had accumulated and been opened and sorted and left in neat piles on his desk by one of the clerks. Now he went methodically through it, determinedly putting out of his mind the prospect of the following day, when Miss Hatchings was to give evidence, when Gabriel was to cross-examine, when he himself would go into the witness box and attempt to account for the four most extraordinary years of his professional career.

The remainder of the afternoon passed very quickly; at about six o'clock he was brought out of the comfort of routine by the entrance of a clerk bearing a plain white envelope with Herbert's name handwritten upon it in capital letters. It was not the time for their normal postal delivery, nor was it a telegram. Inside was a single sheet of paper on which was written:

WHAT ABOUT THE DEATH OF MILLIE'S MOTHER?

Herbert stared at it blankly. It meant nothing to him. He turned the sheet of paper over. There was nothing else written on it. He could not recall that Millie's mother had figured in the story in anything other than a passing reference. He took one of a row of pristine copies of the book off the shelf behind him and looked through the by now familiar story. Millie's mother was mentioned now and again as a saintly guiding influence upon the mouse; the story did not seem to contain any information as to how or when she had met her demise. Herbert continued to flick idly through the pages, musing again on what success and trouble the book had brought him, culminating in the ordeal before him the next morning.

He recalled wistfully the beginning of it all: Elsie's joy when she had first read the tale, bless her, and he saw her small hands clutching the original manuscript to her chest in the carriage on the way home. It seemed unimaginable now that that manuscript had lain around his daughter's nursery and then been casually borne back and forth by Herbert himself as he did a bit of editing on the train to and from work. Not that it had needed much, too well and carefully written for that; but even the best of authors repeats the same word in consecutive sentences and misspells something now and again. It was also slightly too long; he had cut one or two short descriptive passages, he remembered, and a couple of paragraphs that had made Elsie cry, thinking them a little too strong for small children. And then it flooded back to him: just what he had deleted from the original manuscript, safely stowed away for years in the office safe; forgotten in the overwhelming, staggering success of the published book and the hurricane of work it had created for his business. What it was that had made Elsie cry...

'Burton!' he shouted to his secretary. 'The safe keys! Quick, quick! The safe keys!'

The great safe that contained the deeds and money and the most valuable manuscript Moore's would ever hold, was opened up.

And, in a short paragraph remaining only in the original manuscript, locked away from all eyes, lay the answer to the question in the letter – unknown to anyone except Herbert Moore and the real author of *Millie the Temple Church Mouse*.

27

By the time of the luncheon adjournment the next day, it could not be denied that Susan Hatchings had proved to be a good witness, entrusting herself to the capable hands of Sir Vivian Barton but playing her part in answering his careful questions with a pleasing combination of shyness and frankness. Even the coy glances and the fluttering hands seemed to convey a picture of appealing femininity to the stolid gentlemen of the jury. Nor could it be denied that, under Sir Vivian's expert guidance, her story hung together.

Susan Hatchings recounted her growing interest in the romantic history of the Temple Church coupled with her own deeply held religious belief and her mission in life to inculcate those beliefs in her charges; the provision of a typewriter by her kind employers, subsequently thrown away, but with no distinguishing features that she could recall; the rapidly growing story; the use of another name on the manuscript. No, she did not know why she had chosen that name, it had just come to her. And she had never thought of herself as an author; the very idea had made her feel so dreadfully shy. Her plan for a last visit to the church that had inspired her masterpiece; the beloved manuscript in her bag, brought so she could make any little adjustments on the train on the way home; and then the anguish of discovering the tear in her bag; the manuscript gone; and ultimately, the loss overtaken by the illness of her dear mother. It was not until after her mother's death, her move from the Isle of Mull to Edinburgh and her return to a normal life, that she learned of the staggering success of her book. She had been amazed. And appalled.

'Why appalled?' asked Barton.

'Oh, Sir Vivian, all the things that had been done in my invented name, and not in any way I would ever have agreed to; all the toys and pictures and such and the dreadful commercialisation of my story. I wrote it for God, Sir Vivian – to help children understand His message. What has happened to my story cannot be undone, but I want God and His New Church to benefit and no one else.'

Vivian Barton sat down, well satisfied with the impact of this on a now visibly sympathetic jury. It was in his view a highly satisfactory culmination to his case. The afternoon would bring Sir Gabriel Ward's cross-examination, but Barton did not think much of Gabriel's chances.

When at last Sir Gabriel Ward KC rose to his feet that afternoon to confront Miss Susan Hatchings, the first questions he asked her could not really be said to be a cross-examination. There was in them no challenge or hostility, merely gentle confirmatory elaborations to questions already asked and answers already given. Gradually, Miss Hatchings began visibly to relax, and with her relaxation came a certain confidence. And, very gently, Gabriel nurtured it with questions that seemed to arise more from genuine interest than from than any desire to catch her out.

'It seems,' he said at last, 'that when you describe Millie as your mouse, that is indeed how you feel about her?'

'Oh, yes,' Miss Hatchings simpered.

'And her life and adventures must indeed feel graven on your heart?'

'Oh, yes, part of my very soul,' said Miss Hatchings, looking earnestly at the jury.

'Thank you,' said Gabriel, with a friendly smile. 'Just one more matter and then I shall trouble you with no further questions. I am not sure whether you are aware, Miss Hatchings, of the processes of publishing? Did you know, for instance, that books are very carefully read by publishers and edited to correct, for instance, minor errors – spelling mistakes, for example – and sometimes to make other small changes?'

'Oh, dear,' trilled Miss Hatchings, casting a flirtatious eye at the jury, 'have I been caught out in spelling mistakes, Sir Gabriel?'

'No,' he said. 'But a small change was made to the text; an incident was omitted from the published version. It appears nowhere but in the original manuscript. Can you tell us what that was?'

There was a silence that grew long enough to be a little embarrassing.

'Well,' said Gabriel, 'perhaps I can assist you.'

The judge and Sir Vivian Barton gazed fixedly at him. Both knew that Sir Gabriel Ward KC, in the midst of a cross-examination, would not be assisting a witness without some strong motive for doing so.

'The incident,' said Gabriel, very deliberately, 'concerned the death of Millie the Mouse's mother.'

And Susan Hatchings, lulled into euphoria by the preceding gentle handling, now grasped the lifebelt with all the naivety of an inexperienced witness.

'Oh, of course,' she cried. 'Yes, yes... the death of Millie's mother!'

'You recall it?' said Gabriel, deceptively casual.

'Yes, of course, of course,' she repeated, elated to have the finishing line in sight.

'Are you sure?'

'Of course.' She beamed at the jury as the pit yawned in front of her.

'In that case, Miss Hatchings, will you assist the jury by telling them the manner of Millie's mother's death?'

This time the silence lengthened until it became excruciating. The gentlemen of the jury sat forward in their seats, their confidence in Susan Hatchings suddenly wavering. The lawyers all stared expressionlessly ahead. In the press row, even the most hardened of the newspaper reporters were transfixed in the moment, pens stilled. The entire court seemed to be holding its breath.

In the long silence that followed, Susan Hatchings turned red, then white, then grey, as motionless as a statue in the witness box, and the silence grew and grew and grew as deep and inexorable as the hole she had dug for herself.

Mr Justice Anderson put down his pen and looked at Sir Vivian Barton with an imperceptibly raised eyebrow.

'Sir Vivian,' he said, 'would you like a moment with your client?'

The court rose.

Outside in the corridor, Susan Hatchings subsided onto a wooden bench and Barton bent solicitously over her. To one side and at a respectful distance, Gabriel waited with his solicitor and client.

'What is happening, Sir Gabriel?' said Herbert, his voice sharp with anxiety. 'Why has the judge sent us away? Surely we are now going to win?'

'Sir Vivian is evaluating his position,' said Gabriel calmly, 'and advising his client accordingly. We must wait and see.'

After them had flooded the press and public, now agog for the next instalment in the unfolding drama. And with them, from his seat in the gallery, came the Reverend Blair.

Susan Hatchings leaped up and ran towards him. Her hands were outstretched, her face contorted with a passionate yearning, terrible in its vulnerability. She grasped his sleeve and fell at his feet in a position of abject supplication. He attempted to loosen her grip but she clung on desperately, and so was dragged along by his unwavering progress down the corridor.

The Reverend Blair, his face impassive, quickened his step and at last detached her clutching hand from his clerical sleeve so that she fell at his feet. Very deliberately, he stepped around her, and still without speaking or any discernible expression, made his way down the corridor, his dashing figure slowly diminishing into the shadows of the vast building, his footsteps ringing on the tessellated floors long after he was out of sight, humiliating in their steady, remorseless retreat.

Lying where she had been so ignominiously dropped, Susan Hatchings began to emit a noise that could not be described as a sob or a cry or even a scream: a long, low keening, its ghastly resonance thrown back from the great Gothic arches of the corridor, its echoes catching up with it until the sound rolled continuously in a solid wave of suffering. The scene was so unutterably pitiful that it paralysed and silenced the crowd of observers, gossips and cynics, lawyers and bystanders alike.

Vivian Barton at last approached the huddled figure and gently lifted her onto her feet. An usher approached with that centuries-old panacea of the Royal Courts of Justice, a glass of water. But Susan Hatchings seemed unable to take it, or even to stand without Barton's sturdy support. Between them she was carried into one of the small consultation rooms that led off the corridor and the door was closed on her humiliation.

It was some twenty minutes later that Barton emerged and strode over to the usher. 'We need a doctor,' he said brusquely.

'There is Dr Broom in Harley Street who attends if any of their lordships is taken ill,' said the usher. 'Shall I call him?'

'Not that kind of doctor,' said Barton.

Unhappy scenes are not uncommon in the Royal Courts of Justice, where strife is the normal order of events and the passions that drive it are daily exposed; but the scene that ensued half an hour later as a now silent, strait-jacketed Miss Susan Hatchings was borne out of the building by white-coated attendants, was almost unprecedented.

'Wait!' Herbert Moore called out suddenly as the little group passed by. 'Wait! Where are you taking her?'

One of the warders looked back over his shoulder. 'Hanwell, sir, I reckon.'

'Wait,' Herbert cried again. 'What is Hanwell?'

'County Lunatic Asylum.'

And they were gone, two huge, uniformed men, carrying a slight figure between them so that her legs dangled and did not touch the ground, her blue eyes staring straight ahead like those of her own Dolly.

'My God, Ward,' said Vivian Barton to Gabriel who stood soberly by. He removed his wig to mop his brow.

'What a scene, my dear boy,' he said. 'Poor woman. Made the whole thing up you know, to enslave that cad of a man. Absolutely ghastly… never seen disintegration like it. Better go and tell the judge, eh?'

'Wait!' cried Herbert Moore yet again. 'This cannot be the end. Who is she, Sir Vivian? How did she know so much about the writing of the story? Who is the true author of *Millie the Temple Church Mouse*?'

Barton shook his head. 'Couldn't get a word out of her, Mr Moore, not after the first anguish. Only howling for the reverend. All those women after him, she said, so that she had to have something extra to give him. Wanted him to have all that he wanted; wanted him to want her. All truly pitiful, I am afraid. And then she descended into raving incoherence and afterwards that hellish catatonic state. I doubt you will ever get much sense there.'

The usher approached. 'His lordship enquires what is happening, Sir Vivian. He asks if you want more time?'

'No further time needed,' said Barton sombrely.

Back in court, amidst the robes and wigs, the formal language, the elaborate courtesy, Gabriel waited to feel the solace he usually found in the familiar formalities that conclude a trial, but it did not come. He had brought about that terrible grief. The sword had been put into his hand. He had wielded it, and destroyed a woman's happiness in the process. He had done his job and the truth was that his cross-examination had carried with it an element of enjoyment – not in the unmasking he had inflicted but because he had been the architect of that dramatic moment. Now he felt another emotion niggling at him, but did not try to identify it. He hoped it was not shame.

Remotely he heard Barton's explanation to the judge: Miss Hatchings was very unwell. She had withdrawn her claim to authorship and with it her case.

'And the costs of this abandoned trial?' queried the judge. 'The customary order of the loser to pay the costs?'

'No,' said Gabriel. 'I have discussed this with Mr Moore. We make no claim for costs in the tragic circumstances.'

'Very proper, Sir Gabriel.' And Mr Justice Anderson turned to the jury, thanking them all for their service, telling them no verdict was required from them and that they were discharged. Then, as an afterthought, with a whimsical little smile he said, 'Sir Gabriel, the jurymen have listened attentively to a difficult and distressing case. I daresay they feel some curiosity, as I confess I do myself, as to the manner of Millie the Mouse's mother's decease. May we be enlightened?'

Gabriel got to his feet again.

'My lord,' he said slowly, 'it occurs to me that the answer to that question is now worth many hundreds of thousands of pounds. It is the one test of the veracity of any future claims of authorship. I hope your lordship will understand if I respectfully decline to answer you.'

And so it was over. Or had just begun. In the afternoon sunshine they stood on the steps of the courts, Gabriel and Dawson and Herbert Moore, in a curious state of ambivalence such as Gabriel had never known at the conclusion of a case so resoundingly won.

He had revealed Susan Hatchings' lies, but he had not discovered the true author and Herbert Moore was still in legal limbo. Before their eyes a woman had descended into apparent madness and taken her secrets with her into that oblivion. How had she known enough of the background to the writing of the story to claim it for her own? How had she known that she was safe from challenge from the true Harriet Cadamy? Above all else, who was Harriet Cadamy?

Those who had been sitting in the public gallery emerged from the Law Courts. A few stared admiringly at Gabriel as he stood on the steps. He looked away assiduously; unlike many of his colleagues, he did not court the then fashionable interest in prominent members of the Bar. Among the group was Theodora Dunning. She paused to speak to him.

'A splendid result, Sir Gabriel. I thank you for allowing me to watch.'

'I fear,' he said, 'that it must have been a disappointment to you that we did not need to argue the legal implications, Miss Dunning, since Miss Hatchings failed to establish authorship.'

'Indeed yes,' she said with something approaching warmth, 'but nonetheless a forensic triumph. A meticulous cross-examination culminating in that devastating last-minute thrust. It was a privilege to listen to – so cunningly and subtly done.'

And after giving him her thin smile, she walked away as Sir Vivian Barton approached them, his urbane equilibrium restored.

'I am off home to the blessed innocence of my beloved brood,' he said cheerfully, tipping his hat. 'Nothing more soothing, I find, than getting home in time to tell the bedtime story.'

Gabriel bowed politely; he could not, off-hand, think of anything he would find less soothing.

Barton chuckled. 'Well, well, each to his own,' he said tolerantly. 'A job well done, if I may say so, Ward. I wish you goodbye until the next battle. And I wish *you* good luck, Mr Moore.'

'Is there nothing anyone can do to prevail upon Miss Hatchings to enlighten us?' said Herbert Moore, impatient with these professional courtesies.

'It seems unlikely,' said Gabriel. 'I fear, Mr Moore, that you will probably have to wait and see whether the real author comes forward to claim her work.'

'Or *his* work,' said Vivian Barton with a wink, and with his airy wave, he descended the steps.

Herbert looked distractedly after him. 'That is true,' he said. 'Harriet Cadamy could be absolutely anyone, man or woman, old or young, living anywhere. And meanwhile I have unleashed Millie the Mouse and she seems to grow bigger and bigger by the day. What on earth shall I do, Sir Gabriel? I cannot now restrain her success, but it seems I cannot claim it either. Millie the Mouse has become a monster.'

'If you are asking my professional advice, Mr Moore,' said Gabriel, 'then it is that you do nothing. Sign no more contracts. Keep that manuscript in your safe. And just let her grow.

Although,' he added with his little snuffle, 'you might be wise to refrain from any more active promotion.'

'But this trial will be all over the newspapers!'

'It will inevitably cause something of a stir, but I think you will find that it is Miss Hatchings' attempted claim and its unhappy background that predominates. Of course there will be speculation, but you are used to speculation about Miss Harriet Cadamy. You must take it in your stride, Mr Moore. The situation has after all simply reverted to that with which you have lived for the last four years.'

'But I feel now that I have somehow cheated someone,' said Herbert. 'Yet I do not know who or how. It is – it is—'

'"Money which ought not in justice to be kept", 'said Gabriel. 'I know, Mr Moore. But then you must ask yourself to whom, in justice, should you give it?'

Herbert Moore shook his head and offered his hand.

'I should thank you for what you have done, Sir Gabriel,' he said, 'and hope that the answer to that is somehow granted to me.'

———

Gabriel crossed the road to the gates of the Temple; and there, propped up beside them, was the familiar solid figure of Constable Wright.

On his face was an expression of bashful triumph; in his hands a pair of immaculate black gentlemen's shoes. The kind of shoes worn with formal evening clothes; the kind of shoes handmade on a custom last; the kind of shoes immaculately polished after every wearing by a valet or under butler. The kind of shoes that the Lord Chief Justice of England might wear.

28

'Where did you get them?' asked Gabriel.
      'I got 'em,' said Wright, 'off Broadbent's feet.'
'And Mr Broadbent?'

'I found him, Sir Gabriel!' Constable Wright was glowing with pride. 'And where do you think he was?'

'In the flowerbed after all?' said Gabriel with a snuffle.

'No, sir. I've been looking and looking ever since then. I couldn't think how he could have just gone like that. Where do men completely disappear to? I thought. The grave? I'd investigated that as best I could. But then I suddenly thought: I know where else men disappear to. I wondered if he came to and got picked up in the park for begging. It is in the Metropolitan Police patch so we wouldn't know. Then I remembered Tufty.'

'Tufty?'

'My friend from school what joined the Metropolitan. And I thought to myself, I'm damned – sorry, sir, it slipped out – if he didn't once tell me St James' Park was on his beat. So I went and looked him up and I was right. They'd picked Broadbent up for begging. He was in a right state, coughing and shivering. Tufty's a kindly chap and they had an empty cell so Tufty bunged him in it to keep him off the streets for a few days.'

'Didn't they notice his footwear?'

'They did, sir. Couldn't really have missed his shoes, given the state of the rest of him. And asked him about them. When he was fit to say anything at all, Broadbent said he had found them.

They didn't believe him but they had no report of any missing shoes to pin on him.'

Wright paused while he tried to phrase his next observation tactfully. 'Of course, the Temple insisting on a week's private investigation meant the Metropolitan know nothing about the exact circumstances of the Lord Chief Justice's death. In the normal course of things, the City Police would have informed them.'

Gabriel refrained from comment. He would save that for Sir William Waring.

Wright, buoyed by his success, had not in any case waited for an answer. 'We police get to know their ways, sir, the vagrants and the loose women and the drunk and disorderlies. Night after night, banged up in the cells, then the Police Court, magistrate fines them exactly what they've got on them, and back they goes on the pavement. All a bit pointless if you ask me.'

'Indeed,' said Gabriel, 'and a troubling dilemma, Constable Wright. Should it really be the business of the law to keep inadequates off the street?'

'Not everyone we arrest is an inadequate,' said Wright, his confidence growing once he was discussing his own world. 'Mostly they're just poor. And as for the rest, you'd be surprised. I've picked up a famous actor in the Strand before now, and Tufty tells me a few years back his colleagues bagged a Cabinet Minister twice and a retired judge three times. Not,' he added, 'that you saw *them* in the Police Court. Oh, no. Quite different treatment they had. All hushed up and no more to be said.' He hesitated. 'Doesn't seem fair really, does it?'

Gabriel looked rather quizzically at him. 'You are quite the socialist, Constable Wright.'

'Don't let my mother hear you say that, sir. Anyway, Broadbent is all right now. I called for some backup and brought him back to his burrow under Moore's Bookshop. Don't want the Metropolitan Police to get the glory by arresting him on their patch, do we? Not that I needed backup, he came meek as a lamb and is there now, painting his new placard.'

'That does not suggest a guilty conscience to me. What about the shoes?'

'Still claims he doesn't know who they belonged to. Refuses to say where he got them from. We've given him a knock or two, but he still won't say. Would you like to come and have a word before we takes him off?'

Gabriel hesitated. His week of enforced detecting was over. He had complied with Sir William's demands. He was released from the investigation he had so reluctantly undertaken, and surely also from the threat to his home. He was outside the boundaries of the Temple, and the suspect was not a member of that august body but just another Fleet Street vagrant.

He was surprised to find the suggestion of continuing involvement in the mystery utterly irresistible.

'Detective Inspector Hughes has just arrived from Old Jewry HQ, sir, and there are two constables guarding Broadbent.'

Walking back down Fleet Street towards the bookshop, Gabriel told Constable Wright of Meg's confession in the garden. 'And it seems,' he concluded, 'that little Meg was quite right when she thought he was unwell.'

'You did ought to have told me before now, sir,' said Wright reproachfully.

'I know,' said Gabriel. 'But it seemed to me that, while Mr Broadbent was missing, I should do what I could to save the girl's position. But now...'

'Now it is all clear enough. It's the gallows for Broadbent.'

They had reached Moore's.

Sitting outside was a villainous figure: Gabriel could not help noticing, with the intention of teasing Constable Wright about it later, that Broadbent's ears were very protuberant. He was stout and bald, with one front tooth missing and a black eye. The former looked long established; the latter was oozing fresh blood. He wore a ragged suit and ancient woollen mittens. The trousered legs sticking out in front of him ended in feet clad in the filthy remnants of thick woolly socks from which his naked big toes protruded defiantly.

The placard lying beside him had been completed. There was now a curly question mark after the words 'What are judges for?' And beneath had been written the answer: 'To find the truth.'

'That, I fear, is your mistake,' said Gabriel, diverted, as always, by a legal point. 'The answer is that they are there to provide certainty.'

'Ho,' said Mr Broadbent. 'Even if what they're certain of is not true?'

'Even then,' said Gabriel.

'And no appeal? The jury says I am guilty and so I am? Although I'm not. And a judge puts me in prison when I didn't do nothing wrong?'

'Perhaps one day we will have a Court of Appeal for criminals,' said Gabriel. 'But even then, you know, in the end certainty will prevail. More than we need truth, Mr Broadbent, we need certainty. And truth is such an uncertain commodity.'

The two burly policemen who stood, truncheons at the ready, either side of Broadbent, shifted uneasily at this incomprehensible philosophical interchange. Detective Inspector Hughes merely looked impatient; just what he had expected — a lot of airy-fairy, clever-clever nonsense that had fair taken in young Wright.

Passers-by skirted round the group and averted their eyes from Broadbent; vagrancy and drunkenness, lamentably common on the streets of London, held no interest or novelty. Someone, no doubt, would remove him.

Broadbent attempted to mop his bleeding eye with his filthy sleeve. Really, thought Gabriel, I shall have no handkerchiefs left soon. He thought wistfully of the one now reposing in Meg's apron pocket as he extracted his spare from his pocket; a gentleman always has a spare, Nanny had said, and he always did. This he proffered silently to Broadbent.

'I fear you have sustained a recent accident,' he said gently.

Broadbent rolled the functioning eye while mopping the other one.

'No accident. I have been attacked by His Majesty's Constabulary and a crying outrage it is in this day and age. Don't I have any rights?'

'No,' said one of the policemen briskly. 'This here is Sir Gabriel Ward KC. Now you'd better start singing.'

'Mr Broadbent,' said Gabriel, coming straight to the point, 'the shoes removed from your feet by Constable Wright: were they the Lord Chief Justice's shoes?'

'Ho no. I had them made for myself by Lobb of St James'. Just for the evenings, don't you know?'

One of the policemen cuffed him hard.

'It's lucky,' the old man continued in a conversational manner, 'that they was a size ten. I'm a nine and a half myself, but my old socks made them fit lovely. They will be sorely missed. Any chance of 'aving 'em back?'

Gabriel's tone was grave. 'Mr Broadbent, you seem to be treating this matter with a strange degree of levity. Do you not appreciate that you stand in danger of the gallows?'

'The gallows? For pinching a pair of shoes? In 1901?'

'For murder,' said Gabriel, and realised that, although of course everyone knew that there was no other means by which Lord Dunning had met his death, it was the first time he had uttered the word, in all its stark and terrible force.

'*Murder?*' exclaimed Broadbent. And while the policemen looked cynical, it seemed to Gabriel that, just as he had heard occasionally in court, the truth rang out despite the tramp's gruff voice, with a purity and clarity that were unmistakable. '*Murder?*' Broadbent said again. 'Who's been murdered?'

'Had you not heard,' Gabriel said, 'that Lord Dunning was stabbed to death in the Temple the night before you went missing? And that when he was found, his feet were bare?'

'I've been drunk in a flowerbed and then banged up in a cell,' Broadbent replied simply. 'Well, I'll be damned.'

Suddenly he roared with laughter. 'Dead without his shoes, eh? That can't have done the old bastard's dignity much good.' Then, as the seriousness of the revelation suddenly dawned on him, 'Hang on a minute… you're not suggesting—'

'Where did you get the shoes, Broadbent?' said Wright.

There was a silence.

'Answer him,' ordered Detective Inspector Hughes sharply.

'I won't,' said the old man with spirit. 'I knows my rights and you can do as you please.'

'Broadbent, we know you were in the Temple on the night of Lord Dunning's murder,' said Wright.

Broadbent remained defiant. 'I don't know how you think you know that. I'm saying nothing.'

Gabriel put a restraining hand on Wright's arm, impressed by what he perceived to be Broadbent's valiant attempt to conceal Meg's role in events.

'Mr Broadbent,' he said, 'if I were to suggest to you that you will not admit to being in the Temple because you are protecting somebody else, would I be correct?'

Broadbent looked wary. 'And if you was correct, wot then?'

'Mr Broadbent, I will not let the girl come to harm,' said Gabriel steadily. 'You will not help either yourself or her by refusing to speak.'

There was a pause.

'All right. Wot if I was?'

'Were you?'

'All right. I was.'

Detective Inspector Hughes nodded at Wright. 'Albert Broadbent,' said the constable, and before his eyes there floated the glorious announcement that would appear in the *Police Gazette*. 'I am arresting you on suspicion of the murder of the Lord Chief—'

'Wait, wait, Constable,' said Gabriel. 'Until we hear what he has to say.'

'And quite right too,' said Broadbent with dignity. 'Don't you be so hasty, young man. Sir Gabriel here who is an eminent lawyer will tell you that once you have arrested me, you cannot interrogate me without cautioning me. And then I might not say anything at all. Now, do you want to hear my story or do you not?'

'We don't want to hear no stories. We want to know where you got them shoes.'

'Well then, I found 'em on the steps of the garden in Inner Temple, neatly placed together with the socks inside 'em. And please God they are a size nine and a half, I says to myself. But good though the Almighty is, he couldn't quite manage that. A ten they were and a mite too big for me.'

'So you stole them?' said Hughes.

Gabriel was beginning to take rather a fancy to Broadbent and rather a dislike to Detective Inspector Hughes. His forensic instincts aroused by this bald accusation, he intervened.

'I wonder if perhaps you were thinking of the law of abandonment, Mr Broadbent?' he said helpfully. '*Res derelictae*, you know. The finding of an object over which there are no apparent rights of ownership vests ownership in the finder.'

Broadbent was no fool. 'Ho yes,' he said. 'That is exactly what I thought. *Res* wot you just said. Abandoned, I thought, and no crime if I takes 'em, so I ups and takes 'em. No idea who they belonged to and never saw the owner that night, if owner the Lord Chief Justice was, not with or without his shoes on.'

'And the fact that you had a grudge against him and he was found next morning with the Inner Temple carving knife stuck through his heart is by the by, is it?' said Hughes.

Broadbent ignored him and peered steadily, if blearily, at Gabriel.

'I have an alibi for the murder, Sir Gabriel, wot is cast-iron. As you well know, if your source is who you have hinted it to be, I was in the Temple Church that night.'

'I am aware,' said Gabriel, 'that you were – er – escorted there at around ten o'clock, and that your dinner was provided at just before midnight. I cannot regard that as a cast-iron alibi, I am afraid.'

'Nine-thirty or thereabouts I come in. I knows that 'cause I saw the clock on the *Evening Post* offices shortly before.' Broadbent added in an aggrieved tone: 'Since you lot have failed to get the Temple clock repaired, what I always tells the time by when I hear the chimes in Fleet Street, it is a sorry state of affairs for a man without a pocket watch and only one clock on the *Evening Post* building. Anyways, I gets in and a little while later I sees the vicar come in with another man and they had a wander around the church, and some good while after that I was provided with me sustenance.'

'And what was the time by then?'

'I have no idea,' Broadbent responded blithely. 'I fell asleep and there being no clock in the church and me 'aving no watch of my own on account of my personal circumstances.'

'You appear to have left the church at some point to – er – replenish your footwear.'

'I went to relieve myself,' said Broadbent with dignity, 'and, being a decent man, I went to do so through the railings into the flowerbeds of the gardens. There was the shoes, a gift from heaven, and back I went to the church feeling thankful, and tried them on. Just perfect, they fits, with my old woolly socks for lining. So I tosses the silk socks into the Poor Hamper by the door, and a very nice touch I thought it was.'

Gabriel tried hard not to snuffle.

'And then I was given me dinner and then I was locked all night in the Temple Church until next morning.'

'Locked in the church?' said Gabriel sceptically. 'Mr Broadbent, you will have to do better than that. I have lived in the Temple all my adult life and the church has not once been locked in all those years.'

Broadbent was undeterred. 'So you may say, but I can tell you there is some funny goings-on in the Temple Church at night, Sir Gabriel. Quite gave me a nasty turn, wot I saw there. Hardly like to talk of it, even now. Blimey, I said to myself, either I've had a drop more than I thought or this is a very sinister happening, the meaning of which I don't like to think about. Very uncomfortable it made me. I'm a simple man, Sir Gabriel. I don't like libations and sacrifices and such.'

'No indeed,' said Gabriel in his calm way. But he thought uneasily of the mutilated fish Wright had found on the floor of the church and the constable's speculations as to a mysterious secret society. 'It sounds most unsavoury. Might I ask you to elaborate a little?'

Broadbent leaned towards him and lowered his voice confidentially.

'Just after I had me sangwidge, a woman come in, and though my sight is not what it was, she was right up close to where I was hiding in me pew and—'

'A *woman*?'

'Yes, in a long blue dress, all over patterns, and red shoes. Slipped in, holding aloft a blue and white bowl in both her hands, and crept very slow towards the altar. And she laid down the bowl beside it, very careful and ceremonial, and then she said things—'

'What things?' demanded Constable Wright.

'I couldn't hear but they fair chilled my blood. Whispering things, low down on the ground she was. Just an 'uddle in the shadows,' he added poetically. 'Then she gets to her knees and she seems to be praying, and then up she gets and—'

'And?'

'Out comes this great key and she shuffles over to the door and out she goes and then I hear the grinding of the key turning in the lock and I am alone. Chilled me so I dursn't move for a minute, paralysed I was, but then I starts up and goes and tries the door.' He paused dramatically. 'Locked fast! Locked in with whatever that woman had raised. Horrible the sensation was. Who knew what ghastly apparition was lurking among them dark pillars?'

Constable Wright looked impressed. Gabriel looked inscrutable. Broadbent, satisfied with the attention of his audience, though rather conscious of the anti-climax that was to follow, continued his tale.

'And that bowl lay there and I was transfixed by it and I seemed to see movement around it, slinking sneaking movement, just stirring in the darkness. I couldn't see properly and though I listened out there was nothing but silence to hear. It was all in dark shadow. Could I approach that altar? I could not! But then I pulls myself together. Buck up, my lad, I says to myself, you're in the House of God and no harm will come to you. And I settles down in me pew and the next thing I knows I'm asleep. In the morning I tries the door and, lo and behold, it's unlocked and out I goes. I waits until the porters open the Great Gate for the milkman, and out I slips while they're getting the empty churns for him.'

He drew to a triumphant close. There was a pregnant pause.

'It is a remarkable story, Mr Broadbent,' said Gabriel slowly.

'Very remarkable,' echoed Hughes. 'And I don't believe a word of it.' He drew in breath and put on a deep, official-sounding voice. 'Albert Broadbent, I am arresting you on suspicion of the murder of the Lord Chief Justice…'

It was all over in moments. The hovering police van was pulled forward; the horses' heads held; and the two constables grasped Broadbent under the armpits and propelled him into the back of the vehicle.

There was a curious poignancy about his resigned acquiescence. He sat in the back in a dejected huddle and caught Gabriel's sympathetic eye.

'Well, Sir Gabriel,' he said, 'I hopes a noose around the neck of an innocent man is certainty enough for your precious legal system.'

The door slammed before Gabriel had time to reply, though in truth he had no answer.

Seeing his expression, Hughes rushed into defensive speech.

'Well, did *you* believe that story, sir?'

'No,' said Gabriel. 'Not for one moment, Detective Inspector Hughes. But I did believe in his own belief. And I believe his story should be investigated.'

'Investigated? How do you propose we should investigate an alibi of ladies making sacrificial devotions in the Temple Church? Should we go and research witches' covens in Fleet Street? Or perhaps you had in mind wizards in the Royal Courts of Justice? The man is a drunk and halfway blind. I never heard such a load of nonsense.'

He stuck out his hand to hail a passing hansom cab and nodded at Wright.

'You can go off home now, lad, and I'll see you in the morning. We'll have had a confession to murder out of the old boy by then and all tied up in ribbon.'

Gabriel's voice was quite suddenly almost unrecognisably authoritative. 'Go carefully, Detective Inspector Hughes. You may take the view that Broadbent has no rights, but remember your own duty to the law.'

Hughes flushed deeply, opened his mouth, closed it again, and then without another word stepped into the cab. Gabriel watched it trundle away.

'Well, Constable Wright, we seem to be dismissed. Would you care for a dry sherry?'

Constable Wright felt rather like a dog who discovers he has two masters and is uncertain which to please; but the inspector had taken himself off, and here was Sir Gabriel with whom he had so far shared his theories. The prospect of sherry (for which he was gradually acquiring a partiality) and confidences was irresistible.

29

They sat together in the book-filled room in 4 King's Bench Walk and Constable Wright balanced his half-full glass on top of the very legal tome in which a few days before Gabriel had been researching the law of sanctuary.

He had about him an air of tentative triumph. 'There, Sir Gabriel, it is all fitting together.'

'Fitting together?'

'Yes, sir. I cannot quite work out how, but don't you think that Lord Dunning's bare feet and the woman's sacrifice in the church and the mysterious Little Dinner and the bloody hand-marks on the wall of One Crown Office Row and Mr Broadbent's hatred of judges are beginning to point somehow in the same direction?'

'No, Constable Wright. I do not.'

'No, sir?'

'No, I think they are all pointing in quite different directions.'

'But which directions, sir?'

Gabriel shook his head. 'I think they are actions that, if followed through to their beginnings, will be simple pathways into the human heart. If we only understood better the ways of the heart, we would find our way through this puzzle quite easily. It is to the psychology we should look, Constable Wright.'

'Psychology, sir? What is that?'

'What we used to call mental philosophy, Constable, a subject gaining in interest and body of work.' Gabriel gestured to the bookshelves behind him. 'Psychology is the study of the workings of the mind. That is what you were doing when you worked out how to find Mr Broadbent.'

Wright looked pleased. 'Blimey, sir.'

'Let us first look at his account of finding the shoes. Let us assume they were found by him as he says, placed neatly side by side by the garden steps with the socks tucked into them. Don't you think it would seem most likely in those circumstances that Lord Dunning took them off himself? And, if so, he may well have taken them off by the garden from where Broadbent confesses to having – er – removed them. If Lord Dunning returned from the garden to find them gone, he would have tried to find them, one assumes, by walking about on the Temple paving. He could thereby have sustained the minor abrasions on his feet found by the police surgeon.'

'Yes,' said Wright, still puzzled. 'But why ever on earth would he have taken them off in the first place?'

'Ah, now that is where the psychology comes in, and that question is one to which, somewhere, we must be able to ascertain the answer. Forget such exotica as humiliations and rituals, Mr Wright,' said Gabriel, 'why do people take off their shoes in real life?'

He shuffled through the narrow alleyways of books to his shelves, and his eye ran along them as he talked.

'The Greeks went barefoot to signify their freedom; the Romans, on the other hand, expressed their superiority by putting on shoes; English monastics took theirs off again in reverence to God; the Imperial Japanese also took theirs off, in order to express humility towards humans of a perceived higher status. And little children tear them off in their innocence and… yes, humility. I think that might be the answer, humility and innocence. There is a tenderness about bare feet, is there not? *"Every evening from thy feet / Shall the cool wind kiss the heat."*'

PC Wright was regarding him with astonishment. Gabriel, talking half to himself, appeared to have forgotten him.

Struggling to understand these meandering thought processes, Wright was anxious to help.

'The only tenderness I know is the rough old seams on my boots chafing when I am on the beat. Plenty of times I want to take off my boots on the beat, sir. Sore as anything, my feet get.'

Gabriel snuffled. 'Not that sort of tenderness.'

But Wright was now pursuing his own channels of thought. 'I'm just a working man in police-issue boots. The Lord Chief Justice would have his shoes made for him. I can't see him having to take 'em off because his feet hurt.'

At Wright's words somewhere in Gabriel's mind there was an echo. Who else had talked to him of feet sore with work? Suddenly, he had the answer. Annie! Annie, sitting on a stool in chambers to polish the brass door furniture. And with it came all in a rush the other thoughts that had been circling like birds in his mind and at last alighted – all, so to speak, on the same bough; and the bough was Annie standing on the doorstep before the corpse lying face to the wall, and screaming, 'Oh no, oh no.' Annie's ongoing anguish, surely disproportionate to the discovery of a dead stranger. Her sister Mrs Bugg's remark: 'It was the feet that upset her most, you know. On and on, she kept sobbing: "The feet, the feet."' And then Annie's voice in painful enquiry to Gabriel himself as to the identity of the culprit: 'It was a wicked person that did such a thing to him.' No, the emphasis was wrong; it had not sounded like that; that was not quite what she had said. And Gabriel heard in his head her quiet voice saying: 'It was a wicked person that did such a thing to *him.*' As though she had known the victim. Annie, who had been in the Temple the night the Lord Chief Justice had died, moonlighting in Paper Buildings, down by the garden.

'Constable Wright,' he said, getting up from his wing chair with what, for Gabriel, was almost a spring, 'we have a visit to make.'

30

Annie was scrubbing the stone passageway in Crown Office Row prior to leaving for her evening job.

She came into Gabriel's room reluctantly at his request and sat on the edge of a chair, but from his first question her account seemed to come quite easily to her, as though she had been expecting to make it.

'I had been doing my cleaning job in Paper Buildings on that night. And when I opened the front door to put out some rubbish, a lady was standing on the steps and she said, "Is it Annie?" And I said, "Yes, ma'am," and she said, "Haven't you worked in the Temple a long time?" And I said: "Yes, ma'am. Thirty years, ma'am." And she said, "Did you work here when you were young?" And I said "Yes, ma'am, when I was very young, in a different chambers in this building." And she said, "Did you know the young man who was a pupil barrister there…"'

But here Annie's voice trailed to a halt.

'Yes?' said Gabriel. 'And did you?'

She nodded. There was silence.

In this silence Gabriel felt acutely uncomfortable. To him this territory was an unknown country whose borders he had never had the least desire to cross. But still he felt impelled to go on, to edge a little further despite the sensation of ice cracking beneath his feet.

'Annie,' he said at last, 'was that young pupil barrister Norman Dunning?'

She nodded again. The silence deepened. It must have been something in his face that made her suddenly rush into speech again.

'It was nothing wrong, sir. It was – I was very young, sir, only fourteen, and Mr Dunning – I used to clean his pupil master's room. He never said anything wrong to me, but one day I dropped the coals and he helped me to pick them up and after that sometimes he talked to me a bit. He worked ever so hard, but he found the law work difficult and then there was his father, sir, he worried on at him so, sir, and he wasn't very happy at home, and I understood that: neither was I, my mother left us, and my father was always on at me. So we – we—'

'You became friends?'

She looked shocked. 'Oh, no, Sir Gabriel. How could we be friends? I was the laundress. But sometimes Mr Dunning worked late and when I was leaving he was too, just a couple of times a week, and we would walk around the garden in the dark and the peace before going home, and we'd talk a bit – and I would take off – I would take off…'

'Yes?' said Gabriel with a sinking heart at the prospect of what embarrassing revelations might follow. 'Take off…?'

'My shoes,' she whispered.

'*Your* shoes?'

'My feet were always sore, sir, mainly 'cos I had to wear my sister's old shoes; and Mr Dunning would say, "Take them off and cool down in the grass, Annie, that's what I used to do when I was a schoolboy." And every time I would say, "You do it too, Mr Dunning, then I shan't feel so foolish." But no, he never would. So he would walk on the gravel path and I would walk on the edge of the grass in my bare feet.'

'But, Annie,' said Gabriel, 'this was all thirty years ago. What has it to do with the lady you met on the steps on the night of Lord Dunning's murder?'

Annie looked doubtfully at him, groping for the words to describe the sordid, suffocating little conversation with the shadowy woman on the steps of Paper Buildings; the cut-glass accent, the imperious challenge in it, the knowing cynicism with which she had held out a gloved hand full of sovereigns, a lot more than Annie had ever seen at one time or would ever see again in her life.

'She said she would pay me, sir, to say to a newspaper that Mr Dunning had – had – made me do wrong when we went for those walks all those years ago. I was shocked, sir.'

'So am I,' said Gabriel. 'It was a wicked thing to ask you to do. What did you say to this lady?'

'I said no, sir. I said it wasn't true and I wouldn't do it,' said Annie simply. 'She was very angry and said some cruel things, sir. But then, all of a sudden, she looked at her watch and went away and left me there on the steps of Paper Buildings.'

'I am very sorry, Annie,' said Gabriel, 'that you should have been subjected to such an unhappy incident in the Temple. Did you recognise the lady?'

She shook her head. 'She was very grand, sir,' she whispered.

'No,' said Gabriel gently. 'You were the grand one, Annie.'

She twisted the corner of her apron. Looking at her, Gabriel waited; he knew there was more. He knew when to give the witness time. They sat quietly and then, as though answering a question, although none had been uttered, Annie continued.

'When she had gone, I went back inside and finished my work and put on my coat and hat. Then I walked down the steps and I stood looking at the garden and I was remembering, sir; and then someone came to stand beside me. A tall gentleman – in his evening clothes, he was. Whoever is this? I thought. And he said just – just what the lady had said, but in such a different voice: "Is it Annie?" And it sounds just like a fairy story, but it was Mr Dunning, sir. I knew he had become a very grand and important judge; I heard it in the Temple, but I never thought any more about him except to wish him well in my head. But there he was. And he recognised me! I was that pleased to be recognised, sir, all those years later. It was such a strange coincidence – after all that time and just after I'd been asked about him. And I was so startled and still so upset by what the lady had said to me that I just burst out with it and told him all about it. And I don't mind admitting, I cried a bit, sir, and Mr Dunning, I mean – I mean, Lord Dunning – he was very kind and he said I wasn't to worry any more about it. And he said he would always be grateful to me, sir. That it would have lost him his job if I had told such a lie as she wanted me to.'

She hesitated and then went on wistfully: 'And we began to talk again and to remember when we used to walk around the garden when we were young. Mr – Lord Dunning opened the gate to the garden and said to me, "We will do it once more." And he asked, "Do your feet still hurt, Annie?" "Yes," I said, "they've never stopped." And he laughed and said, "Take your shoes off then and walk on the grass." And I knew he was remembering just like me, and I don't know how I dared, but I said just like I used to, "You do it too, sir, then I shan't feel so foolish." And of course it was a little bit of a joke, sir, just saying what I used always to say, and I could scarcely believe it—'

'But he did?'

'He did, sir. Bent down just as though he was anybody and took off his shoes and socks and left them on the steps and then he said: "I never would, would I? Well, this is to say thank you." And we walked across the grass, sir, and we had a little chat about our families, and then he looked at his watch and it was eleven-fifteen and he said, "Time I went home, Annie," and back we walked to the steps, sir, and his shoes and socks were clean gone.'

'So that was how it happened,' said Gabriel.

'It spoiled things,' said Annie sadly. 'He was very embarrassed, and very upset. He said, "The best thing you can do is to go off home, if you please, and leave me to sort this out." So I pulled on my own shoes that I had put in my bag, and though I hardly could bear to leave him there in all his fine things and with bare feet, sir, I went home. I felt bad all night and then when I came in to do my work next morning...'

'Yes,' said Gabriel. 'It must have been a very great shock to you, Annie. I am sorry.'

'Was it the lady took his shoes?' she whispered.

'I think not,' said Gabriel.

'Was it her who killed him?'

'We do not know who killed him, Annie,' said Gabriel. 'But you have provided me with important information that will help to find the killer. You may have been the last person other than the murderer to see Lord Dunning alive.'

'How did you guess about Annie, sir?' enquired Constable Wright later.

'I did not *guess* exactly,' said Gabriel. 'I just tried to remember all that I knew from my books and to apply psychology to the facts; it is the only way I can think of to be a detective. There is nothing new about the human experience. The answer to their motivations must be there, somewhere, already there, in all the written learning we have access to, if we can only grasp it. The quotation I recited to you was from a Quaker poet, a chap called Whittier, written fifty-odd years ago now. His poem "The Barefoot Boy" uses bare feet as a symbol of innocence. And then you talked of your own uncomfortable boots and I remembered Annie's comments about her feet. And Cinderella's bare foot in the fairy story... the prince and the servant girl. And that made me wonder, was there some link between the Lord Chief Justice and Annie? But I could not make sense of the analogy when it was Norman Dunning who had bare feet. Then I recalled the depth of Annie's grief when his body was discovered and felt sure she was somehow connected. She has been the only one, you know, to show real grief.'

'It's a rum story,' said Constable Wright rather helplessly.

But to Gabriel it did not seem so much rum as touching. Norman Dunning's quixotic gesture, this private humbling of his pride and status in gratitude, was not what Gabriel would have expected of him. He tried to transport himself into Dunning's life, so different from his own. As a young man, bowed down under the expectations of his family, he had struggled with intellectual demands that to Gabriel were quite literally as easy as breathing. And he had somehow found with Annie a bond of understanding that bridged their backgrounds, something that had survived in a thread of memory underlying the relentless duty of high office. And so, when he wanted to convey true gratitude, he had done this curious thing, a flouting of the conventionality that had been his god. How curious people were, Gabriel thought, and for a moment, quite unexpectedly, the back of his throat ached. What a patchwork of complex underlying emotions they felt. How little he knew about any of them.

But one of them, unfortunately, he thought he did know about. He must seek out another interview with Lord Justice Wilson. He tried to put out of his mind the social and professional embarrassment involved in such an encounter with the memory of their last one still hanging over him, a cloud that must be dispersed.

31

When Gabriel's arrival at his rooms was announced the next morning, the judge leaped from behind his desk with a gasp of apprehension and then drew himself up defensively like a man facing a firing squad.

'Forgive me,' Gabriel began slowly, 'if I ask you a question of seeming irrelevance, Judge. I do assure you it is not. I believe I may be able to relieve your mind. I think I am correct in recalling that you told me you and Norman Dunning were pupils together in the same chambers?'

'Why, yes, we were.'

'Had you by then met your wife?'

'We were childhood sweethearts,' said Lord Justice Wilson. 'Our parents lived next door to each other. There has never been anyone else for me. She has made me the man I am.'

It occurred to Gabriel that this was a doubtful achievement on Lady Wilson's part.

'I wonder,' he said instead, 'whether you have – shall we say – youthful memories of Norman Dunning at that time?'

'He struggled with the complexities of the law, if that is what you mean,' said Wilson. 'And I recall he did not get on well with his father, the late Mr Justice Horace Dunning.'

'Were you aware of any confidante or companion of his at that time?'

The judge's puffy face took on a disapproving expression.

'Believe it or not, he had a dalliance with the little chambers laundress. Pretty young thing, but that was no excuse. Shocking business. No harm in having fun outside one's class of course, but not with the Temple servants. And she was little more than a child. Quite unacceptable. Disappearances into the garden at night and that sort of thing. Shameless.'

'Perhaps,' said Gabriel, 'it was not shamelessness but innocence. Sometimes they bear a close resemblance.'

Lord Justice Wilson made an indescribable scoffing noise.

'Did your wife know about this?' asked Gabriel.

'Everybody knew,' said Wilson simply. 'Well, everybody of our young set at the time. I am surprised you did not, Ward.' He made this last observation in a slightly sneering tone that made it clear he was anything but. 'I am sure I must have told Louisa. I thought it quite disgusting. A very long time ago now, of course. Why do you ask?'

Gabriel hesitated. He could not go on letting the man think his own wife might be a murderess but now it came to it, he was reluctant to tell Lord Justice Wilson Annie's delicate story. He could imagine it now: the judge's incredulity mixed, if he could be persuaded to believe it, with a degree of contempt for Norman Dunning for not having, after all, tumbled in the shrubbery with Annie. He decided to be selective about what he divulged.

'The laundress's name is Annie Proctor,' he said. 'I am afraid that your – that Lady Wilson may have had an encounter with her on the night of the murder.'

'*An encounter?*'

'A meeting. Not by design; at least not on Annie's part. She opened the front door of the chambers she was cleaning that night and your – a lady was waiting on the steps. One whom she did not know. The lady accosted her. She offered Annie a very large sum of money to tell a newspaper of her youthful friendship all those years ago with Lord Dunning.'

'Friendship!'

'Friendship,' confirmed Gabriel calmly. 'Forgive me, Judge, but do you think the unknown lady could perhaps have been your wife? Such a story would have ruined Lord Dunning; he would certainly have had to stand down as Lord Chief Justice, the position demanding the appearance of irreproachable morality, at least publicly, if not always privately. Can you perhaps conjecture,' he added diffidently, 'why after all these years Lady Wilson might have thought of such a plan?'

The judge's head was in his hands. His response was muffled.

'Poor Louisa. What have I led her into? I am ashamed, Ward. I fear I may have – that I have inadvertently… A couple of weeks ago I had a drink with the Lord Chief Justice at the Garrick Club; we got talking as one does, it was all quite jocular. He said, "It will be a long time before anyone steps into my shoes." Oh, God, that phrase – but it is what he said. And then he continued, "I propose to go on until I am at least eighty."'

'And you repeated that to Lady Wilson?'

'May God forgive me, I did, in some despair. I do not mind admitting to you, Ward, I have wanted that job for many years. I was in waiting, so to speak. But when Dunning is – was – eighty, I would have been close to that age myself. It had never occurred to me he would not step down in a few years. And Louisa…' He groaned. 'How do we know she stopped at bribery?'

'We know,' answered Gabriel, 'because of the rest of the story that Annie told me. After her interview with the woman who had accosted her, and after Lady Wilson had returned to her carriage and resumed her journey home with you, Dunning was still alive, as Annie can confirm.'

'How on earth would she know?'

'Because,' said Gabriel evenly, 'she met him by chance a little later and was with him for some half an hour, until eleven-fifteen. And because we know from Dunning's watch that he died at eleven-twenty-five.'

The judge's eyes popped. 'Good heavens! Are you telling me the thing with this woman was still going on? After all these years?'

'I am telling you nothing of the kind,' said Gabriel, quite sharply for him. 'And the irony is that, had your wife known fate was shortly to hand to her on a plate the result she sought, namely the post of Lord Chief Justice falling vacant, she would not have made her clumsy attempt to bribe Annie.'

The judge winced.

But then another thought struck him. 'The socks! What about Dunning's socks?'

Gabriel shook his head. 'You need not concern yourself with the socks. They are part of someone else's story.'

'But will this servant talk?'

'No,' said Gabriel. 'Annie Proctor is a decent, honourable woman who holds Norman Dunning dear in her memory. She will not *talk*, as you put it.'

The judge had the grace to look abashed. But then he put on his pomposity like an overcoat.

'As one of His Majesty's judges, pledged to observe the utmost integrity, I need hardly tell you that I knew nothing of this enterprise by Lady Wilson.'

'You are right. You need not tell me that.'

'Nor do I need to emphasise the extremely confidential nature of what you have now divulged to me as far as my wife is concerned.'

'Nor that.'

'Nor to assure you that the inappropriateness of Lady Wilson's conduct will be made very clear to her.'

'That is… understood.'

'Thank you.' It was very stiffly said. 'I am grateful to you.'

'May I add something without meaning any impertinence?' asked Gabriel. 'We men – we lead such enriched lives. All the aspirations we are permitted and encouraged in and the opportunities we receive to realise them — I wonder if perhaps Lady Wilson might feel a little happier if she had an ambition of her own to pursue.'

Lord Justice Wilson looked puzzled. 'She has the house and children.'

Gabriel bowed politely.

'And she has me.'

Gabriel bowed again.

Lord Justice Wilson rang for his clerk to show Gabriel out without another word.

But in the hansom cab on his way home that night, he thought very hard indeed about a lot of things all mixed up together until they became a kind of refrain, whirling around in his head to the rattle of the wheels and clopping of the horses' hooves. Of that moment of utter horror when he had thought his Louisa... Of the numerous servants in his house and the children away at school and of his long hours of work and his all-encompassing ambition. And then he thought of Gabriel's gentle voice. Above all, the irony in Gabriel's last bow.

And when at last he mounted his steps, took out his front-door key and prepared to confront his wife, although he looked the same pompous, stolid, unimaginative man who had left the house that morning, Lord Justice Wilson did not feel at all the same inside.

32

Albert Broadbent, meanwhile, remained incarcerated in his cell and his story of observing sacrifices in the Temple Church remained uninvestigated by the police. It seemed plain to Gabriel that Broadbent had indeed seen and experienced something unusual and that these events took place in the Temple Church. Who, in real life, thought Gabriel, knows the most about that church? The Reverend Vernon-Osbert. And in the highly unlikely event of the church being locked, who would have been the most obvious custodian of the key? Vernon-Osbert. But surely, of all people likely to wish to exclude those members of the Inner Temple who had reason to seek solace in the church at night, he was the least likely?

That night very late, before he retired to bed, Gabriel went to the Temple Church himself to see if the door was locked. He could not imagine why it should be, but if it was, it might support Broadbent's version of events.

The night was dark, and the moon obscured behind cloud. Eerie zebra stripes of shadow cast by the elaborate casing of the gas lamps fell across the terrace and the Temple held, along with its usual centuries-old romance, a curious menace. From Sir William Waring's ground-floor office one steady light beamed out. It was nearly midnight. Walking along the Terrace, Gabriel glanced curiously through the window. Around a desk sat a huddled group of men, their faces illuminated like those in a caricature of the Gunpowder Plot. Through the open sash cigar smoke drifted out, overpowering the scent of the flowers beneath; and in the still air the men's voices were just audible, although Gabriel couldn't make out what was said.

He crept a little closer until he stood on the edge of the bed beneath the window. *Really*, he thought to himself, *can I, a senior member of the Bar, possibly be standing in a flowerbed, spying on the Treasurer in the middle of the night?* But the thought, though it caused him to give a little snuffle, did not inhibit him. He peered cautiously into the room. In the smoky, lamplit interior, the Treasurer Sir William Waring sat with Sir Vivian Barton KC, Lord Justice Wilson and Lord Justice Brown. Gabriel could now readily identify individual voices and their words.

'…It would have been the occasion of the century, had Dunning agreed to help,' said Lord Justice Wilson. 'Just think of the glory and the honour.'

'Though, most sadly, as things turned out, that help would never have materialised,' said Brown.

'No,' said Sir William Waring grimly. 'As things turned out, the disloyal bastard got his just deserts.'

'Come, come, Sir William.' This time it was Sir Vivian Barton's warm, fruity voice that spoke up. 'That is a little strong. The poor man has come to a tragic end.'

Sir William got up from the table and walked over to the window. He was so close Gabriel could have touched him. Backing hastily under the cover of a shrub, he peered incredulously at the face he knew so well, now almost unrecognisable in the grip of venom.

The voice became softer, yet somehow more menacing in its softness. 'It makes no difference. Dunning let down the Inner Temple. He failed us when we turned to him. He could have achieved great distinction for us. He could have enhanced our legacy. And he refused to help. I feel nothing but loathing and the coldest disdain for him.'

Inside the room there was an uneasy silence; outside, Gabriel stepped back involuntarily from the almost palpable malice that drifted out, together with the alluring smoke of the Havanas, and seemed to pollute the air with something horrible.

The contrast between the civilised, if somewhat conspiratorial, scene and the Treasurer's icy denouncement made Gabriel feel as though quite suddenly he had seen a curtain drawn back, to reveal not the expected familiar view but something quite different and shocking.

Shaken, he made his way to the church. Next to it, the Reverend Master's beautiful eighteenth-century house was in darkness save for one faint light in Vernon-Osbert's study. This reassuring sight came as a relief after the shock of the scene he had just witnessed. Gabriel thought with affection of the old clergyman living peacefully with his cat and his God.

Grasping the great iron ring on the Norman door of the church, he pushed hard. He thought fleetingly of the mysteriously robed woman Broadbent insisted he had seen. When the door yielded, what or who would be revealed? But to Gabriel's astonishment it did not yield. The door was locked, as Broadbent had insisted it had been on the night he had slept there. The welcome of its church was one of the Temple's great traditions. The mystery seemed to be deepening. Gabriel had a strong sense that he must find the key – in more ways than one.

33

As a result of Miss Susan Hatchings' claims to the authorship of *Millie the Temple Church Mouse* and the sensational collapse of the trial, sales of the book, to Herbert Moore's embarrassment, had soared even higher. Gabriel had been correct in his prediction that interest would centre on Miss Hatchings rather than on the true identity of the author. The assumption was still generally made that Miss Harriet Cadamy was indeed the gentle, reclusive old lady whom Herbert had so effectively created. Miss Hatchings was seen as the villainess of the piece, seeking to take advantage of Miss Cadamy's wish for privacy and falsely laying claim to her work and identity.

What Gabriel had not predicted, however, was the impact on the public of the mysterious 'fact' that had enabled him to discredit Susan Hatchings so effectively. Whipped up by the newspapers, readers embarked collectively on a game to guess the way in which Millie's mother had died. It was a peculiarly pointless guessing game. Poor Herbert was inundated with letters. Millie's mother had been eaten by a cat; she had been poisoned by the Temple Church verger; she had been run over by a passing carriage in the Strand; she had died gracefully in her nest of old age. Every theory under the sun was advanced in a curious mixture of humour and prurience. Herbert lay determinedly low and answered none of the sacks full of letters containing ever more exotic theories.

The precious manuscript was moved from the safe at Moore's to the security of the strongroom at Hoare's Bank situated opposite. Moore's itself became a different place, the rewards of success plain for all to see. The quaint old-fashioned shop was now glossy and slightly intimidating, with a uniformed porter at the door to vet all visitors to the premises.

The nature of the business was changing too; despite Herbert's struggles to maintain his reputation as a specialist legal book-seller, he had to rebut constant submissions by aspiring authors of children's books. Invitations to social events poured in from the fashionable world of mainstream publishing. They were hard to resist. There was no real reason why he should resist them. And yet in the back of his mind ran the phrase that, according to Gabriel, a judge had once uttered in a long-forgotten case: 'money which ought not in justice to be kept.' Harriet Cadamy haunted his dreams; Millie the Mouse dogged his work. He did not know whether he should court publicity because it might reveal who Miss Cadamy really was, or whether he should shun it for the same reason. He did not know whether the knowledge would bring him peace or destroy all he had worked for. He only knew he had to find out.

———

Looming behind the uncertainty and unhappiness that had over-taken him, there was a new ordeal for Herbert. Two days after the trial had ended, beginning with a special Saturday matinee performance for children, the theatrical adaptation of *Millie the Temple Church Mouse* was to be performed for the first time.

The Savoy Theatre was shining with the light of hundreds of incandescent electric light bulbs. On that rainy afternoon, with more light reflected off the wet pavements around it, it seemed to be its own spotlight and the vast numbers congregating outside it, players themselves. The open doors threw out a blaze of illu-mination; on either side of them were flaming electrified torches and above the torches the name of the play gleamed through the rain in golden letters: *Millie the Temple Church Mouse*.

Inside were the assembled papas and mamas, the governesses and aunts and grandparents, and everywhere the children, dressed in their best, clutching their toy Millies and the hot hands of their grown-ups, all surging into the theatre and settling into the blue velvet of their seats. And the excitement mounted until it seemed almost tangible, a great rolling presence in the auditorium, uniting the wriggling, giggling, whispering and rustling audience into one being who very gradually, as the theatre filled, became hushed with anticipation.

High up in an opulent box close to the stage sat Herbert Moore, every inch the successful publisher, dashing, handsome, urbane, apparently carefree, and beside him his wife and his little Elsie, both a credit to him, emblems to an admiring crowd of the family values of *Millie the Temple Church Mouse*.

'And who is the dry little man beside them?' whispered a lady in the audience to her neighbour in the stalls. Her neighbour happened to be Maud Rentoul, exquisitely dressed in green silk and emeralds, accompanying her two immaculate grandchildren who were each, inevitably, clutching one of the very newest deluxe models of Millie the Mouse. Maud was agog for gossip, her opera glasses already busily scanning the audience like a vulture after prey. She was particularly interested to see if dear Frederick and Louisa Wilson were there, and more to the point, whether they appeared to be speaking to each other. But now she forgot this intriguing titbit in favour of an opportunity to display a superior knowledge of her fellow members of society.

'*My dear*, don't you know? It is Sir Gabriel Ward KC. Quite, quite brilliant, they say, but *reclusive* to a fault. And, it has to be said, rather *dull* in conversation. I am *amazed* to see him here, my dear. He is, you know—'

But whatever scurrilous gossip she was about to convey was lost in the collective intake of breath among the audience as the gold satin curtain went up.

Maud Rentoul could not be more amazed by Gabriel's presence than he was himself. When the invitation from Herbert Moore had arrived in his chambers, he had scarcely glanced at it before putting it on what was known as Chapman's pile. This he handed every evening to the clerk with the same snuffly joke: 'Thank you, Chapman. Pay the bills and say no to all the invitations.'

But on this occasion, on catching sight of the topmost card, his clerk had hesitated.

'Are you sure, sir?' he had said. 'It is to be quite an event. They say it may make theatre history.' He added tentatively, 'It is the Savoy Theatre, sir, part of the hotel. You go just a little way down the Strand, hardly out of the Temple at all, sir. Five minutes' walk, if that.'

'Thank you, Chapman.' Gabriel spoke rather stiffly, a nerve touched. 'I am well aware of the location of the Savoy.' But he casually retrieved the invitation from Chapman's pile and looked at it reflectively. He had liked Herbert Moore and the curious nature of the case still preoccupied him. And the Savoy was so close. Perhaps…

And so it was, for the first time in a good thirty-five years, that Gabriel watched a theatre curtain go up to reveal the set. There were the great soaring pillars and arches of the Temple Church recreated on the stage, the flimsy cardboard and plaster transformed by the lights into its solemn stone.

The critics sat in the front row: cynicism nicely honed, expectations determinedly low, pens at the ready. And then they were swept away along with the rest of that enraptured audience into a world of make-believe in which critics did not exist; a world that united them with every child who was present. And they, like the children, laughed and cried and cheered and sang, and forgot what was real and what was imaginary and where the two met and where they divided again.

The diminutive and very famous actress who had competed with every other famous actress in England for the privilege of spending two hours under blazing lights encased from head to toe in grey fur, exceeded all expectations. The well-loved characters and much of the dialogue of the book were faithfully adhered to. The supporting roles were filled by more famous actors and actresses of the day: the Lady in the Hat, the Fat Judge, the Funny Old Gentleman, the Kind Vicar... all prancing and panting and preaching and twirling and falling over, which made everyone laugh, and everyone cry when the same characters expressed unhappiness. And then, in a silence that became almost holy, each character turned to Millie the Mouse for comfort and understanding. The religious message was conveyed principally by a choir of mouse angels swinging dizzily across the stage on trapezes, tails flying, furry, be-tinselled wings outstretched. And the audience, young and old, vowed inwardly that from now on they would love their neighbour and do as they would be done by, and turn the other cheek.

I am not sure whether I have just witnessed a children's play, or a pantomime, or a religious meeting, wrote the one critic with sufficient wits left to put pen to paper for the morning edition. *Suffice it to say it was one of the most wonderful pieces of theatre I have ever seen.*

When the gold satin curtain had risen and fallen twenty times to an audience that would not let the actors go, when palms were burning and voices growing hoarse, when the theatre was momentarily in pitch darkness, a new cry was heard.

'Author! Author!' the audience demanded. 'Author! Author!'

A single blazing spotlight appeared and dipped and wavered its way across the gold curtain until it reached the middle. There it steadied and fixed like a great shining hard-edged piece of tin, illuminating a small portion of the dusty wooden stage, now strewn with flowers, and a larger portion of the golden curtain.

'Author! Author!'

For a minute the spotlight held; and then for another; and another; until five long minutes had passed.

Still the clamour was heard: 'Author! Author!'

In the box above, Herbert Moore craned forward in his seat, his hands gripping the balcony rail. The audience held its collective breath.

At last, as though giving up in despair, the shining orb quivered and dipped and wavered and was extinguished, and the house lights went up.

Herbert Moore turned to Gabriel. 'I thought that was the moment. It *was* the moment. And now it has passed and I feel we shall never know. Don't you feel that, Sir Gabriel?'

There was a little pause.

'I don't know,' said Gabriel slowly. 'And I am very probably quite wrong. But I am just beginning to wonder about one possibility.'

Slowly, the crowd pressed its way out of the theatre. As he squirmed his way through them, a hand smote Gabriel on the shoulder and he turned to see Sir Vivian Barton.

'Good to see you, dear boy,' he said. The Barton family all shone; Vivian with goodwill and prosperity, his wife because of the blue silk of her best dress, the seven little Bartons with scrubbing and excitement.

'I spotted you up there with your erstwhile client,' Barton went on. 'You were on the right side in that case, Ward. A splendid play. But no closer to the identity of the author, eh?' And he winked.

'Perhaps just a little closer,' said Gabriel.

'Oh-ho! Tell me more. In fact, come with us — we are off to the hotel for cake and ice cream.'

Looking at the seven faces, Gabriel could only too vividly imagine them in the restaurant at the Savoy covered in cake.

'Oh, *no*,' he said in involuntary horror, 'I thank you but I couldn't *possibly*.'

He raised his hat and bowed as best he could in the crush before he resumed his slow progress across the foyer. Emerging from the doorway where more crowds were sheltering from the rain, he encountered Lady Dunning with Theodora, Percival, Seraphina, Claud and the governess.

'I hope that you enjoyed the play?' he said to the children.

Seraphina removed her thumb from her mouth. 'I liked the mouse angels,' she declared.

'They were not mice   they were ladies dressed up,' said Percival instructively. 'And they were not really angels either.'

'They *flew*,' said Seraphina.

'That would certainly seem to be conclusive,' said Gabriel.

Percival opened his mouth, caught his aunt's eye, and closed it again.

The Dunning carriage drew up in the Strand and Miss Murray, a wet figure huddled against the rain, herding her charges under a large umbrella out onto the pavement, sneezed dismally and, while fumbling in her bag for a handkerchief, dropped on the wet stone kerb a small volume. Gabriel bent politely to pick it up for her, but by the time he had straightened up again, the carriage was moving out into the heavy traffic.

Never one to resist a book, Gabriel peered at the leather spine. It was a copy of *Jane Eyre*. So poor Miss Murray chose to escape into the world of another governess, one who experienced passionate romance and a happy ending. No harm in that, thought Gabriel. I, too, read to escape; and dreams are so often more satisfying than the reality that awaits us when we stop reading.

He slipped the book in his pocket to be returned later and made his way slowly back to the peace of the Temple, green and fresh from the rain. There he took off his raincoat and hung it on the hook behind the door and forgot all about Miss Murray's dreams bound in leather and tucked into the pocket. It was not until it rained the next day, and Gabriel had need once again of his raincoat, that the astonishing information contained within the book came to light.

34

On the Monday, when the first news page of the normally sober *Times* newspaper was dominated by a caption quite two inches high, which proclaimed 'Mouse Triumph', and the latest skirmish in the Boer War was relegated to the second story, Herbert Moore turned up unexpectedly in Gabriel's chambers. Ushered in by Chapman, he did not look like a man who had doubled his fortune overnight. Flinging himself uninvited into the client's chair, he buried his head in his hands.

'Tell me what I can do for you, Mr Moore,' said Gabriel, fearing for his next linen handkerchief. Once again he found himself the recipient, as seemed to him his fate, of an outpouring of anguish.

Herbert Moore felt he could not stand it anymore. Saturday afternoon and this morning's adulation were the final straws. Last week he had visited Hanwell County Lunatic Asylum and seen Susan Hatchings.

Gabriel looked disapproving.

'You are no longer my client, Mr Moore. But had you been, I would have told you that was very unwise. What could you hope to gain?'

'That she might yet give me some clue as to Harriet Cadamy's true identity. And then I pity her so, poor woman, left to rot in that place. A dreadful punishment for a failed deception. That lonely life; that dreadful man. But I could get nothing from her, Sir Gabriel. Hysteria is the diagnosis. Do you know that they incarcerate women for years who suffer from it? That place! Oh,

I do not say they ill-treat them as such, but I felt – I felt – all hope was gone as I walked through that door. And do you know what the warder said to me? "The gutter is only a stumble away." And it is true, Sir Gabriel. It might be me. It might be you.'

'My dear Mr Moore,' said Gabriel in his dry, logical way, 'we are both of us eminently sane, we have neither of us laid claim to authorship of a famous book we did not write and, in the unfortunate event of either of us becoming unwell, we can both afford to be restrained in private and comfortable secure accommodation.'

Herbert smiled sheepishly. 'I do not mean to sound over-emotional.' He hesitated before adding, 'But there is *so much* money… There are better places – I could help – but do I have the right to spend some of the proceeds in this way? Are they mine to disburse? If I were to pay for her to be looked after and it should emerge, what would the papers make of that? What would people think? What would the real Miss Harriet Cadamy have to say about it? I fear it might be looked upon as some sort of admission that she is in truth the author of *Millie the Temple Church Mouse*. Or look like a reward for dishonesty. But then again, she did not want the money; she did it for the love of that dreadful man. Oh, dear, I find it all so confusing.'

He came to a halt and looked piteously at Gabriel.

'These are not questions for a lawyer. And as for what people think, you have not mentioned the one person who can point you to where your moral duty lies.'

'Who is that?' said Herbert Moore eagerly.

Gabriel snuffled. 'Millie the Mouse.' Standing up, he held out his hand in farewell. 'Or to put it another way,' he said, 'I should follow your heart, Mr Moore. I think it will lead you in the direction of your proper duty.'

35

Miss Murray was not happy in the Dunning household, nor had she been since the day of her arrival, twelve months previously. The stuccoed grandeur of Stafford Terrace oppressed her and she found the relationships within it unfathomable.

Superficially, all seemed to be as the governess had expected. The domestic rhythms ground on, as in all large London households, like the slow unending revolutions of a vast millwheel, its continuance ensured by the servants who ceaselessly cleaned and polished to keep at bay the smuts and smoke of the city clamouring constantly to be let in at doors and windows; who washed and laundered; who prepared and cooked and served.

Against this backdrop the life of the family in the public parts of the house continued normally, each member moving across a stage daily set for them by the assiduous stagehands to whom none of them gave a thought.

Lord Dunning went to court every day; Lady Charlotte Dunning shopped and visited and was visited; Theodora, a forbidding presence, wrote letters and read books and answered all domestic queries. They entertained or were entertained lavishly.

Quite frequently, however, a storm broke; there were raised voices, hastily suppressed, and slammed doors. Sequestered for most of her time in the schoolroom on the third floor of the house, Miss Murray was never quite sure between whom these violent yet muffled exchanges took place. But she was uncomfortably aware of some deep reservoir of suppressed emotion here that was beyond her comprehension and that she could not define. She only knew that it made her afraid.

Lord Dunning she seldom saw. Lady Dunning was kind in passing but quite indifferent to the comfort and entertainment of a governess. Theodora was formidably distant. The large domestic staff kept a respectful distance.

And then there were the children, the only people for whom she had even a notional significance. Claud was still in the care of a nursemaid. Seraphina, a biddable enough little girl, did not seem to have taken to her; she did not want to be cuddled nor did she want to confide in her. If she needed comfort, she turned to her beloved toy Millie and her thumb, or to her Aunt Theodora. She was dutiful but unenthusiastic in the classroom, and happiest on her own outside it.

As for Percival: in the short time in which he had been in Miss Murray's care, he had quite unintentionally subjected her to the closest to torture she had ever known. It was not that he was badly behaved or disobedient or lazy. On the contrary, he was attentive and eager to learn. But Miss Murray found the incisive, and very vocal, logic to which he subjected her every utterance almost intolerably irritating.

Sometimes, looking at Seraphina's curly head as she bent submissively over her sums while Percival earnestly sought clarification of each unfamiliar word he read, Miss Murray wondered how much longer she could put up with it. Had she but known, similar thoughts, though expressed a little differently, were going through the minds of both children. Theodora's assessment had been correct. Miss Murray, clever though she was, failed to inspire as a teacher; and the youngest inhabitants, too, had been affected by the indefinable tensions within the house.

It seemed to Miss Murray that only knowing little Percival – not above listening at doors, she suspected – really understood the inner workings of the household.

'Do not trouble your mama or your aunt today,' she said to him when the air of oppression seemed to her unendurable. 'They are both a little tired.'

'Mama is bored,' said Percival dispassionately. 'She told Papa so. And Aunt Theodora told him she was thwarted. What does thwarted mean, Miss Murray?'

'Be quiet, Percival,' said his governess.

'I think Mama hates Aunt Theodora,' the boy continued with relish. 'And I think Aunt Theodora hates Mama and Papa.'

'Go to your room at once, Percival!' said Miss Murray, who rather thought so too.

Lord Dunning's death had of course been a terrible shock for the entire household; but with it had come a certain peace, and it was with a surprising rapidity that Miss Murray's uneventful routine had resumed its course.

The impact on the occupants of the schoolroom when Sir Gabriel Ward KC was ushered in by the parlourmaid that Monday afternoon, was extraordinary. Seraphina was round-eyed; Percival instantly gleamed with curiosity and conjecture; Miss Murray was speechless with astonishment.

'Forgive my intrusion,' said this vision politely. 'Miss Murray, Lady Dunning has been kind enough to permit me to request a private word with you.'

'With me?' repeated Miss Murray.

'Indeed yes, if I may. Could we perhaps leave the children for a moment?'

Percival was well aware that there was only one reason why gentlemen wished to be left alone with ladies.

'Are you going to kiss Miss Murray?' he demanded.

It would be hard to say which of the two adults was the most disconcerted by this question. Miss Murray blushed a fiery red;

263

Gabriel's head retreated into his collar like that of a surprised tortoise. Percival's fascinated gaze was fixed on his governess's scarlet countenance, while his mind revisited the interesting facts he had assimilated the previous week from Papa's encyclopaedia in relation to dilation of the blood vessels and its causes. While he attempted to remember the description of capillary flow, Gabriel ushered Miss Murray into the next room and closed the door firmly behind them.

His decision to return to the governess the book she had dropped outside the theatre two days earlier had not been easily made. Having discovered the potentially sensational information it contained, he had forced himself to make the journey to Stafford Terrace. He could not trust the emotionally involved Herbert Moore, whose business this undoubtedly might be, to approach the subject with sufficient tact. That only left Gabriel himself.

And so he had drawn deep from his inner well of courage to enable him to close the door of 4 King's Bench Walk, press it carefully three times, negotiate the paving stones of the Terrace and, having reached Fleet Street at last, to put up his hand, as he had watched Wright do on the previous occasion he had visited the Dunning household, and give the cab driver the address with a fair amount of authority.

Lady Dunning had received his unexpected visit with a degree of interest when she thought it concerned her, but on learning the purpose of his errand, gave no thought to the oddity of Sir Gabriel Ward making the journey in person to return the governess's lost property. Without further questions being asked, Gabriel had been ushered up the stairs to the schoolroom.

He had not given much thought in advance to the way in which he would approach Miss Murray. Their previous encounter in the churchyard did not suggest she would be disposed to be helpful. Now they were alone, he looked doubtfully at her before plunging in.

'I believe this is yours,' he said, digging the book out of his pocket. 'You dropped it when leaving the theatre the other evening and had gone before I could hand it back to you. *Jane Eyre*... and if I may say so, a most attractive copy. Are you fond of Miss Brontë's other novels?'

Miss Murray collected herself. 'I am very familiar with them all,' she said stiffly. 'I felt I would like to reread *Jane Eyre*. It is my favourite. I am most grateful that you should have troubled to return it to me.'

Gabriel wondered how he could put her at her ease. Perhaps the children were the way.

'How are your charges progressing, Miss Murray?' he said. 'It must be hard for them to bear their father's death.'

'They will learn. They will not be the first children to lose a parent.'

The remark, so quietly spoken, was nevertheless unmistakably sharp. She caught his look of surprise. 'I am sorry,' she said. 'I should not have spoken like that. It is just that I lost both my parents when I was very young. I was brought up in St Saviour's Orphanage.' She gave a very small smile. 'Perhaps that is why I feel a certain sympathy for Jane Eyre.'

'Indeed yes.' Gabriel was beginning to warm to her. 'How did you find your present position?'

Amelia Murray's expression softened. 'Indirectly, through one of the patrons of the orphanage, Lady Brown. She helped me get my first post and I have worked for several lawyers' families before this one. Though none,' she added, 'were quite as grand.'

Again, Gabriel thought he caught in the quiet voice a satirical note. Miss Murray bent her head and her confidences seemed to be at an end.

Gabriel wondered how best to approach his subject. Sometimes, with a witness, it was best just to plunge in and hope to take them by surprise.

'Miss Murray,' he said, without further preamble, 'what is your connection with Miss Susan Hatchings?'

She looked at him blankly. 'I have none.'

Gabriel opened the little book and showed her what he had discovered written in violet ink on the flyleaf: *This book belongs to Susan Hatchings.*

The governess blinked. 'I am sorry, Sir Gabriel, I have no idea how her name came to be in this book.'

'But where did you get it?'

Miss Murray looked relieved to be able to proffer something positive. 'It was in the small bookshelf in the governess's bedroom. I had not even noticed the inscription. I hope I have not done wrong? I assumed that the books had been provided for me to read.'

'A very natural assumption,' said Gabriel kindly, 'and I am sure it is the correct one. I think I must speak to Lady Dunning again before I leave.'

He hesitated and then picked up the little volume now lying on the table.

'I wonder if I might borrow this? I will very happily send you another copy just as pleasant to the touch and eye so that you may continue reading.'

A little reluctantly, Miss Murray indicated her acquiescence.

The interview seemed to be over, but Gabriel lingered. There was something... something about this young woman he could not reach.

'Forgive me for mentioning it, Miss Murray,' he ventured tentatively, 'but you seem a little uncomfortable. I fear Lord Dunning's death has made this an unhappy household for the staff.'

'Oh, it is not his death that has made it unhappy,' she exclaimed. 'That has made it far better. It was before that it was so dreadf—' She broke off. 'Oh, no, what I am saying? I do not mean that… The children – I must go. Excuse me, Sir Gabriel.'

She stumbled to the door.

'You are still very red,' Percival observed dispassionately when she re-entered the schoolroom.

Downstairs, Gabriel found Charlotte Dunning alone in the morning room. She was even less informative than the governess.

'I have no idea why this name is in the book. Nor, if it comes to that, have I any idea where the books in the governess's bedroom come from,' said Lady Dunning. 'I suppose they must buy them themselves, poor things.'

'I believe,' said Gabriel tentatively, memories of Percival's boast outside the Temple Church vivid in his mind, 'that there have been a number of governesses?'

'Yes,' said Charlotte distractedly. 'Yes, two before Miss Murray. It is dear little Percival, you know…'

'Would you be kind enough to furnish me with the details of those two ladies?' Gabriel persisted.

'Details? Why, I scarcely recall them. The first was quite an elderly lady called Miss Davey, just to help Nanny really. She was with us for about a year. I believe she retired then, to one of those seaside places. Was it Brighton? No, though it did begin with a B…'

'Bognor? Bridlington? Bournemouth?'

'Bournemouth! That was it. I went there with my mama once. Such a pretty place! A charming pier, I recall. And such lovely sands.'

'And the other lady?'

'What other lady?' Lady Dunning's butterfly brain was far away.

'The second governess?'

'Oh!' Her pretty face became a little disgruntled. 'She was not very suitable. Young and flighty. And there was an incident. I was out at the time. Norman dismissed her. I do not recall where she went. Theodora manages the staff in consultation with the housekeeper. She will know. She is out at present.'

'Might I perhaps speak to the housekeeper then?'

Charlotte rang the bell.

The housekeeper was helpful and efficient. On hearing the nature of the enquiry, she fetched her housekeeping book, turned briskly to the back and ran her finger down the names listed there.

'Miss Davey,' she confirmed. 'Now in Bournemouth. And Miss Harrison,' she said with some triumph. 'Employed here until Miss Murray replaced her last year. She went to a position in Greenwich, though whether she is still there, sir, I would not be able to say. I have both addresses.'

Had Charlotte Dunning's mind not been so firmly fixed on her dressmaker's appointment, it might have occurred even to her that Sir Gabriel Ward's interest in the ownership of a book from her governess's shelf was a little odd. But as it was, she wanted only to bring the interview to an end, and saw Gabriel ushered out with some relief.

Bournemouth and Greenwich. Gabriel was aware of his own limitations. The information he required might just as well be in Bolivia and Greenland. He had never been to either of those places and, in terms of being outside the boundaries in which he was comfortable, they were pretty much indistinguishable. Not the most assiduous attention to the little rituals he adopted to make travel tolerable to him would enable him to travel to Greenwich, let alone Bournemouth.

Gabriel did not discuss with anyone the self-imposed boundaries of his life, nor the consequent restrictions on his freedom, nor why they were essential to him, though he knew that Chapman knew of the rules and routines, knew they became more rigid when a big case was coming on, or when Gabriel was tired or feared that some event might in some way disrupt them. Constable Wright, it seemed to him, had also, if only subconsciously, deduced both the physical limits of Gabriel's contribution to the murder investigation and that those limits were imposed upon him by the same mind that enabled him to travel so very far in his imagination.

The difficulty on this occasion was that Wright, while he could legitimately be requested to help undertake investigations in pursuit of the murder case, could not really be requested to waste police time on a matter related to Gabriel's legal practice.

When the problem was put before him later in the day, he too seemed doubtful. 'Detective Inspector Hughes would not like that at all, sir. Not trips off when Broadbent is being interrogated and it's all up in the air.'

'I have not forgotten poor Broadbent's plight. Indeed, I am working very hard to alleviate it.'

'I tell you what, though. I am due two days' leave, sir, what I was saving up…'

And so it was arranged.

36

'Due two days off?' said Detective Inspector Hughes. 'What do you want to do with them? Some young lady, eh?'

Wright blushed.

'Sir Gabriel has asked me to go to Bournemouth. And then the next day to Greenwich.'

'Bournemouth? Greenwich?'

'Yes, sir. In relation to one of his cases.'

'What the devil have his cases got to do with you?'

'It is just a few questions, sir. I don't mind.'

Hughes raised his eyebrows, pursed his lips and shrugged; a characteristic combination with which he liked to convey superiority.

'They're your days off, lad. You can do what you like on them. Should you stumble in passing upon another candidate for the murderer of the Lord Chief Justice, perhaps you would let me know. Meanwhile, I will have another go at extracting a confession from the one I've got.'

Wright smiled perfunctorily at this little pleasantry. The nature of his private investigation for Sir Gabriel was unsensational, to say the least. Sir Gabriel had not even told him what he was supposed to find out, over and above a few enquiries as to the nature of the two ladies' duties, and only his kind heart, and a growing regard for Gabriel, had made him agree to help. In truth, Wright was heavily preoccupied with the death of the Lord Chief Justice and the mystery surrounding it. His curiosity was initially aroused by the information that both the ladies he was to find had been employed in the Dunning household. But it died on hearing that this had been a considerable time ago, which seemed to him therefore to have no relevance to the murder investigation. He had little interest in Sir Gabriel's everyday work, which he thought both dull and obscure.

Nor did he share Herbert Moore's love of railways, and so he embarked on a train from Waterloo station to Bournemouth Central with little interest in his method of travel and nothing to occupy his mind but the death of the Lord Chief Justice and the fate of Broadbent.

Since his arrest, Broadbent had remained incarcerated in the cells beneath Old Jewry police station and, had it not been for the seriousness of the charge, would have been reasonably satisfied to remain there. A dry mattress, bread and tea for breakfast and porridge for dinner were luxuries to be grateful for. But over these relative comforts lay the shadow of the noose, and in spite of his natural optimism, in his abject loneliness the prisoner could not help dwelling on the horror that the future seemed likely to hold for him. As the days passed, Wright had noted uneasily that the porridge was beginning to come back from the prisoner's cell untouched and that Broadbent was sliding into despair.

Detective Inspector Hughes had been informed of the progress of Gabriel's enquiries; he was now well aware, thanks to faithful reporting by Constable Wright, that Broadbent's explanations with regard to his presence in the Temple, his sojourn in the church, his discovery of the shoes by the garden steps, the ultimate fate of both the shoes and the socks, were all borne out by the stories told by Meg, Annie and Maud Rentoul. He was prepared to accept that it was unequivocally the case that Lord Dunning had divested himself of his own shoes and socks, that Broadbent had stolen them, and that he had been secreted in the

Temple Church by Meg during the evening. Any jury would, he thought, reach the same conclusion.

But there the detective inspector's credulity ended. He remained convinced that Broadbent had stabbed the Lord Chief Justice to death at twenty-five-past eleven and had thereafter returned to the Temple Church and remained there until the morning. Attempts had been made to match Broadbent's hand with Wright's photograph of the bloody palm print left at the murder scene. But Broadbent's thick gnarled old palm was worn by two years' hard labour in prison as well as by scavenging on the streets. The attempt had proved inconclusive. The evidence against him remained the age-old combination of motive and opportunity.

The motive was clear, and of the opportunity Hughes had no doubt. His fondly held personal theory was that Broadbent had left the church at around eleven o'clock in the evening to relieve himself, had stolen the shoes while the Lord Chief Justice was engaged in what Hughes described as shenanigans (and best not say what he thought about *them*; the Lord Chief Justice indeed!) in the garden, had secreted himself until Dunning had left Annie at eleven-fifteen. Broadbent had then stabbed him in an act of revenge at eleven-twenty-five, returning to the church and receiving, from the innocent Meg, a few minutes before midnight, a beef sandwich with all the *sang-froid* of the wicked murderer he was.

Broadbent's alibi was tenuous in the extreme, the inspector had pointed out to Wright. With no way of telling the time, the suspect had no way of proving that he was in the church when Dunning met his death, nor indeed of giving them proper information about any of his movements that night. True, it might be that his account of seeing the Reverend Vernon-Osbert with another man tallied with the accounts of Vernon-Osbert himself and Sir Vivian Barton. But

Broadbent's account of being locked in the church and of subsequent events there was simply nonsense; and even if true, it did not mean that he had not murdered the Lord Chief Justice at eleven-twenty-five.

In vain had Constable Wright suggested that if Broadbent's account proved to be true, it was not only suggestive of the overall veracity of his account of the night in question but also of quite independent goings-on in the Temple, which might be pertinent to the murder. In vain he told him the story of the mysterious fish. Detective Inspector Hughes was not minded, he told Wright, to waste his time following up a crazy vagrant's story about libations and sacrifice, whatever they may be, and that was all there was to it.

'And there is no shifting him, Sir Gabriel,' Wright had reported back in worried tones. 'Meanwhile Broadbent is banged up in fear of his life and it doesn't seem quite right to me, sir, not to investigate what he says.'

'There is some force in the inspector's position,' said Gabriel, determined as ever to be objective and fair-minded, 'since the most reliable timing we have is from Meg's statement: she is very clear about the time she left the kitchen and also when she took Broadbent his sandwich in the church. She left at a quarter to twelve and she would have taken barely five minutes to reach the church. If she arrived at ten to twelve, it is clearly possible for Broadbent to have stabbed the Lord Chief Justice at eleven-twenty-five and then returned to the church for his sandwich.'

'But how reliable is she, sir?'

'She strikes me as being very reliable; and furthermore, she says she looked at the clock before she left. She does not know, of course, that she is tightening the noose around Broadbent's neck. She is simply telling the truth.'

'Perhaps the clock was wrong,' said Wright hopefully.

'I thought of that, Mr Wright,' said Gabriel with a snuffle. 'What my nanny would have referred to as grasping at straws.' He explained about Reginald, the kitchen wall clock that was always right and wound weekly by Mrs Bugg.

'What does she say about when Meg left?'

Gabriel shook his head. 'Poor Meg is the last person to leave the kitchen every night.'

'Well,' said Wright, abandoning this tack, 'can't we somehow look at Broadbent's story about the church?'

'Perhaps we can, Mr Wright,' said Gabriel soberly. 'I will have to give it a great deal of thought. And there is another loose end I wish to tie up, if I can only find a suitable opportunity to do so.'

———

As Constable Wright rattled and shook along the track to Bournemouth that opportunity presented itself to Gabriel quite unexpectedly. This morning he was in court making a short legal application for an upcoming case in the Court of Appeal. He found it had been listed, coincidentally, in front of Lord Justice Brown.

Having withered his bumptious young opponent with the diffident courtesy that was his trademark, Gabriel asked the usher if he might have a private word with the judge.

Lord Justice Brown was sitting behind his desk with a barricade of law reports ranged in front of him.

'I hesitate to trouble you,' Gabriel said in his gentle way, 'but there is a matter personal to you that I wish to discuss.'

Brown stiffened visibly. Gabriel plunged in. 'I hope you will forgive what may seem to be an intrusion. The police constable who has been assisting me with my investigations had occasion to go to St James' Park police station in relation to a vagrant who had been arrested for being drunk and disorderly—'

Lord Justice Brown flung down his pen and gripped the arms of his chair. 'What do you know?' he demanded.

'Nothing,' said Gabriel apologetically. 'It is just that I have had a lifetime of putting together little pieces of evidence. It has become a habit, I am afraid. I was told that a retired judge had been picked up a couple of times for being drunk and disorderly. Your father was a most distinguished judge and he retired mysteriously young. And you are a lifelong teetotaller, an unusual characteristic for a barrister, and became quite upset when you were teased about that fact by the Lord Chief Justice. And then you were very angry when he further called you a chip off the old block. You, too, are a distinguished judge. Why should such an observation make you angry unless perhaps you feared that the remark was a reference to some other character-istic of your father's than his distinction as a judge? You were so upset, I surmised, that you walked about for a very long time after the Little Dinner—'

The judge broke in, his voice harsh. 'It got worse and worse, Ward. He loved the law, you know. We had to make him give it up. It would not have remained hidden much longer. We did our best, Maria and I. I think he did his best too. It defeated us all, Ward, like a – a – form of possession. There was degrada-tion such as I cannot describe. He would be lost for days. That is how he ended up in a police cell. That was some time after he retired. The police were very good about it. The story never came out, thank God. He died in dignity at home with us a year or so later.'

He looked piteously at Gabriel. 'It is a taint, Ward, and one I may have inherited. If anyone knows, I will not be deemed fit for this post, let alone the one to which I aspire. No, not *aspire* – for which I am destined. But now when you, as a senior member of the Bar, are consulted as to Lord Dunning's successor…'

'As to that,' said Gabriel slowly, 'I have no idea who will be appointed. I see no reason for your father ever to be mentioned in that context.'

The judge bowed his head. 'I am very grateful to you, Ward. I shall not forget this kindness.'

He looked profoundly relieved. But it occurred to Gabriel that if Brown believed that the Lord Chief Justice's remarks at the Little Dinner had been a reference to his father's drunkenness, it might well be a motive for murder.

As he left, he looked back thoughtfully at Lord Justice Brown standing behind his desk. The burden of high office seemed to weigh him down like a physical presence, as all-enveloping and constraining as the wool and ermine in which he was encased.

37

That night Gabriel went again to the church. This time the moon was so bright that the gas lamps were outshone. Sir William Waring's windows were in darkness. As he passed them, he thought of the extraordinary scene he had witnessed there four days previously, and wondered again what it could possibly mean. The very brightness and clarity of the ancient silent buildings seemed somehow sinister. He hastened towards the church.

As its dark bulk loomed in front of him, monumental in the moonlight, its buttresses casting the blackest of shadows across the churchyard, he saw, in the great arch of the Norman doorway, the outlined figure of a man.

Gabriel pressed himself against the buttressed wall. In the silence he could feel his own heart thudding and wondered if it was audible. The sudden sound of metal grinding on metal was loud and shocking.

There, clearly illuminated, huge iron key in hand, was the Reverend Vernon-Osbert. The two men recognised each other at the same moment. There was no escape from the circumstances that confronted them.

'Good evening,' said Gabriel. 'Why are you locking the church door, Vicar?'

'Oh, good evening, Sir Gabriel! You quite made me jump! Just a breath of air on this lovely moonlit night! And then a nightcap! Would you share one with me, Sir Gabriel? I can offer you a glass or two of a very pleasant 'ninety-three Château Margaux.

You have quite a palate, have you not? I think it may inter-est you; really, a very passable vintage – though not of course quite as good as the 'seventy.'

'But why are you locking the church door?' persisted Gabriel.

'Oh, no, no, you're mistaken. The key is merely in my hand, I'm just putting it in its safe place—'

Gabriel reached past him and turned the iron ring. The latch lifted but the door did not yield.

The two men stood regarding each other in the moonlight.

'Sir Gabriel,' said Vernon-Osbert, and his voice trembled a little, 'had you felt the urge to pray? I would be so loath to think you had been excluded—'

'I have no urge to pray,' said Gabriel. 'I have an urge to know why you have locked the church door.'

Vernon-Osbert was now quivering with distress.

'May we perhaps speak inside?' said Gabriel more gently.

Reluctantly, Vernon-Osbert inserted the great key, turned it and slowly pushed open the door. Notwithstanding its weight, it swung almost silently on its hinges.

In spite of himself, Gabriel felt a spasm of apprehension, a curious desire to turn tail and run. Which of Constable Wright's feverish imaginings would be revealed? he wondered. What Bacchanalian orgy? What secret ritual? What sacrilege?

But the interior of the church was deep in its customary, friendly silence. Gabriel indicated the nearest pew and sat in it, gesturing to the space beside it.

'Well?' he said.

Vernon-Osbert sat but did not speak, so Gabriel took the lead. 'I think I should tell you that this is the second night in the last few days I have tried to gain entry to the church and found it locked. Traditionally, it is always open, is it not? What harm could come to it at night in the heart of the Temple?'

The vicar sighed heavily. 'Sir Gabriel, it pains me to confess that I have locked it every night for the past four weeks.'

'But why?'

'It was a personal matter. Oh, dear, please do not press me, Sir Gabriel!'

'I must press you,' he replied steadily. 'A man's life depends quite literally upon your answer.'

'It was for Delphinium.' Vernon-Osbert sounded close to anguish.

'Delphinium?'

The vicar looked reproachful. 'You have seen her many times, Sir Gabriel. She always attends Evensong and Sunday services. My Persian Blue?'

Gabriel now recalled the majestic cat, draped across a pew, a vast and threatening ball of bluish fur amidst which a down-turned mouth, a snub nose and an enormous pair of malevolent amber eyes, were just visible.

'I am really so very deeply attached to her,' Vernon-Osbert said earnestly. 'She is such a dear cat, Sir Gabriel, and we all have our weaknesses, do we not? I fear Delphinium's is a fatal attraction to the Middle Temple's ginger tom. I blame him very much; he is undoubtedly the instigator, and Delphinium pays the price. Sadly, that is the way of the world, is it not?'

Gabriel bowed helplessly, this social comment rather beyond his own experience.

'And this is the second time. On the last occasion, the Treasurer was very angry and I fear for his reaction if he learns she is now in a similar predicament.'

'What on earth has it to do with the Treasurer?'

Vernon-Osbert looked deeply unhappy.

'It is twofold. The Treasurer does not like cats; they bring him out in a rash and make him sneeze. But it is also a financial issue.'

'Financial?'

'Yes. You see, the Treasurer has been very much pleased with the substantial increase in the amount in the collection every Sunday, thanks, of course, to the popularity of *Millie the Temple Church Mouse*. Sir William has great plans to foster this. He feels that the presence of Delphinium in the Temple, looking – looking – well, perhaps a little fierce to those who do not know her, sends the wrong message to lovers of Millie the Mouse.'

Gabriel suppressed a snuffle, and Vernon-Osbert, mistaking the sound for one of alarm, came close to tears in his earnestness.

'She is not at all fierce, Sir Gabriel. It is merely the cast of her countenance. And I cannot but feel that the welfare and happiness of a real cat should take precedence over a fictional mouse. But I cannot persuade the Treasurer to share my point of view. So far he has allowed me to keep her, but I fear he will use Delphinium's latest transgressions as an excuse to get rid of her. And this time there are *eight kittens*. So far, I have managed to conceal her condition and I have found homes for all the kittens, but at present of course they cannot leave their mother. And so – and here I hope I have not done wrong – I have kept them all hidden in the church.'

'But why lock it?' said Gabriel. 'Did you suppose they would break out?'

'No, no, and during the day when I am constantly about the church there is no difficulty, but recently Sir William has developed a habit of walking about very early in the morning and – how can I best put it?'

'Prowling?' offered Gabriel. 'Snooping?'

Vernon-Osbert looked shocked. 'Not snooping; he is merely taking an interest in all the doings of the Temple. But perhaps for a week or so, it would be desirable if he refrained from – from—'

'Nosing about in the church?'

'Well, yes. Delphinium has settled with her kittens just behind the altar where we keep the spare candles, and a very sweet sight it is. Should Sir William have tried the door, I intended to tell him I had locked it inadvertently.' He looked solemn. 'I must answer to my God for that planned deception. I feel deeply ashamed, Sir Gabriel.'

'I cannot think that God will have difficulty forgiving such a small sin,' said Gabriel in his gentle way. 'Am I to understand that you locked the church door on the night that the Lord Chief Justice was murdered?'

But Vernon-Osbert plainly yearned to unburden his conscience further.

'I did, Sir Gabriel, and I am haunted by the knowledge. On that particular night, I saw a dark figure sitting on a bench on the other side of the courtyard, by the old pump, you know. I could not tell who it was, nor did I approach. I simply locked the church and went home. But now I feel a terrible sense of guilt. What if one of the barristers, one of the souls that are in my especial care, was summoning the courage to pray to his God about some worry or transgression? And then tried to enter His house and found it barred? I feel I cannot forgive myself for such a sin.'

'God will forgive it,' said Gabriel sturdily, since he knew that that was what Vernon-Osbert required of him; and then, as was so often the case, his own logical mind took over from the demands of emotional comfort. 'And anyway, there is no reason to suppose the figure was anything other than a tired old barrister having a rest, or an inebriated young one asleep.'

Vernon-Osbert shook his head but nonetheless gave a watery smile.

'But in light of what you have told me,' Gabriel ventured, 'may I ask you to recount to me once more your movements on the night of Lord Dunning's death? You left the Treasurer's

Little Dinner with Sir Vivian Barton and you went to the church together?'

Vernon-Osbert nodded emphatically. 'Oh, yes, just as I told you. I had left the papers for my morning meeting there. And we left together and of course I could not lock the door then – he would have thought it most strange – and so I returned later.'

'And no one else was aware of your – er – strategy in relation to Delphinium's plight?' probed Gabriel delicately.

The vicar hesitated. 'No one but the Lord Chief Justice,' he said. 'While we were drinking our sherry before the Little Dinner, I told him very quietly that Delphinium had erred, and where I had concealed her.'

'But why on earth should you tell the Lord Chief Justice?' exclaimed Gabriel in bewilderment.

'He liked cats,' said Vernon-Osbert simply.

Recognising the obscurity of the fellowships formed by mankind, Gabriel abandoned this tack.

'When you returned to the church for the second time, did you go in on that occasion?'

'Just for a minute, to say goodnight to dear Delphinium and to leave her a little supper. And I knelt to say a prayer.'

'And what time was that?'

Vernon-Osbert shook his head. 'I really cannot tell you. I need very little sleep, so I potter for hours and lose all sense of time at night. I left the Little Dinner at about ten, I wandered over to the church with Barton and we admired the effigies in the moonlight. I think I got home about half-past ten. I read for a long time, I recall, and wrote some letters. It must have been very late…' he trailed off helplessly. 'I really cannot tell you any more.'

Gabriel looked at the anxious face and fluffy halo of white hair, and light dawned.

'You may feel this is a curious question,' he said slowly, 'but would you mind telling me what you were wearing when you made that second visit?'

Vernon-Osbert looked a little shy. 'I thought that I would wait until the Temple was quite quiet, so I made myself ready for bed while I waited for the right moment. It is, as you know, a matter of yards from my home to the church and it was a most salubrious night. I was wearing my blue embroidered dressing gown and the red Morocco leather slippers my sister bought me for Christmas.'

'And Delphinium's supper: what did you put it in?'

'In one of my old willow-pattern bowls.' By now Vernon-Osbert was looking thoroughly bemused.

'Thank you,' said Gabriel. 'If your conscience continues to trouble you as to your actions that night, Vicar, you may tell it you have just helped save a man from the gallows.'

As he turned to leave, a last thought struck him. 'I suppose,' he said with a snuffle, 'that the herring also is now explained.'

38

Gabriel's credit in the Inner Temple kitchen could not have been higher. His kindness to Annie on the night of the murder had won Mrs Bugg's heart; his championing of Meg had engendered in the girl a fierce loyalty; and now, to compound it all, Mrs Bugg purred with grateful satisfaction at the sight of her Ruby's Fred scything the Temple lawns in his new position as one of the under-gardeners.

The kitchen expressed these emotions in the way it knew best. Gabriel had begun to find on his doorstep, wrapped in the Temple's fine linen and nestled in wicker baskets, all kinds of small freshly baked tributes, and when he passed the kitchen window there was a frequent summons from Mrs Bugg for a cup of coffee and a scone hot from the oven.

On this morning, however, Gabriel made his own uninvited but now less timid entry. Mrs Bugg sat at the vast kitchen table with a pencil, paper and a perplexed frown.

'Now, gentlemen have good heads for figures,' she announced. 'How many eggs do I need, Sir Gabriel for seven hundred puddings if one pudding takes three-quarters of an egg?'

'Seven hundred, Mrs Bugg? Good gracious me. Is an army to descend upon the Inner Temple?'

'For the ball, Sir Gabriel; for the "Erf Alla Pegasus".'

'What ball?'

'There now,' she said cheerfully. 'And the Treasurer especially told me not to say a word. But you won't repeat it, I know, sir. There is a ball to be held for the coronation of the new King, the biggest we have ever held, sir, and the cooking all to be done under my instruction, though never have I known numbers like it, and there are to be new recipes and the menu in French, though it would be fancy in any language. And this is my new egg recipe, named after the Pegasus emblem of the Inner Temple.'

'Ah,' said Gabriel, enlightened '*Oeuf. À la*. You will need five hundred and twenty-five eggs, Mrs Bugg. Why is the ball a secret?'

'Not the ball, Sir Gabriel, but I believe there are to be special plans, I don't rightly know what. Very exercised the Treasurer is, excitable-like and mysterious. Now what can I do for you, Sir Gabriel?'

'I wondered,' he said diffidently, 'whether you might be able to supply me with a little corn starch?'

'Corn starch, sir?'

'Just a cupful.'

'Go on with you,' said Mrs Bugg, and it was a testament to Gabriel's mounting regard for her that his inner lawyer stayed silent.

'If you need any cooking done you have only to ask us,' she continued reproachfully.

'That is very kind but I was not intending to make gravy, Mrs Bugg,' he snuffled. 'I wanted it for a little experiment.'

'Bless you,' she said unaccountably. 'It is in a tin in the pantry. Just you pop into the scullery and ask Meg to find it for you.'

Meg was scouring pans but she wiped her soapy arms and went to fetch the tin of corn starch.

'How are you getting on, Meg?' Gabriel enquired on her return.

She gave a shy smile. 'Very well, sir, thank you, sir. The Treasurer gave me a warning but I am to stay here. How is Mr Broadbent, sir? When will they let him out?'

Gabriel hesitated. 'I am doing my best.'

'Is he getting a proper dinner, sir, where they've got him? Could I send him something in, do you think?'

Gabriel met her innocent gaze and, feeling uncomfortable, tried not to think of Broadbent's filthy, damp cell and rejected plates of porridge.

'I am not sure that would be allowed, Meg,' he said, and again, 'I am doing my best.'

She nodded, consoled. She was too young to know that the best of even a grand gentleman like Sir Gabriel Ward might not be good enough.

'Will you be lunching in Hall, Sir Gabriel? If so, you will need to hurry, sir. It it is one o'clock already.'

'Good gracious, Meg, is it really?' exclaimed Gabriel. 'How fast my morning has gone by and I have a great deal of work still to do. I must bid you goodbye.'

Automatically, he extracted his pocket watch from his waist-coat and peered at it in his myopic way; it read twelve-thirty.

Meg had returned to the sink, her slight figure silhouetted against the light from the narrow window in front of her.

'You are ahead of yourself, Meg,' said Gabriel. And then, as she turned enquiringly towards him, he looked past her and out of the little window and saw, at last, what was most easily visible to Meg. Not Reginald the kitchen clock that was always right, but out of her window, across the detritus of cloths and scourers on the window ledge. Across the dark alleyway that led between the kitchen window and that of the clerks' Room in Gabriel's own chambers. And straight into the window that illuminated one side of Chapman's room where the grandfather clock stood.

The very clock that Chapman had adjusted a short time ago so that it ran half an hour fast, so as to ensure that that insuffera-ble puppy, the Honourable Cecil Haynes, arrived punctually for his hearings in the Law Courts.

39

'And so,' he said, not without some triumph, to Constable Wright that evening, 'it was all quite simple. No supernatural dramas, I am afraid, Constable Wright, just human nature at work. No rituals or covens; just an elderly vicar who loves his cat. No lies or subterfuge; just Meg looking at a different clock from the one we had naturally assumed it to be.'

'And what is to become of her?' asked Wright.

'Well, in order of importance: the Treasurer's pudding will no longer be cold because it was put in the servery half an hour early. Meg will no longer stand waiting at the gate and wondering why her father is so late. And, of course, Mr Broadbent will not hang because he has a verifiable alibi for the murder of the Lord Chief Justice.'

He got up to pour Wright another dry sherry.

'Meg let Broadbent into the Temple not at ten o'clock in the evening, as she believed, but at nine-thirty as Broadbent said. She eventually left the kitchen not at eleven-forty-five, as she believed, but at eleven-fifteen. She arrived at the church five minutes later. So, while Inspector Hughes thinks Mr Broadbent was stabbing the Lord Chief Justice, he was in fact tucking into Meg's beef sandwich. And just to tie his alibi up with a neat bow, we now know he was indeed locked in the church all night and there witnessed what he said he witnessed. So, all in all, as far as Meg and Mr Broadbent are concerned, I believe it is a happy ending.'

'But still no one knows who murdered Lord Dunning.'

'Not quite yet,' said Gabriel. 'Now tell me what you have learned in Bournemouth and in Greenwich.'

Constable Wright fished from his pocket a little notebook.

'That looks very professional,' said Gabriel.

Wright looked horrified.

'Oh, no, sir, this is not my Notebook. This is just *a* notebook, so to speak. I could not write in my police notebook, official-like, sir, when I was just doing a bit of questioning for one of your cases. That would not have been at all proper, sir.'

'Quite right. Go on, Constable.'

'Well, Bournemouth first, and Miss Davey. She was an old lady, sir, reminded me of my granny. Knitting away she was, with a cat on the rug. Gave me a ginger biscuit.'

He began to warm to his theme. 'She has just the one room and, my word, it was full of things. A great big bookshelf full of children's books and little china animal ornaments everywhere and framed photographs of all the children she had looked after. She was with the Dunnings before Claud was born, when the little girl was a baby and Percival was quite small; shared duties with the nanny really, though she helped with his first letters and sums.'

'Were there photographs of Percival and Seraphina?' asked Gabriel.

Constable Wright paused. 'No, sir, not now I come to think of it. But Miss Davey didn't seem to care much for the Dunning family. Perhaps that explains it. She was with them for under a year and then she retired.'

He looked doubtfully at Gabriel.

'There wasn't really very much more, I'm afraid.'

'Why didn't she like the family?'

'Nothing she could put her finger on, sir. She said Lady Dunning seemed unhappy; a lot younger than Lord Dunning, wanted to be out every evening. And Lord Dunning, he was very disapproving — always on about his family name and being a judge and so on. And Miss Dunning was very satirical, didn't get on with her brother, inclined to make clever digs, Miss Davey said. In fact, she said, not very ladylike, and needed a husband to tell her so. Miss Davey's intended died in the Crimean War, and she never looked at another.'

'I would have hoped, as an educationalist, Miss Davey would have had more enlightened views on the role of women. What about Miss Harrison in Greenwich?'

'Miss Harrison is employed by a gentleman in banking. I had to see the lady of the house and ask permission to speak to Miss Harrison. Then of course she wanted to know why. I didn't say I was a policeman, of course. It wouldn't be right when I was doing it private-like for you, sir.'

'Very proper,' said Gabriel gravely. 'What answer did you give?'

'I told the truth,' said Wright with dignity. 'I said I was making enquiries on behalf of an eminent KC in relation to one of his cases. Quite impressed she was and summoned Miss Harrison down and left us in the morning room.'

He drew in his breath.

'Quite a funny one is Miss Harrison, sir. Did you know the Dunnings dismissed her?'

'It was mentioned,' said Gabriel. 'Did she tell you why?'

'Oh, yes, indeed, very talkative she was. A real gossipy one and most of it spiteful, if you know what I mean, sir.'

Gabriel thought of Maud Rentoul. He did know what Wright meant.

'She was employed by the Dunnings when Percival was just six and stayed until last year. Apparently, she came in from taking the children to Kensington Gardens one winter afternoon when the lamps in the house had not been lit, and as she came through the door she heard the muffin man's bell just down

Stafford Terrace. She left the perambulator in the middle of the hall with little Claud in it, to go out and buy some muffins for the children's tea.'

'No very dreadful crime committed so far,' Gabriel said.

'No, sir. But Miss Dunning came running down the stairs in the dim light and fell over the perambulator. She sent it flying and, trying to save herself, put her hand through the glass window on the inner hall door; cut herself badly, had to have stitches and all, but that was not the most serious thing. Little Claud was thrown out of the perambulator onto the tiled floor. Nearly knocked him out, poor little mite, and you can imagine the uproar, sir.'

'Indeed yes.'

'Lord Dunning arrived home and found Miss Harrison in hysterics, and Miss Dunning holding little Claud. The child was crying and covered in blood. By the time Lord Dunning had discovered the blood was not Claud's, the little boy had calmed down though he was a bit poorly for some days. Miss Harrison was dismissed. Reading between the lines, sir, I suspect buying the muffins had taken her a good old while.'

'And did you learn anything about Miss Harrison's life with the family before this incident?'

'Oh, she was only too keen to tell me, sir. According to her, nobody in the household liked anybody else. Tension between Lord Dunning and his wife, and between Lady Dunning and her sister-in-law. And at the end of her time there, some terrible rows between Lord Dunning and his sister, apparently. But I have a feeling Miss Harrison quite enjoyed all the strife in the household. Very pleased she seemed with her connection with the Dunnings; he was appointed Lord Chief Justice while she was in post and she told me she felt quite superior to the other nannies and governesses she met in Kensington Gardens. She went there every afternoon. I shouldn't think there is much they didn't know about the Lord Chief Justice's family!'

Gabriel nodded thoughtfully.

'Oh, and she rattled on about young Master Percival too, sir. He and his friend Harold, they sound little cautions, sir: chased the pigeons in the park, stole an old man's hat, rolled Seraphina in the mud. Miss Harrison couldn't take her eye off them for an instant.'

Wright looked apologetic. 'I was not very sure what I was trying to find out, so I just let her run on, sir.'

'Letting people run on is a very good policy, Constable Wright. And you have told me all I needed to know. Thank you very much for giving up your free time to assist me in this way.'

Wright looked bashful. 'What now, sir?'

'Well,' said Gabriel, 'I have some visits to make. And then we shall see.'

40

The next morning Gabriel made his way to Sir Vivian Barton's chambers in Fig Tree Court. The late-night meeting he had overheard in Waring's room had preyed on his mind. He did not knock on the window this time, though he saw Barton bent over his desk. Instead, he sought a formal announcement from Sir Vivian's clerk.

For such a large, self-confident man, Barton looked a little discomfited to see him. Gabriel wondered how to begin but in fact he had no need to. Leaning back in his leather-covered desk chair, Barton unbuttoned his waistcoat, extracted a case, offered a cigar to Gabriel, who declined, and took one himself.

'I am glad you have come, Ward. You and I have known one another a long time, and I confess that for the last few days I have been very uneasy.'

Gabriel squinted through the cigar smoke and waited.

Sir Vivian launched in with a rush of words. 'It is about the Treasurer's Little Dinner. I have been feeling that perhaps I should have been more forthcoming when you asked me about it. He set such store by secrecy that it seemed churlish not to indulge him. You know what Waring is. More self-absorbed than my six-year-old, and the Inner Temple and his status within it are all that matter to him. What is it, Ward, about some men that causes their positions to go their heads?'

After a moment, since Gabriel said nothing but continued to look encouraging, Barton ploughed on: 'The Lord Chief Justice is dead. Sir William Waring keeps secrets. I thought the two wholly unconnected; I still cannot believe they have any relevance to each other. And yet— I am no sneak, Ward, as I hope you know, but Sir William Waring's petty little secret has become – a burden suddenly. I want to share it, and to be told I am talking nonsense.'

'Well,' said Gabriel with a dry smile, 'I am frequently paid to tell you that you are talking nonsense. I will make an exception and do it for no fee at all this morning.'

Barton smiled too but still looked uncomfortable.

'When we walked around the garden, Ward, I described what happened at the Little Dinner as fatuous plotting. If Waring wanted to hug his little plan to himself, I was happy to let him; but now – well, something has happened to make me feel different.'

He leaned forward and lowered his voice. 'The Treasurer asked Vernon-Osbert, myself and Lords Justices Wilson and Brown to form a Coronation Ball committee, with himself as chair. The Little Dinner on the night of the Lord Chief Justice's death was its inaugural meeting. Dunning was invited too – unbeknown to us until we arrived.'

'But the ball was not to be a secret, surely? Why, Mrs Bugg was only yesterday calculating the number of eggs needed for one of the dishes on the menu.'

'Well, believe me, Ward, the cost of eggs is the least of the Treasurer's grandiose plans. Seven hundred invitations are to go out; the whole thing will take many months to organise; judges from all over the world are to be invited – from Australia, New Zealand, Cape Colony, Natal, Newfoundland – I forget where else. And, closer to home, the entire senior judiciary and the Lord Chancellor and the Lord Chief Justice of Ireland. Distinguished guests to be met, of course, on the Terrace by the Treasurer, and the ball to commence and end with the "Coronation March". Grenadier Guards to direct the crowds and the dancing, a hundred pounds' worth of flowers and the garden illuminated with fairy lights – tastefully, as the Treasurer hastened to inform us. Bugles to announce the beginning of each dance—'

'As a resident of the Inn who values his sleep, I don't like the sound of that.'

Despite his earnestness, Barton grinned. 'You will be there too, dear boy, spinning around in the valse and the polka with the best of us!'

'Somehow I don't think so,' replied Gabriel firmly. 'But what did the Treasurer want from the Lord Chief Justice?'

'There was one guest missing off the list: the one it is all to be about.'

'Good God! You cannot mean…?'

'Yes, our new King; known to like a party, our new King.'

'But surely that was aiming impossibly high? In the coronation year, with the Palace itself and every great institution of London holding events? Distinguished we may be, but a very small cog in a great imperial power that will be putting on a vast show to the world.'

'Precisely what His Majesty's private secretary had pointed out when Waring made his suggestion. So Waring wanted the Lord Chief Justice to make an approach; he thought Dunning, given the seniority of his position, might be able to exert influence. But when the plan was put to him, Dunning wouldn't play.'

'And did he say why not?'

Barton shrugged. 'You knew Dunning. Not much in it for him apart from a lot of trouble. Waring was very put out, of course, and made it plain he thought it was a poor show. But the Lord Chief just shrugged it off and, as you may recall, I left early. I cannot say I considered it much at the time, and after we heard of the poor devil's murder I never gave it another thought.' He drew heavily on his cigar. 'Until we met again the other night for the second meeting of the committee. Ward, I don't know how to describe Waring's attitude to Dunning's death. The obscene dismissal of that dreadful tragedy; the venom! It was really quite – quite abnormal. And most unnerving. I have been worrying about it ever since. And yet, it seems so utterly inconceivable I keep trying to push it to the back of my mind.'

He looked intently at Gabriel. 'I can scarcely believe I am asking this question – you will doubtless think I am mad – but nonetheless, Waring's attitude was so extreme, I feel compelled to do so. Have you checked his alibi for that evening, after the dinner?'

'It might be said he is one of two who do not have one. You and Vernon-Osbert left the Little Dinner early; your wife can confirm that you were home by eleven. So you have an alibi.'

'I have another seven little alibis,' said Barton with a deep chuckle, 'all engaged in a clandestine feast in bed, the scamps, until I got home and put a stop to it.'

'Vernon-Osbert is – technically, at least – without an alibi for the time of the murder; he says he went home to his study.'

'It would take a lot more than that to make me think old VO murdered the Lord Chief Justice. The old boy was hardly a knife-wielding maniac even in the vigour of his youth, and he's pretty decrepit now!'

'Indeed,' said Gabriel. But he thought fleetingly of Delphinium, and the depths of a love so profound as to lead this devout clergyman to deception and dereliction of duty. Men, he thought uneasily, were unaccountable.

'Lord Justice Wilson was picked up by his wife at eleven,' he continued. 'Lord Justice Brown left with them and was seen by them to leave the Temple.' No need to share with Barton the curious story of that odd lost hour in which Lady Wilson had tried to advance her husband's career, nor of Lord Justice Brown's long walk while he wrestled with his past.

'And the Treasurer?'

He has rooms near the Hall, as I'm sure you know. He tells me he finished a glass of port and went up his internal staircase after the dinner.'

'So, any alibi was a pretty one and not likely to see the light of day, eh?'

'Just so,' said Gabriel, and the two men smiled at each other in perfect understanding.

Vivian Barton brushed the ash from his waistcoat.

'Well, well. Off my chest, dear boy,' he said. 'You are the detective. You will no doubt do as you see fit. Just thought I should add another little piece to the jigsaw.'

'Thank you,' said Gabriel drily. Fond though he was of Barton, he reflected that this airy handing over of any responsibility was rather typical of him. 'A jigsaw that is proving to be quite perplexing. The fact is that Sir William was extremely angry with Dunning and he has no satisfactory alibi that we know of.'

But Barton, clearly feeling he had discharged his duty, changed the subject.

'What about your other mystery?'

'My other mystery?' Gabriel looked his most inscrutable.

'Yes indeed, the identity of Miss Harriet Cadamy?'

'That is not "my mystery". It was a case and it is over. It is of no further interest to me.'

'And I am the Emperor of China,' was Barton's parting riposte. He showed Gabriel out with a wink and his airy wave.

41

A nd then, as they sometimes do, a number of events occurred all at once.

Two days later, a discreet ambulance drew up outside an anonymous door in Wimpole Street and Miss Susan Hatchings was assisted from it. Here she was to reside with two other lady patients and three nurses. From her pleasant room she could see the garden, and by her chair was the perambulator containing Dolly. Although still silent, she had been observed by the nurses to smile when she heard one of her fellow patients playing the piano and in these gentle surroundings there seemed some hope for her recovery.

With reluctance Detective Inspector Hughes, on being informed of all the evidence that now supported Broadbent's overnight stay in the Temple and of the alibi provided by Meg, was brought to acknowledge that he was innocent of murder.

'We'll charge him for theft of the shoes. The old devil will get six months' hard labour, and then he'll be back to being a pest in Fleet Street,' he grumbled to PC Wright.

'He says the shoes were abandoned, sir.'

'And who put that into his head? What did I tell you about barristers?'

Wright looked nervous. 'Sir Gabriel Ward is a very clever lawyer, sir. Do you think perhaps—'

'Oh, very well, very well,' snapped Hughes. 'Release the man back onto the street and have done with it. I have enough to do finding the real killer without worrying about it anymore.'

On the same morning that Broadbent resumed his place on the steps of the Law Courts holding a new placard, the paint still wet, which read 'Whosoever sows injustice will reap calamity', the Lord Chancellor in his inscrutable wisdom and with no consultation whatsoever, summoned Lord Justice Bradley to his room in Whitehall and appointed him as the new Lord Chief Justice of England.

Lord Justice Bradley (by now, principally thanks to Maud Rentoul's wide dissemination of the theory, generally thought to be the model for the Fat Judge in *Millie the Temple Church Mouse*) was kind, clever and popular, if a little elderly for the job, and so devoid of ambition that he could scarcely believe his ears when the Lord Chancellor informed him of his decision. On hearing the news, Lady Bradley, who, to the disapproval of many, had built for herself quite a reputation as an *avant-garde* artist, roared with laughter, planted a congratulatory kiss on top of her husband's bald head and went back to her new painting of a pig in a bonnet.

Lords Justices Brown and Wilson, encountering one another in the judges' corridor of the Royal Courts of Justice shortly after the news had broken, avoided and then caught each other's eye, and for no reason at all involuntarily shook each other by the hand. They followed it up with an early dinner at their club where they spent an enjoyable evening tearing apart Lord Justice Bradley's intellectual capabilities, not to mention the artistic merit of his wife's pictures.

Lady Brown heard the news with her usual sweet resignation. Lady Wilson had been told that very day that, quite in her own right, she had been made a member of the committee of the Royal Horticultural Society (having applied with the strong encouragement of her husband), and so minded the dashing of his dreams rather less than might have been expected.

Delphinium's kittens were about to be sent to their new homes, two of them destined for a life of rough love from Sir Vivian Barton's seven children. Delphinium herself, released from the unwelcome demands of motherhood, resumed her prowlings around the gardens, her taunting on Sir William Waring's windowsill and her flirtation with the Middle Temple tom doomed to flower into one inevitable result, or perhaps eight.

And Sir Gabriel Ward made one more visit.

———

The journey to Stafford Terrace, Kensington was slowly becoming familiar to him, and the anxiety engendered by straying outside the precincts of the Temple correspondingly less. Despite this, as he sat in the cab that conveyed him there, his heart was pounding. He had two people to visit.

'I have come to see Miss Theodora Dunning,' he said to the butler. 'But before I do so, I wonder if I might have a quick word with Miss Murray?'

The butler showed him impassively into the morning room. The governess, once summoned, stood quietly by the door, her hands folded in front of her, her remarkable eyes wary.

'This is the last time I shall trouble you, Miss Murray,' said Gabriel. 'We lawyers, you know, we like to tie up loose ends. Forgive me for putting it thus, but you are a loose end.' He snuffled and she gave her little half-smile.

'I have thought about our conversation when I came to ask you about your copy of *Jane Eyre*. You told me you had been unhappy in this house. And you showed an obvious affection for only one person: Lady Brown. The morning that Lord Dunning's death was discovered, I think you went to St Saviour's expressly to see Lady Brown. It was a Tuesday, her regular day at the orphanage. Am I correct? She was a safe harbour? The only one you felt you had?'

Amelia Murray pushed back her heavy fringe and said, seemingly irrelevantly, 'I do not want to read Charlotte Brontë, Sir Gabriel. I want to write like her. I want to be a novelist.' She looked at him with a challenge in her eyes.

'A very laudable ambition,' he said. 'And?'

'I could not write for all the strife in this household. It was like – like some sort of darkness. It pervaded everyone and everything: the adults, the children, every room in the house. I wanted to ask Lady Brown to help me find another post.'

'But then you did not?'

'I could not. I… oh, looking at her, and her pleasure in my achievements, and then at the other orphans… I am one of their proudest stories, Sir Gabriel. Those little girls are told if they work hard they can become governesses in grand families. From nothing, they are given a chance. *I* was given a chance. It felt so… so… ungrateful, I just could not. And so I came away.'

Gabriel said, 'I will not commit my previous error of being impertinent, Miss Murray, by offering you sympathy. But I thank you for telling me.' He hesitated. 'You say things are a little better now?'

'Oh, yes.' She did smile this time. 'I am on chapter seven!'

———

Back in the hall, he followed the butler up the thickly carpeted stairs to the drawing room and greeted Miss Theodora Dunning, sitting down in the chair she indicated and facing her across the fireplace, filled on this summer's day with an opulent arrangement of lilies.

'Miss Dunning,' he began, 'what I am about to say is none of my business. There is no reason why you should respond if you do not wish to do so.'

'You do not sound like a barrister, Sir Gabriel,' she replied calmly. 'Nor like a detective.'

'I am here in neither capacity. I am not engaged on business on behalf of a client; nor am I here because of the enquiries I was asked to make on behalf of the Inner Temple.'

'Then why are you here?'

'I suppose,' said Gabriel, 'as a result of our conversation in the Temple Gardens, Miss Dunning. *Ex aequo et bono* – to the right and good.'

'And what particularly right and good consideration has led you to me, Sir Gabriel?'

'I suppose,' said Gabriel again, 'that I wish you to claim what is rightfully yours, Miss Dunning.'

She would not make it easy for him. 'And what is that?'

He wondered if the beating of his heart was actually audible. He drew from his pocket the little leather-bound copy of *Jane Eyre* and placed it on the work-table in front of her. The leather gleamed gently, invitingly, in the morning light and she picked it up, almost reverently, and cradled it in her hands.

Gabriel smiled. 'You can always tell a book lover, Miss Dunning.'

'It is an attractive copy. It is not mine. I have never seen it before,' she said.

'No,' said Gabriel. 'That is not what I wish you to claim. Your governess dropped it at the theatre premiere of *Millie the Temple Church Mouse*, and I picked it up. May I invite you to look at the flyleaf?'

Theodora Dunning looked inside at the tiny inscription and raised her eyebrows.

'Save that she was the litigant in your trial, I have absolutely no idea who this Miss Susan Hatchings is, Sir Gabriel. Nor how the book came to be with Miss Murray. Nor, as far as I am concerned, why it matters. Though I do appreciate that Mr Moore will have an interest in following this mystery through to a conclusion. Perhaps you would care to make some enquiries of Miss Murray?'

Gabriel sighed and, retrieving the little volume, put it back in his pocket.

'I have already done so, Miss Dunning. And I learned that she found the book on the shelf in her bedroom: the room always assigned to the children's governess. I have caused enquiries to be made with the two previous governesses and I have a little theory that I would like to share with you, if I may. Do you recall the second of the two, Miss Harrison?'

'Indeed yes. An irresponsible young woman who, thanks to a stupid flirtation with the muffin man, very nearly killed Claud.'

'Precisely so. But prior to that incident, her daily routine was, I understand, to teach in the schoolroom in the morning and take the children to Kensington Gardens to play in the afternoons.'

'That is so.'

'And I believe Percival had a particular friend there, Harold?'

'I believe so.'

'I think, Miss Dunning, that little Harold was Harold Mundy, son of the Reverend Mundy, a Canon of Westminster Abbey. And Harold's governess was Miss Susan Hatchings. I think, Miss Dunning, that that is how a book with Miss Hatchings' name on it came to be in this house. Miss Hatchings lent it to Miss Harrison; perhaps they were both in need of a book about a governess who lives happily ever after. And Miss Harrison had the deplorable habit of most people to whom one is unwise enough to lend one's books. She failed to return it.'

'That sounds plausible,' said a perfectly composed Theodora. 'If speculative.'

'That led me to think more about Miss Hatchings. I have always been troubled, Miss Dunning, by the question of how she knew enough about *Millie the Temple Church Mouse* to lay claim to its authorship. And how she knew she was safe from challenge by the real author.'

'And have you reached a conclusion?'

'I have often thought of our talk in the garden during Miss Hatchings' trial, and of our brief meeting on the steps of the Law Courts after that. It is, in my opinion, very likely that the person who, to use a vulgar expression, tipped off Mr Moore by an anonymous letter to the significant point about the mouse's mother, is the true author. The letter arrived in the late afternoon after you had left my company that day. I remember that I watched you drive up Middle Temple Lane and wondered why, if you were going to Kensington, your coachman turned right into Fleet Street, towards Moore's Bookshop.'

'Perhaps I had an errand in the City.'

'Well, perhaps you did. But then, Miss Dunning, when we met on the steps after Miss Hatchings' trial, do you recall what you said? You said that my cross-examination, culminating in what you described as *a last-minute thrust*, was most beautifully done. In my gratification at the compliment, it did not immediately dawn on me to ask myself how you could possibly have known that the information I used had been obtained at the "last minute". Oddly enough, your comment came back to me in the Savoy Theatre, when I was idly considering the impact of praise on the human psyche.'

There was a pause.

'Perhaps I just made an assumption that you saved your strongest question until last,' said Theodora.

'Perhaps,' said Gabriel again, very politely. 'But then, armed with those two perhapses, I considered once more the role of Miss Hatchings in all this. If young Harold Mundy and Percival were in each other's company every afternoon, then so too were Miss Harrison and Miss Hatchings as their governesses. Miss Harrison, I am told, was a gossip. Might she perhaps have heard in this house information that she fed to Miss Hatchings who, as her mind became more troubled, and her obsessions mounted, eventually thought she might use it for her own ends?'

'Information?'

'Yes. Forgive me, but there have been various accounts of unhappy scenes in this house, Miss Dunning, tensions that have reportedly lessened since Lord Dunning's death. I think those scenes were perhaps not as quiet or as private as the protagonists imagined they were. To put it plainly, I think Miss Harrison heard the rows between you and your brother and she made it her business to listen. Indeed, I believe your present governess, though perhaps less eager to learn the reasons, also heard intermittent rows in this house. Things in the household are "better" now that your brother is dead, she told me. I think those rows may have concerned the authorship of *Millie the Temple Church Mouse*.'

The scent of the lilies was overpowering in the warm room. A fly buzzed furiously, trapped in the velvet curtains. Theodora Dunning gripped the arms of her chair. A pulse beat at the corner of her mouth and she closed her eyes.

'Why did your brother prevent you from claiming authorship of your book, Miss Dunning?'

Theodora opened her eyes and said, quite simply: 'I wrote it originally for Seraphina. My own childhood had involved a great deal of church-going and wriggling and boredom, and very little true religion. I wanted her to understand spirituality with all the wonder of which little children are capable. But when I had written it, I felt that perhaps it could have a wider audience amongst the families who then attended the Temple Church. It is, as you know, the church of the law and lawyers. Who better to approach than my brother? So I gave it to him to read and asked for his help.'

She paused and looked rather helplessly at Gabriel.

'I cannot tell you how angry he was, and how contemptuous. Oh, not of the book; I am not even sure he ever read it. He had no objection to my amusing myself with it, providing it remained within the family, but he furiously rejected any notion that it might become public.'

'But why?'

She shrugged. 'Norman was always imbued with a curious, subconscious feeling that he would somehow be found out; that he was not as clever as he should be; that he was in some way wanting. Nothing makes people cling to the conventional like a fear of being found out, Sir Gabriel. It pervaded every aspect of our lives. He was afraid of the smallest unconventionality, lest as a result he was thought to deviate in some way from what a Lord Chief Justice should be. And his family had to comply with those expectations too. The Lord Chief Justice's spinster sister cannot be an author; she has to be simply the Lord Chief Justice's spinster sister. Indeed, we all had to be the Lord Chief Justice's family as a sort of collective entity, without any recognition of individual aspirations or achievements. And, of course, we have never been a family who has contemplated, let alone encouraged, our women doing anything except to marry; certainly nothing in the outside world. I learned that young when I had wanted so badly to become a lawyer. Have you heard what they say my ambition led to?'

Gabriel shifted uncomfortably. He had heard.

'They say I killed Papa with the shame of it all. He died very suddenly, you know, just when my attempts to become a barrister had made my name a laughing stock. Norman blamed me. There were terrible family scenes; I was too young to moderate my emotions in circumstances of such bitter injustice. For the whole of my youth, while Norman was idling about at school and on sports fields, I sat in Papa's study, reading his *Law Reports*. I started with the criminal reports, I am afraid. I was a rather passionate child and the fiction I was permitted to read was so very limited. Those real-life stories of iniquity seemed to me more thrilling than the anodyne literature young girls are supposed to read. And then as I grew older, I realised the great power of reason, the purity of logic – I understood the law better than Norman ever did, Sir Gabriel, not that that is saying a lot. And Papa knew it. It was with me and not Norman that he discussed his cases; yet it was Norman who went to Oxford, Norman who obtained a pupillage, Norman who got through it with a little guidance from me when he was struggling to understand, Norman who had his first brief obtained for him, Norman who made his way up the profession as a result of his family name and a sprinkle of charm, Norman who became the highest judge in the land.'

Her account had come close to being a rant. Theodora realised it herself and broke off.

'Forgive me, Sir Gabriel. It was a very unhappy time for me. It is in the past, but that is why I felt so bitter that this last small opportunity for – for – *validity* was denied to me. Denied, moreover, by Norman who knew so well the limitations of the life I have led. He said that my becoming known as the authoress of such a work when he was in the public eye, occupying such grave office, was undignified. He forbade me to pursue it. But I couldn't entirely abandon the idea of seeing my book published. The only publisher I knew was Mr Moore. I had seen him among the congregation in church with his little girl and so I thought, perhaps, he would like my book. I dared not send it in my name and so I used the names of my nursemaid Harriet and my first governess Miss Cadamy, and I left it on Moore's doorstep.'

Gabriel couldn't restrain a tiny snuffle.

Theodora relaxed a little. 'I heard no more until the day I was walking down Fleet Street and there it was, with a beautifully illustrated cover, right in the middle of Moore's Bookshop window! I think I have never felt such joy, Sir Gabriel.'

'And your brother?'

'He was very angry. I had compounded my errors by defying him. He took a lofty tone. Said that the whole unfortunate episode need no longer be discussed. That once Christmas was over, and Mr Moore had sold the copies he had printed, the matter would be closed. He promised me he would never refer to it again.'

'And then?'

'And then, as you know, *Millie the Mouse* just grew and grew, past all expectations or even dreams. I reached the point where *I* could scarcely believe that I was Harriet Cadamy.'

'But surely, Miss Dunning, with the success of the book came the opportunity to obtain your independence?'

'Had it been a modest success, yes, perhaps. But this! Think of the sensation. The Lord Chief Justice's unknown spinster sister suddenly wealthy and widely admired! For Norman it was unthinkable that my fame and prestige might outstrip his own. He could not have borne it. I already had Papa's death on my conscience.' She paused to regain full composure. 'There were, as you surmised, many bitter arguments. With each new triumph of *Millie the Mouse*, I begged Norman again and again. But he grew only more adamant. Had I claimed authorship, I would never have been forgiven.' She paused again. 'And then, what is independence when you are nearly sixty years old, Sir Gabriel? A loss of all family ties, of all contact with the children I love?'

'Your brother is dead, Miss Dunning,' said Gabriel gently. 'And your book lives and will continue to do so for as long as there are children. It is a singular achievement, and a legacy of which you can be proud. What happens next is for you to decide.'

He stood up and held out his hand. She took it and for a moment he retained a light hold on her own hand.

'I bid you goodbye, Miss Dunning.'

She rang the bell for him to be shown out before giving her thin smile.

'You still have not asked me.'

'Do you wish to tell me?'

'Millie's mother met her demise when she was inadvertently trodden on by the Fat Judge, an incident Millie witnessed. The Fat Judge was the very gentleman she comforted after the death of his own dear wife. It was intended as a lesson in the true nature of forgiveness. I realise now that Mr Moore was correct. It was a little strong for small children.'

Gabriel bowed. And then the butler appeared to usher him back down the stairs.

42

'I should like you to send a telegram, Chapman,' said Gabriel on his return to chambers.

'Yes, sir?'

'To Police Constable Wright at the station, asking him to come and see me here. And to bring with him a small artist's paintbrush.'

Chapman was shaken out of his usual deferential imperturbability. 'Whatever for, sir?'

But Gabriel had already retreated into his room.

Browsing his bookshelves with the usual sense of peace that this activity engendered, he at last extracted from the lowest tier a thin and obscure pamphlet from the Laboratoire d'Anthropologie Criminelle written by one Dr Forgeot.

When Wright arrived, he found Gabriel deep in thought. Silently, the constable proffered a small paintbrush.

'Ah, thank you, Constable Wright. Please do sit down – no, not there,' as Wright began to lower himself into the client's chair opposite the desk. 'Beside the desk under the light with me.'

Between them they manoeuvred another hard chair until it was beside Gabriel's at his desk, where, despite the bright day outside, the lamp was lit.

On the desk was the cup of corn starch he had begged from the kitchen and beside it a small leather volume.

'Are you aware of the technique of lithography, Constable?'

'Is it a sort of picture?' ventured Wright doubtfully.

'Indeed yes. Here is one example,' said Gabriel, gesturing to the wall behind him on which hung an engraving of a map of London. 'It is an old art, developed in the eighteenth century from the Greek, you know, *lithos*, stone, *graphein*, write...'

Wright's eyes glazed over.

'...An oil-based image is put on a surface, originally lime-stone, hence the name, and a solution of gum Arabic in water is applied. The gum sticks only to the non-oily surface and the image that is the oily surface therefore appears.'

Wright began to think about his dinner.

'The same principles apply to the process of rendering the previously invisible visible, such as crude palm prints on a polished surface. The natural oils of the hand leave a latent image that is very difficult to destroy.'

Wright sat forward in his chair, his interest suddenly engaged.

'And this French gentleman has now discovered that the same applies to other surfaces such as paper – ' Gabriel indicated the little copy of *Jane Eyre* ' – or leather.'

Placing it carefully under the light, he picked up the cup of corn starch and sprinkled it very gently over the surface of the book. With even more care, he very gently brushed it off again, using the little paintbrush. There, standing out on the leather surface were a series of marks, and amongst them, clear and firm, was a squareish-oval mark crossed with lines.

'Blimey, sir, whatever is it?' Wright exclaimed.

'It is the print of a human hand, Constable, recently pressed flat on the surface of the book, leaving the imprint of the thenar eminence – that is, the mounded area at the base of the thumb.' Gabriel handed Wright a magnifying glass.

'It has funny lines on it,' he said, peering curiously.

'Scars,' said Gabriel sadly; for they confirmed what he had already known.

Slowly, he opened the drawer of his desk and withdrew from it the print of the hand on the door of 1 Crown Office Row, photographed by Wright on his Brownie box camera. It seemed a long time ago.

He put it on the desk and in turn the two men looked through the magnifying glass at the crooked lines, clear on the palm of the photographed handprint.

'They are the same lines,' affirmed Wright. 'It is the same hand.'

'Yes,' said Gabriel, 'the same.'

'But whose hand, sir?'

'Someone, Constable Wright, with a smallish hand, smaller perhaps than a man's hand; and someone who had sustained quite a serious injury to it. The jagged scars are suggestive of an accident involving broken glass, I believe.'

'Blimey, sir.' The light had dawned on Police Constable Wright. 'Miss Dunning, sir, she put her hand through the window when little Claud was knocked out of his pram.' Wright's words tumbled over each other in his eagerness and anxiety. He leaped from his chair. 'You have cracked it, sir. She must be the murderer!'

'I fear so,' said Gabriel. He felt suddenly very tired.

'But what is the book, sir? How did you get the handprint on it?'

'I went to Stafford Terrace earlier today, Constable Wright, and handed the book to Miss Dunning. No one who loves books can resist caressing a leather cover such as this. I watched her do it and then I carried it away. And I felt like Judas, Constable.'

Wright looked respectfully at him. Gabriel wondered what he would say and waited, it must be admitted, with a certain feeling of triumph amidst his sadness. He, an amateur and unwilling detective, had solved a murder case, after all. But when Wright spoke, it was not that achievement he acknowledged.

'Did you go to Kensington all on your own, sir?'

Gabriel fumbled with the cup of corn starch and averted his eyes from Wright's. He felt suddenly a little hot and shy.

'It was my duty.'

'I am glad, sir,' said the young policeman; and he had the tact to say no more on the subject. 'But what made you think she did it?' he asked.

Gabriel sighed. 'I think that it may be that sane people kill when they think that they have reached the end of some personal road and there is no longer a future for them. That it is simply a void.'

And in his quiet concise way, with no embellishments or diversions, no sentimentality or hyperbole, as though opening a case in court, he told Wright the story of how Millie the Mouse came to be written.

'All the same, sir,' said Wright doubtfully, when he had finished, 'it is a terrible act to commit, for the sake of a children's storybook.'

'Not just for a book,' said Gabriel, and he remembered Theodora Dunning's own word. 'For the validity always denied her. And then, I fear she may have realised that the dreadful nature of her deed meant she could not, even now her brother was dead, justly claim the recognition as an author that she craved.'

'And how did she get into the Temple, sir? And why did no one see her? I thought women were not allowed in there at night?'

'The Regulations specify *unknown women*, Constable. It is intended to apply to a certain class of visitor. A respectable woman in a carriage would not be denied entry, whether a known one, such as Lady Wilson, or even an unknown one. The Lord Chief Justice's sister, in a carriage, or even, curious though it might be considered, on foot, would not be challenged.'

'I dunno how you lot apply all these rules you make,' said Wright, moved to unusual bluntness by the strangeness of the situation. 'They seem to have a lot of mysterious hidden meanings that are intended to make sure the likes of me cannot understand.'

Gabriel snuffled. 'I have seldom heard the rationale behind the rules of society so clearly described, Constable. But in any event, the porters do not seem to have seen Miss Dunning; it would certainly have been worthy of report to us, had they done so.'

'But why didn't they see her?' pursued a perplexed Wright.

'I think that is easily answered. Sight can be – indeed, often is – unreliable: people see what they think they see and believe it to be real. Look at Mr Broadbent, who believed he saw a woman making a sacrifice, when what he really saw was Reverend Vernon-Osbert feeding his cat. Equally, the Temple porters see countless men going about their daily business here and in consequence believe that all respectable visitors entering on foot are men. Do you recall one of them – Wray, it was – pointing out the little wall that meant they could not see the feet of those entering and leaving? Miss Dunning is a rather… linear figure, is she not? In her slender, dark clothes, differing only from the gentlemen coming in and out because of her skirts. And with the little wall obscuring her lower body, her skirts would not have been seen by the porters. She came in when barristers were coming in and out, and then when she left, they saw what they were accustomed to see: a dark figure hurrying up Middle Temple Lane to pass through the gates before they were closed, and who said, as they were accustomed to hearing, "Good night, Simmonds."'

'Well, I never,' said Wright.

Gabriel stifled his inner lawyer and was silent.

It seemed to him inexpressibly sad that Theodora Dunning, who had wanted to be a barrister so badly, had in this extraordinary hour of her life been thought of as one at last.

In the silence that followed, Wright picked up his helmet. 'I must report to Inspector Hughes, sir. We will put the arrangements in place to have her arrested later this afternoon.'

'I think you need not hurry,' said Gabriel.

After Wright had left, he sat on at his desk as the afternoon sun sank a little lower and the shadows lengthened. A breeze stirred the trees in the garden. In the shrubbery Delphinium began her evening prowl and in the kitchens Mrs Bugg and her staff began preparation for dinner. The rhythms of Gabriel's little world continued undisturbed around him but he himself felt as though some internal upheaval had occurred, leaving him drained of energy; all of it expended, for the very first time in his life, on the emotional turmoil of others.

A messenger came up the steps and Chapman brought in the letter he was expecting.

Dear Sir Gabriel,

You knew, I think, when we last met and I am grateful to you for giving me the choice that you did. Laudanum, I have been told, is a peaceful end; certainly preferable to the horror of the alternative.

How? These things are complex in novels and simple in real life. I walked into the Temple and I walked out afterwards. I was not, in truth, very concerned if I was seen or not. Perhaps it was that indifference that led to my success.

Why? Why is of course so much more difficult to put into words. With each triumph of Millie the Mouse, the arguments with my brother became more unforgivable and unforgettable. On that day, the newspapers announced that the book was to be published in the United States of America. I saw the news in an evening edition after Norman had left for the Treasurer's Little Dinner.

It occurred to me that, in the environs of the Temple, after a convivial dinner with colleagues, Norman might be more inclined to listen to me as an individual rather than as his spinster sister; and so I determined to go and meet him and accompany him home. There had been a slight altercation with Charlotte; I had retired early; there was no difficulty in simply leaving the house and hailing a cab. I arrived in the Temple at about eleven-fifteen and walked down Middle Temple Lane unchallenged and through Fig Tree Court, to the little alley leading to the Terrace. I stood there in the shadows hoping to see Norman emerge from the dinner. I watched the kitchen maid leave by the back door. And then, in the opening to the alley, as though in some kind of fantastical and incongruous storybook illustration, appeared Norman – in full evening dress, but without his shoes and socks.

And we descended then, precipitated I suppose by the extreme oddity of the situation, into a kind of vicious chaos; a random exchange of accusations and counter accusations. I had no idea, of course, why my brother was barefoot; I am still unclear. I gathered that there had been some odd intimacy in the garden. But he was almost beside himself, not because of whatever he had been doing there, but because of the social embarrassment of being discovered barefoot, and of what he perceived as the affront to his dignity of having his shoes and socks stolen; above all, the jeopardy to his position, were he to be seen by anyone who mattered. Equally, he had no idea why I was there, and no interest in me save as his possible lifeline. It seemed to me that, as always, everything was subordinated to Norman's interests and Norman's career.

Did I murder my brother because of Millie the Mouse? Because he wouldn't listen to me? Because he had so undeservedly had all that I wanted? Because of the injustice of his rich life compared to my poor one? In a complicated way a little of all those things, perhaps; or perhaps they were all the same thing.

*It was an impulse; a terrible combination of urge and oppor-
tunity in which all the bitterness of our exchanges over the years
became an unstoppable flow. The kitchen window was open; the
carving knives were clearly visible; I grabbed the nearest one and
I stabbed him. It was very easy. He scarcely had time to resist: an
outflung hand; a few steps staggered; and he fell across the doorway of your chambers. It was almost impossible to accept that one
could kill a man with so little effort.*

*I leaned over his body and seemed to see myself doing so. I
could not believe what I had done. But I had blood on my hand,
literally as well as metaphorically. There is a pump near the
church and so I went over to wash. And there I sat and thought
of such impossibly silly things. I wished I were a real barrister,
sitting there as of right, as of* inveterate usage, *as all those
generations of men had done before me. I wished Millie the
Mouse would come and comfort me. I wished I had not killed
my brother. His distinguished position was indeed an unjust
enrichment; but I realised, as I sat there, that to claim Millie
the Mouse as my own after what I had done would simply be to
perpetrate another kind of injustice. And then I went home. The
rest has been torment. Mr Broadbent's incarceration weighed
on my soul. I hope you believe I would not have let him hang.
Yet every day I hesitated to face my dreadful crime. Your visit
was the profoundest relief to me, as is writing this letter and the
ending of my story.*

*And what of Mr Moore? I have no desire for posthumous fame;
nor do I wish Millie the Mouse to be besmirched by the kind of
notoriety that will inevitably be attached to me. Let us leave dear
Miss Harriet Cadamy to her triumph. But to whom, in justice,
should the riches go? Undoubtedly, in some degree, to the man
who recognised the worth of Millie and who has made her the
mouse she now is. And, I think, to Seraphina, to buy her true*

freedom from the very beginning of her life, now, before it is too late. Will you see to it, Sir Gabriel?

Theodora Dunning

Post Scriptum: I have not, during my life, had much opportunity for interesting conversation let alone for invigorating debate. I have much valued our encounters.

Gabriel put the letter in his pocket.

He tidied the papers on his desk, turned the inkwell so that the hinges on its silver top were precisely aligned with the edge of the oaken perpetual desk calendar next to it, and placed his gold pencil (with the lead pointing towards the window) in the shallow tortoiseshell case that housed it. It was nearly six o'clock. He always went home at nearly six o'clock.

The trials of Gabriel Ward continue
Summer 2025

AUTHOR'S NOTE:
WHAT IS REAL AND WHAT ISN'T

The area of London called the Temple, situated between Fleet Street and the Embankment on the north bank of the Thames and between the West End and the City of London, houses two of the four societies of barristers: the Middle Temple and the Inner Temple. The other two societies, Gray's Inn and Lincoln's Inn, are housed a short distance away on the other side of Fleet Street, and have separate historical backgrounds. The four are collectively known as the Inns of Court.

To this day the Temple, Inner and Middle, holds the extraordinary status described in my novel. Although within the boundaries of the City of London, the Temple is a little world of its own, an independent enclave, similar in some respects to the Vatican in Rome. It is free from the jurisdiction of the Mayor and Corporation of London, exempt from all other civil and ecclesiastical jurisdictions, governed by its own parliaments and policed by its own porters in conjunction with, by consent of the Temple, the City of London Police. Nowadays, of course, many of these peculiarities are purely technical, and some, after over 600 years, still said to be arguable.

The Temple Church is a Royal Peculiar and is jointly owned and cared for by the Inner and Middle Temple.

The governance of the Inner Temple, even in 1901, was rather more complex than described in my novel. It has been simplified for the sake of the story.

The Temple was bombed heavily during the Second World War, and so its layout today is different from that described in this book. Those interested in seeing how it looked then can consult the map provided. I have taken a few authorial liberties with the location of doors and windows, but the descriptions are otherwise as accurate as I could make them, as is the way of life described.

There really was a Coronation Ball for King Edward VII, and the description of the arrangements made for it are all based on the real ones, including the fairy lights in the garden which the Treasurer did indeed decree should be 'tasteful'. The plan to invite the royal guest, however, is fictional. Although Mrs Bugg is imagined, her special egg recipe is a real one.

Theodora's attempts to become a barrister are loosely based on an amalgam of applications made by women to all the Inns of Court around this time. These applications were indeed refused, on the basis that, though no law forbade it, 'inveterate usage' dictated otherwise. The first woman to be called to the Bar was in fact an Inner Templar, Ivy Williams, in 1922.

The law of unjust enrichment did not evolve under that name until the 1960s, but its modern-day genesis was first described by an eighteenth-century Lord Chief Justice, Lord Mansfield. Theodora's identification of the importance of the case was therefore some sixty years in advance of legal thinking.

All the human characters are fictional, as is the entire story, and any resemblance to any real person is coincidental.

I like to believe that Millie the Mouse was a real mouse; but if so, she died over a century ago, her soul flew straight to mouse heaven and her mortal remains will now be a mere wisp of dust. Perhaps they lie in a crevice of one of the marble wall plaques on the south side of the Temple Church, erected to another virtuous woman. The plaque reads:

A lady of —piety charity humility chastity constancy and patient suffering—
In brief one of the most virtuous amongst women
and worthy of pious and eternal memory.

ACKNOWLEDGEMENTS

My thanks to my dear Inner Temple for my inspiration.

I also thank my sister Pippa and my friend Joanna for encouraging me not to put this novel in a drawer and forget it.

I am hugely indebted to my agent, Anne-Marie Doulton at The Ampersand Agency, and to my editor, Therese Keating at Bloomsbury, Raven Books. Between them they have been everything I could have wished an agent and publisher to be.

Read on for the first chapter of the
next Gabriel Ward mystery,
A Case of Life and Limb

A Case of

LIFE
AND
LIMB

I

No hint of the horror to come was discernible in the pure snow. It lay pristine on every ledge and roof of the ancient buildings and drifted into the doorways and around the old gas lamps and water pumps. No whiff of corruption in the perfect scarlet berries that hung from the holly bushes in the gardens. No discordance in the robins' song. Through the windows, the soft glow of oil lamps illuminated desks, their occupants deep in studious concentration. Smoke drifted peacefully from the crooked chimneys.

It was Christmas Eve. The Michaelmas term of 1901 had recently concluded. The Temple, that cloistered little area of London in which the lawyers live, huddled together in the ancient chambers that line the passageways and squares around the Temple Church, was slowly emptying. Save for the residents and for the industrious few who faced big trials in the New Year, barristers were leaving for Christmas at home.

The whole scene, thought Sir Gabriel Ward KC, as he picked his way across Inner Temple Terrace, was the very embodiment of a three-dimensional Christmas card. It needed only a few choirboys. As if on cue came that unmistakable sound, the ringing yet muffled swell of joy that is children liberated into snow. A group of small boys, in the innocence of red gowns and white ruffs and the determination of stout boots, tumbled from their rehearsal onto the smooth white lawn of Inner Temple garden and within seconds defaced it with frantic feet and scrabbling hands.

The smallest of the pack hung back and watched the snowballs flying with trepidation. On impulse Gabriel crossed the Terrace and, heedless of his immaculate black kid gloves, scooped up a very soft bundle of snow and shied it gently through the railings at the child's back. He started and turned, and Gabriel removed his top hat and bowed.

'I fear,' he said in his precise way, 'that I have assaulted you. I beg your pardon.'

The little boy smiled, fairly sure this was a joke, and at the sight of that characteristic wide smile that seemed to link ear to ear, Gabriel made a discovery. 'Are you one of Sir Vivian Barton's sons?' he asked.

'Yes, sir; Bertie, sir. The third one, sir.'

'In that case, Master Barton Tertius, as the son of an eminent lawyer, you know that if you are assaulted, you are entitled to damages.'

And Gabriel extracted sixpence from his inner waistcoat pocket and handed it through the railings. The other boys had kept their distance. Gentlemen barristers walking along the Terrace between the Dining Hall, the Library and the Temple Church were an unpredictable bunch. It might be a penny and a pat on the head, but equally it might be a telling-off and a demand to know where your papa's chambers were. But now they gathered round, neck ruffs askew and mittens caked in snow. Sixpence!

'It is for you all to buy toffee,' said Gabriel. 'But remember, Master Barton is in charge of it.'

They tore off in a breathless chorus of thanks; Gabriel noted with satisfaction that Barton was now in the lead.

From his elegantly curtained study window, Sir William Waring, Master Treasurer, head of the Inner Temple, watched the scene with strong disapproval and a complete lack of appreciation of its subtlety.

Really, he thought to himself disagreeably, sometimes I do wonder about Sir Gabriel Ward KC. Throwing snowballs! A lawyer of his seniority and distinction. One of our King's Counsel! In public! I shall speak to him.

He looked at his pocket watch. Time was getting on. Gertrude had visited earlier in the afternoon, heavily veiled for a quick Christmas assignation, and now he was soon to go home to his beautiful house in Chelsea, a testament throughout to Lady Waring's immaculate taste and efficient management of the servants. And Christmas Eve dinner with the family. Dear Amelia and Harriet… both as pretty as pictures, thank God, and their futures thus assured. Indeed, Amelia was to announce her engagement that very evening, and as for Raymond, the Bar was beckoning: a real chip off the old block. A credit to Sir William. None of the nonsense that other men had with their sons. But there, he'd been brought up from an early age to understand his duty to his parents. Waring looked at himself in the mirror above his chimneypiece, smoothed back his already smooth hair and straightened his already straight shoulders. Getting on a bit now, but not bad; Gertrude had no complaints anyway. He sighed with deep complacency.

There was a knock at the door.

'Come,' Sir William barked peremptorily. A maid entered holding a Christmas box of the most attractive kind. Exactly a foot square in all dimensions, it was immaculately wrapped in thick green paper and tied across both ways with a shining red ribbon that finished in a glossy bow.

'This was left on the doorstep for you, Sir William,' she said.

Sir William looked gratified. He would take it home to adorn the top of the already towering pile under the family tree. But even as he resolved this, a doubt entered his mind; it was a rather feminine-looking present. Gertrude was a long-standing feature of his domestic life, with a family of her own and a mania for discretion. She had made no mention of sending him a present earlier and he knew she would not expose him to the embarrassment of taking home something more suitably opened alone. All the same, perhaps…

Nodding dismissal to the maid, he put the parcel on the table, pulled the bow with a satisfying slither, and tore off the paper. Inside was a plain brown cardboard box. When he lifted off the lid, he found enticing layers of tissue paper. Sir William unwrapped them to reveal the contents.

So great had been the expectation of something expensive and good to look upon, that his mind seemed for a moment unable to adjust to what it was seeing. He stared as though paralysed. Then a wave of panic rolled over him. A sharp reflex action caused him to slam back the lid, and he staggered to his chair with a shudder of horror.

A NOTE ON THE TYPE

The text of this book is set in Fournier. Fournier is derived from the *romain du roi*, which was created towards the end of the seventeenth century from designs made by a committee of the Académie of Sciences for the exclusive use of the Imprimerie Royale. The original Fournier types were cut by the famous Paris founder Pierre Simon Fournier in about 1742. These types were some of the most influential designs of the eight and are counted among the earliest examples of the 'transitional' style of typeface. This Monotype version dates from 1924. Fournier is a light, clear face whose distinctive features are capital letters that are quite tall and bold in relation to the lower-case letters, and *decorative italics, which show the influence of the calligraphy of Fournier's time*.